The Federal Civil Service System and the Problem of Bureaucracy

JK
681
.J64
1994

Johnson, ...

The Federal civil
service system and
the problem of
bureaucracy.

$17.95

DATE		

WITHDRAWN

BAKER & TAYLOR

NBER Series on Long-term Factors in Economic Development
A National Bureau of Economic Research Series
Edited by Claudia Goldin

The Federal Civil Service System and the Problem of Bureaucracy

The Economics and Politics of Institutional Change

Ronald N. Johnson
and Gary D. Libecap

The University of Chicago Press

Chicago and London
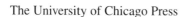

RONALD N. JOHNSON is professor of economics at Montana State University, Bozeman. GARY D. LIBECAP is professor of economics and director of the Karl Eller Center at the University of Arizona and a research associate of the National Bureau of Economic Research.

The University of Chicago Press, Chicago 60637
The University of Chicago Press, Ltd., London

ISBN: 0-226-40170-7 (cloth)
0-226-40171-5 (paper)

Library of Congress Cataloging-in-Publication Data

Johnson, Ronald N.
    The Federal Civil Service system and the problem of bureaucracy:
the economics and politics of institutional change / Ronald N. Johnson
and Gary D. Libecap.
        p.   cm. — (NBER series on long-term factors in economic development)
    Includes bibliographical references and index.
    1. Civil service—United States—History.   2. Bureaucracy—United States—History.   I. Libecap, Gary D.   II. Title.   III. Series.
JK681.J64   1994
353.001—dc20   94–12539
                                                                      CIP

To Cel, Ann, Sarah, and Cap

Contents

Acknowledgments

As is often true with a project of this sort, the motivation to undertake this volume was derived from the theories, empirical work, and ideas of others. Our work here has been greatly stimulated and guided by the writings of Ronald Coase, William Niskanen, Douglass North, Gordon Tullock, and Oliver Williamson. We have also benefited from the comments of reviewers at the National Bureau of Economic Research and the University of Chicago Press and especially from Claudia Goldin's very useful comments on an earlier draft of the book. John Lott's work has also clarified our thinking on many of the points raised in the volume. Parts of this volume have been presented at university seminars, lectures, and professional meetings, and we express our most sincere appreciation for the many suggestions we have received. We also wish to acknowledge financial support from National Science Foundation grant SES-8508924 and from the Earhart Foundation. Finally, we want to thank Sheila Smith at Montana State University for constructing the tables and figures and Hazel Lord and the staff at the University of Southern California Law Center Library for reference support.

1   The "Problem of Bureaucracy"

1.1   Introduction

Cynicism about the federal bureaucracy is widespread. The general public views federal employees as aloof, uncaring bureaucrats who are unresponsive to their requests. Throughout the country, there is a prevailing sense that government is synonymous with inefficiency and waste and that the federal bureaucracy is essentially out of control. Discussions in both the academic and the popular press have focused on the issue of poor productivity and ways to make the bureaucracy more effective and responsive to voters in the provision of services.[1] Indeed, restructuring the federal bureaucracy so that it "works better and costs less" is a major objective of the Clinton administration.[2] In addition to concerns about worker productivity, presidents have also expressed serious misgivings about their ability to manage and direct the bureaucracy in the implementation of policy.[3] President Nixon, for example, felt that the bureaucracy was subverting his programs, and President Reagan repeatedly charged that big government was the problem, not the solution.

Despite all this attention and concern, antibureaucratic sentiments are long standing, and few would claim that substantial progress has been made in addressing the problems of bureaucracy. From time to time, there have been attempts to reform the federal civil service through the installation of new personnel rules that would reward performance and allow for a greater degree of political control over the actions of federal employees. These efforts began in 1905 with President Theodore Roosevelt's appointment of the Keep Committee to investigate ways of organizing the federal government more effectively; they were followed by President Taft's 1912 Commission on Economy and Efficiency, President Franklin Roosevelt's Brownlow Committee in 1936, President Truman's Hoover Commission of 1949, a second Hoover Commission in 1953 under President Eisenhower, President Carter's Reorganization Project of

1977, President Reagan's Private Sector Survey on Cost Control in 1982, and, most recently, President Clinton's National Performance Review.[4]

In each of these cases, recommendations have been made to provide incentives for productivity, to develop procedures for greater control of the bureaucracy, and to eliminate redundant programs and bloated staffs.[5] These efforts, however, have met with entrenched opposition, both from federal employee unions, which stress that civil service rules are in place to guard against a return to the evils of patronage, and from elected officials, who have been wary of implementing major changes in the federal personnel system.[6]

Besides performance, the other major problem of bureaucracy is a lack of accountability. Much of the current discussion of accountability has centered on the latitude available to administrative agencies for engaging in opportunistic behavior of their own in the implementation of congressional statutes and administration policies. Within the literature on this subject, there is debate as to how far agency officials can go in policy making to channel programs and services to favored constituents, to expand agency mandates and budgets, or to act on their personal preferences in ways that deviate from the desires of Congress and the president. Some authors view the federal bureaucracy as acting in self-interested ways to promote agency growth and budget maximization.[7] Other authors emphasize strategic alliances made among the bureaucracy and congressional committees that weaken presidential control of executive agencies and allow for opportunism (see Sayre 1965, 1–3; Kaufman 1965, 57–68). This problem has often been traced to the rise of professionalism in the civil service and the formation of close ties between agency officials and professional interest groups.

A parallel literature has developed regarding the ways in which Congress and the president attempt to constrain the discretionary actions of administrative officials, although congressional and presidential interests can, and often do, diverge. One avenue is through congressional committee oversight of specific agencies (see Weingast and Moran 1983; Gilligan and Krehbiel 1989). Another is through the budget appropriations process (see Fenno 1966; Wildavsky 1979; and Weingast and Moran 1983). A third is through systems of administrative rules for policy making, such as those outlined in the Administrative Procedures Act (60 Stat. 237 [and subsequent amendments]; see also Arnold 1979; McCubbins, Noll, and Weingast 1987; and Wilson 1989). Indeed, some argue that the intricate system of committee oversight, appropriations hearings, and administrative procedures provides a relatively short rein that does not allow federal bureaucrats to stray very far from the wishes of Congress (see, e.g., McCubbins, Noll, and Weingast 1987). Nevertheless, it is fair to say that much skepticism remains as to how much these institutions really constrain the bureaucracy.

In this book, we examine the persisting problem of bureaucracy. Our objective is to identify the forces that have molded the existing civil service system. The analysis offered reveals that, as the federal civil service system developed, a permanent bureaucracy and a vast array of bureaucratic rules were created as the result of conscious decisions by successive politicians. The system was put into place incrementally through executive orders and statutes, following political negotiations among the president, members of Congress, and interest groups, particularly federal employees. Understanding why the federal civil service system has evolved in the way it has, with its well-known problems of productivity and accountability, requires attention to the objectives of elected officials and the confused political property rights that exist over the federal bureaucracy.

As we point out, the U.S. Constitution did not provide either the president or the Congress with clear authority over the federal bureaucracy. Hence, they have competed as rivals to direct the bureaucracy in different ways. In part, the civil service system has been designed to reduce the costs of competition over control of the bureaucracy. This rivalry, however, has also allowed federal employees to figure as a powerful additional interest in molding the civil service system. The book concludes that, given the forces underlying the civil service system, major institutional changes, such as adoption of the full list of programs suggested by the National Performance Review in 1993, is unlikely.

It is ironic that the current civil service system is, itself, a product of an earlier reform movement, one that was aimed at correcting conditions that are reminiscent of today's problems—a federal labor force that was inefficient, wasteful, and, seemingly, out of control. In the beginning, the federal civil service system was based on patronage, and reforms were sought by the president and the Congress to improve productivity in the provision of government services. Later, rules and sanctions were added to limit the president's and the Congress's access to the bureaucracy in order to shield bureaucrats from political manipulation and threats. These protections, however, reduced political control of the bureaucracy and facilitated the rise of federal employees as a third party, with a specific agenda for further structuring the civil service system. Despite the complaints of politicians about the functioning of the bureaucracy, much (but certainly not all) of the current arrangement is as they have wanted it and, indeed, as they have designed it. Recognizing this point helps make clear why meaningful change will be difficult to achieve.[8]

The shift from a patronage system to one of bureaucratic civil service rules was, in aggregate, a major institutional change, one that has important implications for the control and effectiveness of the government labor force. We argue that an analysis of the political economy of the origins and development of the civil service system is essential for understanding the rationale for the current arrangement and how it affects presidential and congressional authority over the bureaucracy and the performance of federal employees. Moreover, analysis of the gradual formation of the modern civil service system provides a case study of the mechanisms by which institutions are created and altered in the political arena. In general, these institutions can have profound implications for long-term economic growth.[9] Analyzing the historical development of the civil service will help in understanding how the system, with all its apparent faults, came to be. Importantly, the analysis provides an explanation for why elected officials, who often run campaigns directed against the bureaucracy, do not support major reforms.[10]

1.2   Political Institutional Change

Until the early part of the twentieth century, most federal employees were hired on the basis of patronage. Patronage workers were expected to be politically active on behalf of their mentors by engaging in campaign work and other partisan activities and by contributing part of their salaries in the form of political assessments. Under patronage, federal workers did not have job tenure, and they were removed routinely after elections, whenever their political benefactors were defeated (see, e.g., Fish 1905; Fowler 1943). Patronage was a popular political institution that generated votes for federal politicians. It was viewed as a means of democratizing the government service. Thousands of individuals applied for positions in the federal government after every election, and the president allotted patronage appointments among members of Congress as a means of building support for administration policies. Once secured through such exchanges, patronage positions were awarded by members of Congress or local political machines to the party faithful as rewards for their partisan services. Under patronage, there was accountability. Loyalty and responsiveness to political mentors were the essential attributes of the contracts between patronage workers and politicians.

The shift from patronage to the current system began with the Pendleton Act of 1883 (22 Stat. 403), which authorized merit hiring for a small portion of the federal labor force. This shift was in response to the problems of administering a growing patronage labor force that had become increasingly corrupt and ineffective. Gradually, the system was extended and modified over the next hundred years, and ultimately it displaced patronage as the principal means of hiring and firing most federal civilian employees. By the 1980s, there were only about 5,000 political appointees in the federal service, less than 1 percent of total civilian employment (see Pfiffner 1987). The growth of the civil service system through presidential executive orders and congressional statutes, however, involved more than expanded coverage. It also involved the adoption of new rules and sanctions regarding work practices, compensation policies, promotion conditions, job tenure, and political activity by federal employees. As such, the civil service system that emerged over time provided the governance and incentive structure for the vast federal bureaucracy that exists today.

It is our contention that the key to understanding the current bureaucratic problems of performance and accountability is the relative political autonomy of the civil service system and the unusual protection that it provides federal employees. Federal civilian white-collar employees are hired on the basis of merit, largely outside the political process. By law, they are not to be explicitly involved in politics. Once beyond a probationary period, federal employees are granted tenure, and it is extremely costly to dismiss them (see Johnson and Libecap 1989a, 1989b). They are promoted within the framework of civil service rules that heavily weigh seniority over merit, and they are paid under a national pay plan that compensates them more than their private-sector counterparts are (see Smith 1977). There is also considerable wage compression within the federal salary structure, making it difficult to create a "rank-order tournament" for federal employees in promotion to encourage labor productivity (see Lazear and Rosen 1981). Further, their salaries are protected from fluctuating political conditions that lead to the growth or decline of their agencies (see Johnson and Libecap 1989a). Given this structure of bureaucratic rules, it is not surprising that there are debates over productivity, shirking, and the extent of discretionary behavior by federal employees.

In adopting merit hiring in the place of patronage, the president and the Congress were responding to the immediate demands of voters. But the very process of institutional change established the prerequisites for subsequent modifications in the civil service system. That is, one phase of institutional change created an environment that either required or facilitated further institutional adjustment. Hence, the process of institutional change in the civil service was one of incremental alteration, in a manner similar to that described in a general context by Douglass North (1990, 89).[11]

According to North, external events and the actions taken by various actors alter the relative costs and benefits of particular institutions and set in motion the forces of change. But institutional change is most often incremental because those interest groups negatively affected resist and because to change the "rules of the game" fully requires changing the culture, customs, and beliefs of members of the society.[12] Information is costly, and, hence, current beliefs about an institution are based on limited information that, factually, may be right or wrong. North conjectures that changing these beliefs is costly and that this condition slows down the process of institutional change.[13]

Given this approach to institutional change, four forces can be identified as underlying the sequential modification of the civil service system. (1) Changes in the political and economic environment facing the president and members of Congress have affected their relative support for patronage. (2) Once established, adjustments in the new civil service system, taken at one point in time, affected the relative positions of the president and the Congress regarding access to and control of the bureaucracy. Because the president and the Congress competed for authority over federal employees, both sought further modification in civil service rules to maintain or to advance their own positions. (3) The actions taken by the president and the Congress often assisted the efforts of federal unions, as a critical third party, in obtaining subsequent additions to the civil service system. The inauguration of the merit system raised the relative returns for federal employees of organizing to lobby for additional bureaucratic rules designed with their interests in mind. Once established, federal unions engaged in lobbying and other political activities that contributed in an important way to the gradual development of the civil service system. (4) Instrumental in promoting the cause of federal workers has been the widespread belief that patronage is evil and that federal workers should therefore be spared from political influence. This conviction remains a powerful factor to this day, and it presents an obstacle to meaningful reform, which is often presented by opponents as weakening civil service protections and reexposing government employees to patronage pressures.[14] The contribution of the federal bureaucracy as an influential interest group in creating and protecting the civil service system is almost totally neglected in the literature; it therefore receives special attention in this volume.

In pursuing the topic of institutional change in the federal bureaucracy, we employ a number of paradigms. We will, for example, borrow heavily from the public choice literature.[15] In that literature, politicians are accorded the same behavioral status as any other individual in society; that is, they seek to maximize their own self-interest, most often by seeking election and reelection. Furthermore, well-organized interest groups are recognized as having an advantage in a representative democracy. These groups focus on narrow issues and tie their votes, money, and support of politicians to those issues. The interaction between politicians and interest groups in the design of the civil service system is a central focus of our analysis. In examining the opportunities for major change in the civil service system, we consider the division of power in the federal government and borrow from a recent literature on "structured induced equilibrium" that focuses on the rules for government decision making (see Shepsle 1979; Shepsle and Weingast 1984; and Weingast and Marshall 1988). The drafters of the Constitution designed a structure that assured that policy would not be overly responsive to the preferences of any one branch of government. This federal structure, however, strictly limits the ability of the president or the Congress to make unilateral changes in the civil service system at any point in time. Third, we rely heavily on the basic property rights paradigm and its implications for the costs borne by politicans in competing for control of the bureaucracy. Finally, we turn to the industrial organization literature to derive hypotheses about the management of the federal labor force and to explain the outcomes of different organizational arrangements.

At the outset, we want to emphasize that this book is not intended to be another exposé of the performance of federal bureaucrats. Nor do we offer a plan for reforming the existing federal bureaucracy. Indeed, as we discuss in chapter 8, there is a sense in which, despite all the complaints, the current institutional arrangement may in fact be relatively "efficient," given the structural constraints of the federal system and the costs of major institutional change.

At this stage, we also wish to emphasize some additional points regarding the federal bureaucracy in order to better understand the debates about the problems associated with it and the modifications that have been made in the civil service system over the past hundred years. Distinctions must be made among political appointees, who hold the top positions in most agencies; senior career officials, who hold positions in the Senior Executive Service (SES) or have top management General Schedule positions (GM- and GS-14 and -15) within the civil service; and the rank-and-file career workforce, who hold positions from GS-1 through GS-13. These three groups have very different incentives for policy administration and operate under different constraints within the bureaucracy. Senior political appointees are designated by the president, with the approval of the Senate. They are expected to help set and to carry out the administration's policy agenda within the bureaucracy. As such, their goals are political—to advance the objectives and interests of the president. Their positions within the bureaucracy are temporary, lasting at most the length of a presidential administration. They lack tenure protection and can be removed at the president's discretion. Senior career officials, who hold leadership positions within agencies, may have a role in the formulation of agency policy; they can also affect policy administration through long-standing ties to congressional committees, contacts with professional groups and other constituents, and management directives to subordinates. Unlike political appointees, they owe no specific allegiance to the administration. Rank-and-file career employees generally do not establish policy, but they are charged with administering it. They perform the routine operations within agencies, have day-to-day contact with constituents, and are often in a position to determine the details of policy application. They have strict tenure guarantees, have no expressed ties to the administration or to Congress, and by law are to be politically neutral. In fact, under the current bureaucratic structure, both groups of career civil servants have, to varying degrees, been placed essentially outside direct presidential or congressional control.

The implications of a well-protected, career bureaucracy for the performance and accountability of government have not been emphasized in the recent literature, which often views the bureaucracy as a single unitary entity.[16] The tendency is to focus on senior officials and their ability to carry out, or their propensity to stray from, the wishes of the president or the Congress. We point out that rank-and-file employees, who are the most shielded from political control by the civil service system, can also contribute to "policy drift." Not only does the bureaucracy matter, but the motives and restrictions provided by the civil service system also vary across the three groups involved. Hence, any analysis of the bureaucracy requires an understanding of the institutional environment, its ramifications, and how it came to be.

In chapters 2 and 3, we describe how the federal civil service system was inaugurated and expanded by the president and the Congress in response to increasing problems of administering a growing patronage labor force. In this discussion, we borrow from the theory of the firm, which addresses the problems of organizational size and the loss of control in explaining the movement away from patronage (see Williamson 1967; Williamson 1975, 117–26). In particular, as the patronage labor force grew after the Civil War, it became more and more costly for federal politicians to monitor the actions of their patronage appointees in order to ensure that the demands of constituents were met. The partitioning of the federal civilian labor force into patronage and merit components allowed the president and the Congress to address those demands while still maintaining patronage where it remained politically valuable. Our analysis suggests that, with the most at stake in improving the overall efficiency of government, the president would be the leader in the adoption and expansion of the merit system.

These changes in the administration of the federal labor force in response to growing organization size, however, created new problems that required further institutional adaptation. In order to constrain political opportunism regarding the use of merit employees, limited job-tenure guarantees and requirements for political neutrality were added by the president and the Congress to the initial civil service rules. A major hypothesis offered in this volume is that these rule changes, followed by the gradual replacement of patronage workers with merit system employees, set the stage for the rise of a new and influential interest group.

In chapters 4–6, we point out that these institutional modifications served to promote the rise of federal workers as an organized, independent interest group with very particular objectives in structuring the bureaucracy. The goals of federal unions, as a special interest, were often not consistent with the objectives of federal politicians, particularly the president. Conflicts over various aspects of the civil service system ensued, but federal unions were able to use the ongoing rivalry between the president and the Congress over control of the bureaucracy to secure favorable legislation and executive orders for their members.

In structuring the bureaucracy, the president and the Congress had an incentive to insulate senior-level officials from political manipulation in the administration of policy. Achieving this goal required shielding them from arbitrary dismissals and limiting the role of political favoritism in promotion and advancement. Federal unions, on the other hand, were concerned about obtaining similar protections and benefits for their membership, which was drawn largely from the rank and file. Because lower-level employees were more removed from policy determination and thereby less likely objects of manipulation, providing them with the same protections and benefits granted to senior career officials was less in the interest of the president or the Congress. Indeed, as these provisions were added to the civil service system, it became increasingly difficult for federal politicians to motivate or to manage the bureaucracy. As tenure provisions were strengthened and bureaucratic rules extended, the ability of politicians to dismiss employees was reduced, weakening their control over the bureaucracy. In chapter 6, we offer a number of reasons for the relative success of federal workers in obtaining higher compensation and job protection in comparison to both private- and public-sector counterparts.

In chapter 7, we examine a number of implications of a highly protected bureaucratic labor force for the performance of government. We suggest that civil service protections for career federal employees both allow and reduce the motivation for opportunistic bureaucratic behavior. On the one hand, since salaries and promotion opportunities for rank-and-file employees are insulated from the effects of agency growth or decline, those employees have less incentive to push for the expansion of agency mandates and budgets in order to advance. These findings bear directly on the frequently stated hypothesis that bureaucrats have a strong incentive to promote the growth of their agency in order to increase their salaries.[17] On the other hand, under the civil service system, the president and the Congress have fewer means of disciplining and controlling the rank-and-file labor force. For particular agencies, mandates can be restricted, budgets cut, discretion curtailed; but, absent fundamental changes in civil service rules, job tenure remains, restrictions on supervisory authority continue, and salaries and promotion proceed along previously established timetables.

The major finding of the volume is that the president and the Congress are unlikely to make sweeping changes in the civil service system. Both, of course, would like to enhance their own control over the bureaucracy. But placing senior career officials more or less off limits to political manipulation in the administration of policy provides significant benefits to federal politicians because it lessens the temptation to act opportunistically. The net benefits to federal politicians of these protections as they apply to lower-level career employees, however, seem to be negative. There are fewer gains from shielding these individuals from political competition and manipulation because they play a more peripheral role in policy formation and execution. In contrast to the rules governing senior-level personnel, the civil service rules that protect these individuals are due largely to the actions of federal unions. But the President and members of the Congress are rationally reluctant to take on this powerful interest group.

Finally, the book argues that a full account of why we should not expect a sweeping change in the civil service system requires an understanding of how the history of federal patronage has been perceived. Patronage in any form has come to be viewed as undesirable. As we discuss in the final chapter, current civil service reformers, academic experts, and, recently, the Supreme Court are convinced that all career government workers must be protected from political pressure. The often-repeated claim is that any adjustment in civil service rules to address issues of accountability and productivity potentially could lead to the unraveling of the system of protections that have been put into place and to a return to the spoils system. Although we believe that this concern is exaggerated, because the president and the Congress have had a vital interest in limiting patronage through the adoption and maintenance of the merit system, the specter of the spoils remains as a powerful break on reform efforts, one that federal unions and their supporters have been able to exploit.

Since 1883, piecemeal adjustments in the civil service system have been made in response to the objectives of the president and the Congress, as they competed for control of the bureaucracy, and in response to the demands of federal employee unions. Through this process, attributes have been incorporated into the civil service rules that have had long-term consequences for the governance and performance of the federal bureaucracy. As this book makes clear, the bureaucratic structure put into place at the behest of these three parties has created the "problem of bureaucracy," and changes in this system will occur at best incrementally.

Notes

1. See, e.g., Sayre (1965), Heclo (1977), Mosher (1979, 1982), Kaufman (1981), Seidman and Gilmour (1986), Knott and Miller (1987), Wilson (1989), and Osborne and Gaebler (1992). These discussions cover nearly thirty years, and it is striking how little the problems have changed. More recent discussions include U.S. House of Representatives (1993) and DiIulio, Garvey, and Kettl (1993). The report of the U.S. House of Representatives' Committee on Government Operations states, "In general, we found that public perceptions—those that waste and abuse are rampant throughout the Federal Government—to be generally accurate. It pervades every agency and hundreds of important programs (1993, v–vii). The committee had examined nineteen departments and agencies. Similarly, DiIulio, Garvey, and Kettl (1993, 62–65) claim that federal programs and bureaucrats have a reputation for cumbersome or unresponsive administration, excessive complexity, and rudeness. In this book, we do not attempt a broad comparison of the performance of the federal government relative to corporations, private nonprofit organizations, or state and local governments. Our concern is with how the institutional structure of the civil service system came to be and its implications for the performance and accountability of the federal bureaucracy. We examine aspects of the efficiency of the civil service system in cahp. 8.

2. The Clinton administration's plan for reforming the federal bureaucracy, submitted to the president by Vice President Al Gore, hopes to remove "useless bureaucracy and waste" and free workers "from red tape and senseless rules" (see Gore 1993).

3. The volume edited by Sayre (1965) offers a number of articles pointing to the political autonomy of the federal bureaucracy and the associated reduced ability of politicians to make the bureaucracy accountable (in particular, see Kaufman 1965). Kaufman (1981) examines the independence of bureau heads and their ties with professional groups. Another examination of this theme as well as a detailed discussion of the protection provided by bureaucratic rules is provided in Heclo (1977). More recently, Mosher (1982), Knott and Miller (1987), Rosen (1989), and DiIulio, Garvey, and Kettl (1993) outline some reforms that would improve bureaucratic accountability.

4. For a discussion of the Keep Committee and the Commission on Economy and Efficiency, see Van Riper (1958, 191–92, 219–22) and U.S. House of Representatives (1912d). The Hoover Commission's report is provided in Hoover Commission (1949). The President's Private Sector Survey on Cost Control (Grace Commission 1984, 343) and DiIulio, Garvey, and Kettl (1993, 8) summarize past efforts to reorganize the federal government. Gore (1993) outlines the Clinton administration's recommendations.

5. The pressures on almost every president to create these reform commissions arose out of broad concerns about the effectiveness and costs of government institutions, rather than solely as a result of complaints by specific constituents that an agency was not providing the desired services. As an indication of just how broad the scope of these investigations has been, the President's Private Sector Survey on Cost Control submitted thirty-six major task force reports and eleven studies of specific items, which the commission argued would bring a three-year savings of $424.4 billion (Grace Commission 1984). Similarly, after examining every cabinet department and ten federal agencies, the National Performance Review recommended reforms that would bring a five-year savings of $108 billion (Gore 1993, iii).

6. The lack of progress has been recognized. The Hoover Commission (1949, v) points to the "scant success" of previous reorganization efforts.

7. See Niskanen (1971), Tullock (1965), and Downs (1967). For discussion of the Niskanen budget-maximization hypothesis, twenty years after it was first proposed, see Blais and Dion (1991). For empirical examination of an aspect of the Niskanen hypothesis, see Johnson and Libecap (1989a).

8. That politicians have been instrumental in the design of the bureaucratic system has been noted by Horn (1988), Moe (1991), and Knott and Miller (1987).

9. For a summary of a broader literature on institutional change and the role of institutions in economic and political decision making, see Furubotn and Richter (1991). Specific work includes that by Davis and North (1971), Williamson (1975, 1985), North (1981, 1990), Eggertsson (1990), Ostrom (1986, 1990), and Libecap (1989a).

10. James Wilson has noted, "No politician ever lost votes by denouncing the bureaucracy" (1989, 235). Yet little is actually ever done to bring major reforms to the system.

11. One institution's legacies to subsequent institutional change often create a sense of path dependence. For discussion, see North (1990) and David (1985).

12. For North, institutions are "the rules of the game in society or, more formally, are the humanly devised constraints that shape human interaction" (1990, 3). They include a variety of arrangements, ranging from informal customs and traditions to formal constitutions, laws, court rulings, and administrative proceedings.

13. A related concept is that of bounded rationality, as discussed by Williamson (1975, 254–55). Some of the implications of imperfect information and bounded rationality for civil service reform are mentioned, but not developed, by DiIulio, Garvey, and Kettl (1993, 2–6).

14. We illustrate this issue in chap. 8.

15. For a survey of this literature, see Mueller (1989).

16. The literature is surveyed in chap. 7. The major contributors to the recent literature on bureaucracy include Tullock (1965), Niskanen (1971), Borcherding (1977), Weingast and Moran (1983), McCubbins, Noll, and Weingast (1987, 1989), Moe (1989), and Knott and Miller (1987). The civil service is given more explicit attention by Kaufman (1965), Heclo (1977), Mosher (1982), and Wilson (1989). Bureaucrats are essentially ignored by others concerned with policy formation and administration, such as Peltzman (1976) and Becker (1983).

17. The implications of these protections are discussed in chap. 7. Our analysis suggests that there is little incentive for federal employees to push for the growth of their agency as a means of advancement to higher levels of authority and pay. The role of agency growth and salaries is stressed in Downs (1967, 11), Niskanen (1971, 38–41), Tullock (1974, 127), and Heclo (1977, 131). For discussion of the budget-maximization hypothesis, see Blais and Dion (1991). The effect of agency growth or decline on salaries and the returns to tenure for federal employees are also discussed in Johnson and Libecap (1989a, 1989b).

2   Replacing Political Patronage with Merit: The Roles of the President and the Congress in the Origins of the Federal Civil Service System

2.1   Introduction

Throughout much of the nineteenth century, federal workers were a valuable political asset. Patronage was the currency of political exchange. The right to place the local party faithful into relatively high-paying federal jobs, making them postmasters or customs officers, was coveted by members of the House of Representatives, senators, cabinet members, and local political bosses. The president, who had the constitutional power to staff executive branch positions, traded these positions to members of Congress, local bosses, and other politicians in exchange for their support on legislation and in reelection.[1] Patronage jobs were known to be temporary, subject to the political fortunes of each worker's benefactor and political party. Not only was patronage an integral part of party politics in the United States, but it was viewed as a means of democratizing the government. Anyone with the right political connections could obtain a government job, at least for a short while.

Nevertheless, in the late nineteenth century, with the enthusiastic support of the president Congress voted to restrict the number of patronage positions that were available. With the enactment of the Pendleton Act (22 Stat. 403) on 16 January 1883, the process was established by which patronage was to give way gradually to merit-based employment. By 1904, only twenty-one years after the Pendleton Act was passed, over 50 percent of the total federal civilian labor force was under merit provisions (U.S. House of Representatives 1976). No longer were federal employees to direct their attention primarily to the political needs of their patrons and party. Instead, they were to provide government services competently and efficiently. Merit, not political influence, was to determine employment. Moreover, after the Pendleton Act, federal workers were gradually extended protection from removal through actions of the president and the Congress. By the mid-twentieth century, they effectively had tenure in their federal positions but were required to be politically neutral.[2] With these changes, most vestiges of patronage that had characterized the organization of the federal labor force since the founding of the Republic were replaced by bureaucratic civil service rules.

From this summary of events, it is clear that the shift from patronage to merit in the federal government represented a major institutional change in the hiring and administration of the federal labor force. This shift to merit is commonly portrayed as a victory by reform groups over an unwilling Congress.[3] According to this view, civic-minded reformers objected to the inefficiencies and corruption alleged to be inherent in a system of patronage, and they worked to deny the reelection of members of Congress who were supporters of the spoils system and to replace them with members sympathetic to reform. Although reform groups played a role in mobilizing opposition to patronage, we find an explanation that solely emphasizes exogenous pressures for institutional change in the organization of the federal force incomplete. For example, the federal civil service reform associations generally cited as major proponents of the shift to merit employment had largely withered away by the end of the nineteenth century (Hoogenboom 1968, 256–67). Even in their absence, however, the proportion of federal employees covered under the merit system continued to expand rapidly between 1900 and 1930. Moreover, the notion that reform groups somehow carried the day against hesitant, elected officials ignores more fundamental forces underlying the shift from patronage—the incentives of politicians to replace a system that was no longer capable of winning electoral support. In our examination of the adoption of the merit system, federal politicians play a central, leading role, rather than a peripheral or reluctant one.

In this chapter, we reconsider the move from patronage to merit in federal employment and demonstrate why the president and the Congress would find it in their interests to restrict the number of patronage positions and to install bureaucratic rules for the hiring and management of federal employees. The analysis, together with the analytic framework presented in appendix A, explicitly links the growth of the federal labor force in the post–Civil War period to civil service reform. It makes it clear why the president would take the lead in reducing the number of patronage positions, even though historically the exchange of patronage had been key in obtaining congressional support for legislation and other policy initiatives. In addition, implications are drawn as to which members of Congress would be most affected by the growing costs of patronage and, hence, would join the president in supporting institutional change. These implications are examined empirically, using congressional votes on major civil service reform legislation.

The overriding factor that changed the way in which federal politicians viewed patronage was the growth in the size of the federal labor force. Commensurate increases in the number of patronage positions raised the costs of negotiating and administering the distribution of the spoils and of monitoring the performance of patronage employees. We describe, and show formally in appendix A, how the president was forced to devote more and more time to the allocation and monitoring of patronage appointments, diverting attention from other executive duties. Similarly, members of Congress were also required to spend more time on patronage issues, including bargaining with the president for positions and seeing that they were filled by individuals who would be obliged to them and who would also advance their political goals. In addition to these costs, federal politicians faced growing complaints from voters that the expanding patronage labor force was not providing them with the services they desired from the federal government. The monitoring problem was made worse by the physical separation of politicians in Washington, D.C., from those at the state and local level, who worked directly with patronage employees. These two groups of politicians had different constituents and conflicting aims regarding the use of federal workers. Scandals, inefficiencies, and corruption associated with patronage employment damaged national politicians in the eyes of business and commercial groups and many voters, while the net benefits of patronage generally remained large for the local party machine.

The shift from patronage, then, reflected a growing dissatisfaction with the spoils system among the president and many members of Congress. These concerns generally have not been addressed by those who previously have studied civil service reform; hence, much that is important to the story has been left out. We argue that federal politicians needed a new means for organizing federal workers and for more efficiently delivering federal services. The personnel rules adopted through passage of the Pendleton Act reflected the desires of the president and the Congress both to reduce the costs of patronage by improving the quality of federal workers and to constrain competition among politicians over the control of federal positions. In the end, the last objective required political neutrality for most of the federal workforce. Our analysis incorporates arguments in the historical literature regarding civil service reform with the economics of organization. We also draw on concepts from the public choice literature in examining the incentives of politicians to move from patronage to merit. This approach provides a more comprehensive explanation for the timing of the shift to merit, the identity of the interest groups involved, and why particular politicians would be responsive to those groups' demands.

2.2 Patronage

Since the early days of the Republic, patronage was viewed as a necessary and useful method for staffing federal offices. The number of positions to be filled was initially relatively small, perhaps 5,000 in 1816, with 500 positions in Washington, D.C. (U.S. Department of Commerce 1975, 1101). The Constitution granted the president the right to fill executive branch offices, and the notion, especially under the Jackson administration, was that these positions should go to the average citizen. There was to be no long-term holding of federal offices, a practice that could lead to the development of an entrenched civil service elite and would be counter to the democratic goals of the new government. The positions were relatively simple ones—postmasters, postal clerks, land office clerks, surveyors, and customhouse employees. The assignment of these jobs became a central element of the early political party structure, which was largely locally based. In his study of the Jacksonian era, Leonard White emphasizes that the connection between national politicians and local party organizations was patronage: "The success of . . . local organizations seemed to depend much more on securing office, contracts, and favors for their members than on campaigning over disputed issues of statesmanship" (1954, 84).

Patronage positions were awarded to the party faithful, who engaged in campaign work and contributed part of their salaries in the form of political assessments. These assessments on the salaries of patronage workers were a means of transferring federal tax revenues to political parties. The payments ranged from 2 to 10 percent of an individual patronage worker's salary, depending on the position held. Solicitation letters were sent by the party to each worker, return envelopes were provided to ensure that payments were made, and compliance was carefully monitored. Those who did not contribute the requested amount lost their positions (Fowler 1943, 157–60). Federal patronage jobs appear to have paid more than the market wage for comparable private positions in order to cover the payment of assessments.[4]

These funds were an important source of campaign financing in the nineteenth century. For example, Louise Overacker (1932, 103–9) states that, in 1878, the Republican Congressional Committee alone raised $106,000 for political campaigns, of which $80,000 came from federal employees. The control of assessment funds rested mainly within the local party apparatus.[5] Thomas Reeves provides an illuminating account of the assessment collection activities carried out by Chester A. Arthur, illustrating the potential for conflict between national and local party officials, as federal employees were often "required to contribute simultaneously to the national, county, local, and now state committees" (1969, 581). Nevertheless, the critical support of local party machines for congressional candidates depended on the latter's ability to obtain patronage positions from the president. The president, in turn, exchanged patronage for promises of support on various bills and policies and for reelection. Those who held patronage positions did not have tenure, and they expected to be (and were) removed routinely after elections, whenever their patrons were defeated. For example, during the Cleveland administration, 43,087 fourth-class postmasters were either removed, suspended, or asked to resign to make room for Democratic party stalwarts (Fowler 1943, 306). These were the rules of the game, and they provided for a partisan federal bureaucracy. When the government was small, patronage provided for close allegiance between appointees and their political benefactors, and as a result the behavior of the employee could be monitored at a relatively low cost. As such, patronage was a standard and generally respected practice for promoting the ideals of equality and social mobility and was the cornerstone for the development and maintenance of the political parties.[6]

So long as the interests of federal politicians and the local party machine coincided, the spoils system was mutually beneficial. To obtain the party's nomination and support in the campaign, candidates for federal political offices were required to permit the machine to play a role in the dispensation of the jobs and favors that they acquired on election and to be responsive to the demands of local party leaders.[7] In return, assessment money was made available for campaign expenses, and the local party boss used the promise of patronage to motivate campaign workers to get out the vote. Jobs were given to those who worked for the organization and voted for the party's candidates. Hence, having a say in who obtained patronage positions provided benefits to members of Congress. Patronage power enhanced their positions within the party and among some voters, and it created a form of political indenture.

Because of the value of patronage employees, a major prize for a party on winning the presidency was access to the spoils. Among the chief patronage positions were those of postmaster, postal clerk, and mail carrier. The provision of postal services was the major activity of the federal government in the nineteenth century. In 1881, for example, 59 percent of all federal employees were in the postal service (U.S. Civil Service Commission, *Annual Report,* 1893, 9, 230). The allocation of these positions among the various competing claimants involved considerable negotiation among relevant members of Congress, the president, and the postmaster general (Fowler 1943, 140–45). The postmaster general was one of the president's chief advisers in political negotiations with members of Congress, providing information on those who had received postal positions, who had requested more, what positions were available, and whose requests were inconsistent with their votes on the president's program. In 1890, there was an average of 250 postal workers per congressional district and some 1,700 applications for those positions (Fowler 1943, 215).

The exchange of valuable patronage privileges was a means by which the president and members of Congress reached agreement on legislative policies. The power to nominate allowed the president to exchange patronage appointments for favorable votes in Congress on various bills, and there was considerable logrolling and compromise. As Theodore Roosevelt noted regarding upcoming bargaining with Congress, "If they'll vote for my measures I'll appoint their nominees to Federal jobs. And I'm going to tell them so" (Van Riper 1958, 185).[8] Although senior office selections required Senate approval, appointments to the more numerous lower-level positions could be made without the consent of the Senate, and there were few restrictions on who could be hired. While it was customary for the president to consult members of the House on appointments to postmasterships in their districts, this "congressional courtesy" implied no guarantee of an appointment.[9] Members of Congress, local party officials, and cabinet officers all sought rights to patronage positions, and considerable time and effort were required to promote their interests (Fish 1905, 173–80).

When Congress and the president disagreed, the president could use the control of patronage to discipline recalcitrant members of Congress. For example, President Andrew Johnson used patronage in an unsuccessful attempt to promote his reconstruction policies at the end of the Civil War. A political ally wrote Johnson, "Our three most important officers as far as patronage and influence are concerned are Collector of Customs, Postmaster, and Assessor of the Third District (Stewart). Each of these offices has a large number of men under him filling responsible positions and daily coming in contact with the people of the city. If all of these officers were sincere and earnest friends of the President, acting in concert in political matters, there would be no difficulty in controlling the city and state. . . . With proper management we will send a full delegation to the next House to support the President, and also a Senator in place of Creswell" (Fowler 1943, 132).

2.3   Changes in the Benefits and Costs of Patronage

2.3.1   Growth of the Federal Labor Force and the Increased Costs of Patronage

The historical circumstances surrounding the shift from patronage to merit are closely related to the size of the federal labor force. In the post–Civil War period, as the economy expanded, becoming more urban and industrialized, demands were made on the federal government to increase the services that it provided. In response, the size of government grew dramatically. Table 2.1 lists federal civilian employment between 1816 and 1911. Although by the end of the Civil War the federal government was the largest employer in the country with 51,020 civilian employees in 1871, within thirty years the civilian labor force was nearly five times larger at over 239,000 employees (U.S. Department of Commerce 1975, 1102–3). Government income and expenditures grew correspondingly. For example, federal receipts, most of which came from customs

Table 2.1   **Federal Government Civilian Employment**

Year	Employment	Year	Employment
1816	4,837	1871	51,020
1821	6,914	1881	100,020
1831	11,491	1891	157,442
1841	18,038	1901	239,476
1851	26,274	1911	395,905
1861	36,672		

Source: U.S. Department of Commerce (1975, 1102–3).

duties, rose from $42,000,000 in 1861 to $393,000,000 in 1891, an increase of over eight-fold (U.S. Department of Commerce 1975, 1106).[10]

With the growth in the size of the labor force, the costs of negotiating, screening, and monitoring patronage positions increased. This new condition strained the personal nature of the patronage staffing process and the political exchanges built around it. Members of Congress and the president often had to meet with job seekers to evaluate their political merits and fitness for their regular assignment. For the president and members of Congress, the allocation of patronage increasingly became a tremendous burden on their time. In 1870, James Garfield claimed that "one-third of the working hours of Senators and Representatives is hardly sufficient to meet the demands made upon them in reference to appointments of office."[11] As the demands of the system grew, the president's role was being reduced to that of a position broker, dispensing hundreds of jobs under great pressure. These duties diverted attention from other, presumably more presidential, responsibilities. In the case of James Garfield, the costs to allocating patronage were especially high. On the morning of 2 July 1881, shortly after having assumed the office of president, he was assassinated by a disappointed office seeker.

Since the president had control over the allocation of patronage, there was more than occasional conflict between the president and members of Congress over appointments and removal. Such conflict, too, became more intense in the post–Civil War period. While members of Congress attempted to claim property rights over patronage positions, the president sought to maintain control over those positions and the range of possible trades with other politicians.

One of the most notorious conflicts over control of the federal labor force involved a battle in 1871 for control of patronage in the New York customhouse between New York senators Fenton and Conkling. Following embarrassing public exposés of corruption associated with the conflict, President Grant attempted to obtain greater authority in patronage appointments at the New York customhouse but met with only limited success. Senator Conkling and the local party machine aligned with him then gradually assumed control of patronage. President Hayes, who followed Grant, continued to try to assert presidential authority over New York customhouse officials. In 1877, Hayes named replacements for a number of key senior positions, but they were rejected by the Senate, and Conkling retained control over the New York spoils. Competition among local machines, the Senate, and the president over the New York customs and postal positions continued unabated through the Hayes administration.[12]

The president's concern about scandals in the operation of federal government facilities reflected more than a desire to maintain control over patronage. It also reflected a growing concern about the image of the president and the effectiveness of the administration in providing government services to voters throughout the country. With narrow constituencies, the local party machine and, indeed, some members of Congress could benefit from an increase in the number of patronage jobs, even if there were complaints from other groups about the efficiency and corruption of local patronage employees. On the other hand, as a national political figure with a much broader constituency, the president was in the position of bearing the brunt of voter anger over poorly run facilities and the fallout over patronage battles. Moreover, lacking effective control over the staffing of particular facilities, the president garnered fewer benefits from the patronage retained for presidential appointments (see Hoogenboom 1968, 155–204; Van Riper 1958, 182–89; and Kaufman 1965, 23–26). Given limitations on the president's time, more appointment decisions were delegated to others, increasing the risk that the political tribute and allegiance paid by patronage workers would be to those who actually distributed the spoils, not the president. To a somewhat lesser degree, members of Congress faced a similar problem in the management of patronage appointments.

The agency problem that the president and members of Congress confronted in the use of patronage workers arose in part because of the personal nature of the services that patronage workers offered local constituents.[13] Those who received benefits from federal patronage workers attributed them to the local party machine with whom they had contact rather than to the federal politicians who provided patronage. As a consequence, local political officials generally were held in high esteem, and this situation encouraged those officials to act independently of Washington. Once federal politicians relinquished patronage positions to lower party officials, they faced a loss of control over their appointments as local officials and the patronage workers, who owed their allegiance to them, acted opportunistically. These problems were aggravated by the fact that the constituents of many national politicians had interests that were different from the narrow, parochial interests of most concern to local party officials.

The agency problem associated with different constituencies and control of the labor force was also compounded by the growing number of federal patronage employees. As the number of workers grew, careful supervision of patronage appointees to ensure that their actions were in the interests of the president and Congress became more difficult. Indeed, by the early 1870s, patronage was seen by a growing number of federal politicians as a major problem for them among voters. High turnover was inherent in the system, and patronage workers had other obligations than the provision of federal services. They arranged political meetings, escorted voters to the polls, and attended party caucuses. For many postal workers, there was little time for post office business.[14] Many workers appear to have been hired just for their ability to pay assessments or to satisfy local political debts.

Business organizations were especially critical of the patronage system since the growing commercialization of the economy in the post–Civil War period depended on the smooth functioning of the postal system for shipments and billing receipts and of the customhouses for the import of intermediate and final goods. Over half the membership of civil service reform associations came from business groups. These groups developed a keen sense of the limitations of the spoils system in providing dependable services. They argued that "the primary needs of the merchants and the great interests of national commerce [have] been constantly surrendered to the demands of the party" (Skowronek 1982, 51).

Scandals and charges of fraud and inefficiency were linked to the country's largest post offices and customhouses. Patronage was blamed, and the president and members of Congress with major federal facilities in their districts were increasingly pressured to reform the system. Administration of customs was also important because tariff duties accounted for by far the largest share of federal government receipts in the nineteenth century. Three-fourths of all customs duties were collected in the port of New York, and the New York customs collector was one of the most powerful federal officeholders. The *New York Times* discussed efforts to improve the performance of the New York customhouse, reporting: "At no point had the defects of the previous method of appointment [patronage] seemed more obvious. . . . The customs service at the Port of New York had been properly considered as the climax of inefficiency and corruption" (24 March 1873). The *Chicago Tribune* reported that the problem of patronage was that "the appointees of congressmen and private individuals are expected to render a dual service, a service to the government and a service to their patrons" (18 November 1882).

The Jay Commission (U.S. House of Representatives 1877), appointed by the secretary of the Treasury to investigate five large customhouses in New York, Baltimore, Philadelphia, New Orleans, and San Francisco, argued that the New York customhouse had a labor force, appointed through patronage, that was at least 20 percent too large. The commission compared the costs and functioning of U.S. customhouses with those in Great Britain, which were staffed by merit service employees and, according to the commission, much more effectively run.

Similarly, complaints were made by business groups against the New York and other large post offices for incompetence in mail delivery (U.S. House of Representatives 1881). They pointed to claims that bags of undelivered mail lay forgotten in locked rooms and that the customhouses in Prussia and Britain were four to five times more cost efficient per volume of work done (Skowronek 1982, 51–55). A merit-based labor force "promised merchants and bankers an administrative system that would 'protect their interests and secure efficient services in the departments in which they were most directly affected'" (*New York Times,* 9 September 1881, quoted in Skowronek 1982, 52).

Because of repeated charges of corruption and inefficiencies in the New York customhouse and post office between 1872 and 1875, President Grant attempted to implement merit hiring at the facilities under a Civil Service Commission that was created in 1871. Appropriations for the commission, however, lapsed after 1875, and it was not until passage of the Pendleton Act that the commission again became active.[15] In both cases, the president met with the entrenched opposition of the New York party machine.

Management problems associated with the growth in the size of the federal labor force appear to have been the major factor behind the increasing dissatisfaction of the president and members of Congress with federal patronage in the post–Civil War period. The notion that control is lost as an organization increases in size is an integral part of the theory of the firm. For example, Oliver Williamson (1975, 117–26) argues that the distinctive advantages of internal organization are impaired and transactional diseconomies incurred as firm size increases. Bounded rationality and specialized communication and decision-making arrangements require new hierarchical layers and costly coordination mechanisms in order to accommodate larger firms.[16]

The linkage between organization size and labor control problems is also made in the literature on government bureaucracy by Gordon Tullock (1965, 142–92), who argues that authority deteriorates within the bureaucracy with increases in the size of the agency. Anthony Downs (1967, 143) points out that, the larger any organization becomes, the weaker is the control over the actions exercised by those at the top. Downs and Tullock emphasize opportunities for deliberate distortion by those at the bottom of the hierarchy.

The argument that control problems associated with the size of the labor force were the major factor in explaining the rise in the costs of patronage and the associated adoption of merit-based hiring is supported by evidence from state and local governments. Civil service reform at the state and city level also began in the late nineteenth century, and the pattern of adoption across jurisdictions appears similar to that observed at the federal level. The most populous states and cities with the correspondingly largest government labor forces tended to be the earliest adopters of civil service reform. According to the Council of State Governments, seven of the ten most populous states by population had adopted statewide merit systems by 1941: New York, 1883; Illinois, 1905; Ohio, 1913; California, 1913; Michigan, 1937; Massachusetts, 1885; and New Jersey, 1908.[17] Of the remaining less populous thirty-eight states, twenty-five, or 66 percent, had no statewide civil service system by 1941.[18]

Records compiled by the International City Managers' Association reveal a similar pattern: municipal merit systems were in operation in all the thirteen largest U.S. cities by 1920, and six of those had merit service rules as early as 1900.[19] Calls for civil service reform in the larger cities followed the decline in the quality of government services under patronage and associated demands by reformers for more efficient government.[20]

2.3.2   The Costs of Patronage and the Changing Economic and Political Environment in the Post–Civil War Period

The rising costs of negotiating, screening, and monitoring patronage workers facing the president and members of Congress owing to the growth of the labor force were intensified by important changes in the structure of the party in the late nineteenth century. Prior to the Civil War, American political parties developed largely as loose confederations of local institutions (see Kolbe 1985; Skowronek 1982; Chambers 1975; Stokes 1975). Indeed, Richard Kolbe (1985, 33) describes early American parties as factions, not well-organized national groups. In this way, the parties mirrored the national economy, which, because of high transportation costs, tended to be a collection of regional economies.[21] Parties focused on parochial concerns to win elections for their candidates, and patronage was used to organize campaigns and to fill appointive offices. Assessments from patronage workers provided local party machines with election and administrative funds from federal tax revenues.[22] Charles Stewart (1989, 26) argues that patronage kept local interests loosely bound in national political parties in the nineteenth century.

In the post–Civil War period, the rural, relatively isolated nature of the American economy began to change rapidly. The economy became increasingly urbanized, industrial, and integrated through lower transportation and information costs, linking labor, product, and capital markets. Per capita income rose. Expansion in the size of markets and technological change brought increases in the size, scope, and complexity of production.[23]

In part, because of the Union success in the Civil War, which established the domination of the federal government over regional interests (the South), and because of the growth of a truly national economy after 1865, politics and political parties began to take on a more national identity. Stephen Skowronek (1982, 39–40) discusses the change in the structure of American political parties in the late nineteenth century. While the earlier role of parties had been to direct the dispersion of particularistic benefits from the federal government downward to the localities, as the century progressed the parties were called on to take a more national role. Social interactions and economic contacts were becoming increasingly national in scope, with a corresponding rise in private interest groups demanding new and more complex services from the federal government that transcended local boundaries. These conditions brought about the gradual and at least relative replacement of the locally oriented party democracy.

Interstate coalitions, such as the Grangers, the National Association of Manufacturers, and the National Civil Service Reform League, lobbied Congress for legislation that they desired. There were demands for the setting and regulation of railroad rates and tariffs to promote domestic businesses and for establishment and enforcement of a sound money supply policy, antitrust law, and meat inspection procedures (to promote exports).[24] Such legislation as the Pendleton Act of 1883, the Interstate Commerce Act of 1887 (24 Stat. 379), the Sherman Antitrust Act of 1890 (26 Stat. 209), the McKinley Tariff Act of 1890 (26 Stat. 567), and the Meat Inspection Acts of 1890 (26 Stat. 414), and 1891 (26 Stat. 1089) was enacted, representing new and unprecedented intervention by the federal government into the American economy. Not only did these groups call for the provision of new services, but they also demanded that such traditional services as those provided by the post office and customhouse be improved. In order to be responsive to these interest group demands and to organize institutional reactions to them, such as the creation of the Interstate Commerce Commission, political parties became more national in scope. This new direction tended to reduce the relative importance of the locally based party and machines, although machines kept a place in local politics.[25]

Tension between local and national party officials increased, as their interests and constituents began to diverge. As Skowronek notes, "[Local] Parties in this context were the cornerstone of an old order, an order that presumed the absence of strong national controls. The hold that the party machines had gained over American institutions would have to be broken before new centers of national institutional authority could be built. The expansion of national administrative capacities thus threatened to undermine party government in the nation that first gave it full expression" (1982, 40).[26]

Support for patronage became a central element in this division. While the local party depended almost exclusively on patronage for campaign funds and workers, the emerging national parties, many members of Congress, and the president were finding that patronage was losing its appeal as a source of votes. Not only did patronage provide an inept and corrupt labor force and prove to be a source of increasing scandal and embarrassment, as congressional hearings in the 1870s indicate, but assessments were also becoming insufficient to fund the growing costs of national, state, and congressional district political campaigns.

Table 2.2 outlines the pattern of presidential campaign expenses for the Democratic and Republican parties between 1860 and 1904. Much early campaigning for political office took place in newspaper columns, with the candidates traveling little. Editors' fortunes rose and fell with the political success of their patrons. Pamphlets about and biographies of candidates were handed out at campaign rallies, organized by local party officials. Candidates for federal offices generally were not in attendance. Widespread barnstorming by federal candidates was introduced by Stephen Douglas in 1860 and became more central to election campaigns as the nineteenth century progressed. As more

Table 2.2   **Expenses for Presidential Campaigns**

Year	Expenses ($)[a]	Year	Expenses ($)[a]
1860	150,000	1884	2,700,000
1864	175,000	1888	2,205,000
1868	225,000	1892	4,050,000
1872	300,000	1896	4,025,000
1876	1,850,000	1900	3,425,000
1880	1,455,000	1904	2,796,000

Source: Compiled from *Congressional Record,* 61st Cong., 2d sess., 18 April 1910, 45:4931, as reported in Overacker (1932, 71) and adjusted by Alexander (1971, 3878).
[a]Current dollars.

and more people had to be reached and greater efforts were made to reach them, costs rose. The table reveals that presidential campaign expenses in 1900 were over twenty times those in 1860, and the latter part of the nineteenth century is generally conceded to have been a period of deflation. As political campaigns became broader and more costly, political parties that had relied previously on patronage assessments turned to contributions from national interest groups and wealthy individuals to fund campaigns for state and federal offices.[27]

Constituent demand for the more effective provision of services by the growing federal labor force, then, coincided with the desire of the president and members of Congress to strengthen the national party and to weaken the local machine. A merit system for federal employment was seen as breaking the hold of the party bosses over political institutions and the patronage labor force and as facilitating the creation of a "responsible" national party system (see Skowronek 1982, 54). George Curtis, a founder of the National Civil Service Reform League and one of the leading critics of patronage, explained that "the goal of civil service reform was not 'merely a system of examinations' for administrative appointments but 'the restoration of political parties to their true function,' which is the maintenance and enforcement of national policies" (Curtis 1887, 358, quoted in Skowronek 1982, 54).

On this same issue, Donald Stokes (1975, 192–96) dates the rise of the modern U.S. party structure from the 1870s, with the concomitant rise of a national party administrative apparatus and institutional changes that weakened the power of the local political machine: direct political party primary elections, civil service reform, the adoption of the secret ballot, and the direct election of senators.[28] The local party had maintained itself through the control of patronage, the collection of assessments, the monitoring of voters through the open ballot, loose registration requirements, and the legislative selection of senators, which increased the role of the local machine in brokering the assignment of Senate offices.

Within this context, the president and certain members of Congress reassessed their position on patronage and civil service reform.[29] Civil service reform was an essential ingredient in, indeed a prerequisite for, this process of change. If the federal government were to respond to new demands or calls for the improved provision of existing services, it had to wrest control of the labor force from the local party apparatus. With the federal government doing more, the organization and performance of federal workers became an election issue for the president and members of Congress, beginning in the early 1870s. The Republican party adopted merit reform as a political plank in 1872, and the Democratic party followed in 1876. Rutherford Hayes was elected president in 1876, after a campaign in which he promised to change the patronage system. Although Hayes did not follow through as completely as reformers had hoped, the New York Civil Service Reform Association was formed in May 1877 to organize political pressure, and the National Civil Service Reform League was organized in August 1881. With the assassination of President Garfield in 1881 and continued controversies over the collection of assessments from patronage workers and those workers' overall performance, civil service reform became one of the principal election issues in 1882.[30]

2.4   The Design of a New Institution: An Analytic Framework

The historical literature on civil service reform portrays the movement either as one of dedicated reformers battling a Congress reluctant to adopt a merit system or as one of skillful incumbent politicians seeking to deny their competitors access to patronage should they lose office. We address these issues in this and the following chapter, and we argue that the president and the Congress had other important reasons to support reform. Influential constituents were demanding alterations in the organization of the federal labor force, reducing the incentives of the president and certain members of Congress to maintain an all-patronage workforce. If these politicians were responsive to constituent demands, the growing public dissatisfaction with patronage in the late nineteenth century should have led to directed efforts for institutional change.

Contemporary analyses indicate that roll-call voting by members of Congress closely reflects constituent interests.[31] This finding is consistent with the postulate that politicians behave as if they were attempting to maximize the votes that they expect to receive in the next election.[32] Although reelection is considered a standard motive for twentieth-century politicians, it appears to have been on the minds of most federal politicians in the late nineteenth century as well.[33] For example, in the 1880 election, 74 percent of the members of the Forty-sixth House of Representatives sought reelection. Of those, nearly 87 percent were successful. Similarly, in the 1882 election, 61 percent of the members of the Forty-seventh House sought reelection, of whom 75 percent were successful.[34]

In this section, the reelection postulate is used to develop implications about which politicians were most likely to favor civil service reform and to explain the choices made in adopting the initial rules for the merit system. As part of the argument, we describe why the president would take the lead in controlling the growth of patronage. Unlike the earlier historical literature, our approach places federal politicians at the center of the civil service reform movement.

For the president and each member of Congress, a decision to alter the long-standing federal patronage system involved a calculated trade-off (in terms of votes) in expected costs and benefits. In the late nineteenth century, members of the House, senators, and the president were subject to voter scrutiny. House members were directly elected in their districts, and voter support for reelection depended, in part, on the popularity of the patronage institution and on how well patronage employees provided federal services. Even though senators were not directly elected at the time civil service reform was being considered, their appointment by state legislatures also depended on the success of their party in elections. Indeed, senators were often state party leaders.[35] Similarly, the president's reelection chances were affected by voter evaluation of the effectiveness of the administration. High-ranking party officials, particularly the president and members of the Senate, bore the brunt of public discontent with the effectiveness of patronage workers.

Despite the increased unpopularity of patronage among many voters in the late nineteenth century, neither the president nor members of Congress could distance themselves from its problems by unilaterally withdrawing from the spoils system. Collective action among politicians was required. If a member of Congress unilaterally withdrew from patronage competition, other politicians would obtain control of the appointments, and the problems of monitoring the provision of constituent services and the blame for the poor performance of patronage workers would remain. Hence, federal politicians had to decide, as a group, whether to maintain patronage or to adopt a more politically neutral method of selecting and administering the federal labor force. Obtaining a group consensus took time. Civil service reform legislation was introduced into Congress and promoted by the president as early as 1864, but no legislative agreement was reached until 1883 with the Pendleton Act.

Public dissatisfaction with patronage, especially in the large postal and customs facilities, would have reduced the popular support received by both the president and members of Congress. But the growth of the all-patronage labor force presented the president with an especially difficult management problem. He had both to improve the performance of federal workers and to control the size of the pool of patronage employees. The ultimate solution to this problem was the adoption of the merit system. While the formal arguments illustrating this management problem are presented in appendix A, the essence of the argument is outlined here.

Under the authority granted by the Constitution for filling executive branch positions, the president held the property rights to patronage. Appointments were traded with members of Congress for support on various policy initiatives. In effect, the president was a monopoly seller of patronage, who sought to maximize the returns from these exchanges. However, the implicit "price," or what each member of Congress was willing to pledge in exchange for patronage, depended on the total number and productivity of patronage workers.

The size of the patronage pool affected what each member of Congress was willing to give up in exchange for appointees because monitoring costs grew with the number of positions. With additional appointees, more effort was required to ensure that they worked on the behalf of their benefactor. Hence, the amount of time that any member of Congress could devote to monitoring limited the number of patronage positions that could be effectively utilized. As a consequence of rising monitoring costs, members of Congress would be willing to give up less to the president for an additional patronage position, yielding a negatively sloped demand curve for patronage. The president could potentially act as a price setter, but, in order to maximize the returns from patronage, a mechanism was needed for restricting the quantity of patronage offered to members of Congress.[36] Prior to civil service reform, the only available option was for the president to increase or decrease the number of direct presidential appointments (appointments therefore beyond congressional control). As with members of Congress, however, there were limits on the number of appointments that the president could use beneficially. With more individuals to interview and positions to administer, the president would have either to invest more time in the process or to delegate responsibility to others.[37] Such delegation of duties would weaken the president's control over patronage appointees and increase the influence of the local party machine.

The president could not unilaterally adjust the total number of patronage workers. The size of the federal labor force was determined by programmatic legislation passed by Congress and the associated staffing of federal agencies. Further, Congress would not support mere reductions in the size of the patronage pool because that would increase the implicit price for patronage paid by each member of the Congress. Hence, to obtain congressional support for limits on the number of patronage workers, Congress had to be offered some form of compensation. Improvements in worker productivity offered a potential basis for exchange. The president, too, was interested in obtaining a more efficient workforce and would be a strong supporter of reform efforts *both* to place restrictions on the amount of patronage and to raise productivity.

One possible solution to the performance problem facing the president and members of Congress was to increase the quality of patronage workers by requiring examinations for those entering federal employment. The allocation of jobs through the political spoils system could have remained in place. Civil service testing had been adopted earlier in parts of Europe, and there had been a number of efforts to implement entrance exams into the federal workforce after the Civil War. Moreover, there is evidence, drawn from evaluations of the effects of the Pendleton Act, that testing to screen patronage applicants would have improved quality and performance. Accordingly, testing *within the patronage system* could have been a means for improving the quality of government employees and potentially increasing their benefit to members of Congress and the president. Testing alone, however, would not have solved the monitoring problem of how patronage workers' time was to be distributed between providing regular government services and partisan activities. By continuing the practice of hiring the party faithful (even those screened by tests), the opportunity remained for the local party machine to divert patronage employees from providing the constituent services desired by Congress and the president to the parochial activities desired by local politicians.

When the labor force was small, the costs for federal politicians of managing the allocation of federal workers' time and effort would have been relatively low. Moreover, voters could have more easily identified patronage workers with a particular federal politician. As a consequence, a vote-maximizing federal politician would have had the incentive to assign jobs to those who would deliver the most votes by weighing the applicant's potential as a local campaign worker, source of assessment funds, and provider of government services.

As the labor force grew, the time costs of monitoring each employee would have risen. Further, while members of Congress had incentives to police the provision of local partisan services, their motivation for monitoring the provision of general government services would have fallen as government became more national in scope and as the size of the patronage pool expanded. The actions of federal workers in one section of the country were more likely to have an effect elsewhere. In addition, a growing federal labor force was more anonymous in the eyes of voters and more difficult to link to any particular national politician, except the president. These factors presented an accountability problem between some members of Congress and voters. As we argue below, however, voter ire would have been directed toward the president and members of Congress from predictable districts.

In the face of these growing management difficulties, the mere testing of job applicants within the prevailing patronage system was unlikely to have seriously improved productivity, although the effect would have depended on the standards adopted. Moreover, with a growing demand for federal services, there were few means of limiting the growth of the labor force. Hence, the monitoring problem would have intensified, despite the adoption of merit testing within patronage. Further, as the numbers of patronage jobs grew, the president would have been under pressure to delegate more of the actual dispensation of patronage to the very department heads who were charged with administering exams and selecting new employees. The department heads, in turn, would have been subject to the political demands of members of Congress and local party officials. This may explain why some of the early attempts to use testing within the patronage labor force that predated the Pendleton Act did not fare well.[38] As a result, merit testing alone was an incomplete solution to the problems of allocation, control, and performance of the patronage labor force faced by the president and members of Congress in the post–Civil War period.

The resolution lay in a new arrangement that involved both testing and removing targeted positions from patronage. Once dislodged from the spoils system, federal employees would no longer be required to fulfill local party duties. Accordingly, the allocation of federal jobs on the basis of test scores instead of patronage considerations would reduce the influence of local party officials among federal workers, lower monitoring costs, and increase output as workers were able to devote their full attention to the provision of government services. If the problems associated with patronage were to be resolved effectively, legislators had collectively to institute a politically neutral system for hiring and administering federal workers.

A decision to support civil service reform involved a trade-off in benefits and costs for each politician, and legislators were subjected to different political pressures in this calculation. Certain politicians could secure greater support from voters by reducing the number of patronage positions. In particular, those politicians most negatively affected by patronage practices would be the ones with the greatest incentive to alter the system. Large post offices and customhouses were considered to be especially troublesome and were the focus of considerable concern in subsequent congressional debate over the Pendleton Act: "The necessity of the application of the system in smaller offices is not so great. The heads of such offices have more leisure, more immediate supervision of each subordinate; and the temptation to use their position for mere political purposes is not so great. The system can readily be extended at any time" (U.S. Senate, "Report," 1882).[39] Accordingly, we expect that legislators from districts with large federal installations would be the most likely to support the adoption of a merit system in place of patronage.

Once a politician decided to support civil service reform, there was still the problem of which positions to remove from patronage. Not all patronage jobs posed the same costs or offered the same benefits. If they acted judiciously to maximize votes, federal politicians would be expected to compare the costs and benefits of placing various patronage positions into the new merit system. In particular, we expect that rank-and-file positions in those large federal facilities subject to voter complaints would be the most likely candidates for placement under a merit system. The performance of these positions critically affected the delivery of federal services, and, because many of the appointments were to relatively low-level positions, they provided few political benefits to federal politicians as patronage assignments. In contrast, the more limited number of high-level supervisory and executive positions, such as first-class postmasters at the largest post offices, were less directly linked to the local party and were patronage plums with high political returns. Hence, we expect that these positions would not be given up in the conversion to a merit system.

In sum, the arguments developed in this section suggest the following implications for the initial design of the new federal labor institution:

1. The new federal labor arrangement would include both testing and removal from patronage.

2. Not all federal positions would be affected by the civil service reform, and the shift to merit would be gradual. The most likely to be included are rank-and-file appointees at large urban post offices and customhouses. High-level appointees would remain within the patronage system.

3. The president would take the lead in promoting civil service reform.

4. Members of Congress from districts with large customhouses and post offices would join the president in promoting adoption of the merit system.

These implications regarding the nature of civil service reform legislation and the identity of the politicians who supported it are examined in the following section.

2.5   Legislation for Merit

2.5.1   Early Efforts to Adopt Merit: The Jenckes Bill

The most serious early effort in Congress to adopt a merit system for the hiring of federal employees was made by Congressman Thomas Jenckes of Rhode Island.[40] The Jenckes bill, which was a prototype for the Pendleton Act, called for the use of competitive examinations for entry into the federal civil service for *all* positions, except those top-level offices named by the president and confirmed by the Senate. The Civil Service Commission was to monitor the selection process. In support of his bill, Jenckes argued that introducing a merit system would "save congressmen and executive officers countless hours wasted listening to office seekers" (Hoogenboom 1968, 28).

Jenckes was a member of the Joint Select Committee on Retrenchment after the Civil War and also believed that a merit system improving government efficiency would allow for a reduction in taxes: "Let us seek to obtain skill, ability, fidelity, zeal, and integrity in the public service, and we shall not be called upon to increase salaries or the number of offices. It is safe to assert that the number of offices may be diminished by one-third, and the efficiency of the whole force of the civil service increased by one-half, with a corresponding reduction of salaries for discontinued offices, if a healthy system of appointment and discipline be established for its government" (*Congressional Globe,* 39th Cong., 2d sess., pp. 838–39).

Jenckes and other civil service reformers looked to Great Britain, where merit-based reforms were being implemented at the time.[41] Indeed, later in 1879, as the campaign for civil service reform continued, Dorman Eaton of the National Civil Service Reform League, the chief architect of the Pendleton Act, wrote *The Civil Service in Great Britain* (1880) to extol the rewards of civil service reforms in Britain and their likely beneficial effects in the United States. The book set a British standard for American legislation and linked the merit system to progress and patronage to provincialism and incompetence.[42]

Despite growing support for some type of merit system for federal workers, the Jenckes bill would have resulted in massive cuts in the number of patronage positions. As the analytic framework in section 2.4 above suggested would be the case, the bill's broad scope was too much for most representatives, and the House voted to table the measure in 1867 by a margin of 72 to 66 (*Congressional Globe,* 39th Cong., 2d sess., pp. 1034–36). The vote to table the Jenckes bill is instructive because of the patterns of support and opposition for civil service reform that are revealed. As Ari Hoogenboom noted, "This vote . . . was surprisingly close and cut across party lines. Although the bipartisan vote reveals no sharp cleavage between political 'outs' and 'ins,' it does outline an urban versus rural pattern. There is an indication of correlation between distance from centers of commerce and decrease of interest in civil service reform" (1968, 31). Hoogenboom's description indicates that, in voting for the

Jenckes bill, those House members with the large postal and customs facilities that were critical for commercial activities would be the most likely to support civil service reform. We examine congressional voting behavior and this hypothesis in our analysis of the Pendleton Act.

2.5.2   The Pendleton Act of 1883

After the failure of the Jenckes bill in 1867, there were various attempts to create a merit-based system for hiring federal workers. The Jenckes bill was reintroduced in 1868, 1870, and 1871, but it did not pass (see Titlow 1979; Van Riper 1958, 68–78). Between 1871 and 1874, there was a short-lived Civil Service Commission authorized by a rider to an appropriations bill (16 Stat. 514 [1871]) and supported by President Grant.[43] The statute authorized the president to establish rules and regulations for the hiring of federal workers to best promote the efficiency of government through the use of criteria that stressed knowledge and ability rather than political ties. It also authorized the establishment of a commission to prescribe the functions of the civil service. Grant appointed seven members to the committee to initiate merit hiring. They drew on the British civil service model to draft rules for competitive examinations for hiring and promotion. These efforts, however, did not lead to a permanent federal merit system because Congress refused to continue the appropriations for the commission's actions in 1874.

A permanent institutional structure for merit hiring did not come until the Pendleton Act was passed in 1883. The original Pendleton bill was submitted to Congress by Senator George Pendleton of Ohio in December 1880. It followed the earlier Jenckes bill, creating a strong Civil Service Commission to administer a merit system. Some constitutional issues were raised, and the bill was withdrawn and replaced by one carrying provisions drafted by members of the New York Civil Service Reform Association and the National Civil Service Reform League (Sageser 1935, 37–40; Skowronek 1982, 64–66). The new bill was reintroduced by Pendleton on 10 January 1881, and hearings were held by the Committee to Examine the Several Branches of the Civil Service. Although the committee recommended passage, no action was taken by the Congress during that session. Action awaited the new president (Sageser 1935, 40–41; Titlow 1979).

The assassination of President Garfield in July 1881 reignited the spoils system as an explosive campaign issue. The New York Civil Service Reform Association took advantage of public revulsion over the assassination to campaign for passage of the Pendleton Act, and the legislation was reintroduced by Pendleton on 6 December 1881 (Sageser 1935, 42–44; Titlow 1979). Congressional debate emphasized the efficiency and economy that would come about with a merit system and broad public demand for civil service reform. Even so, no action was taken on the bill. During the summer of 1882, reform groups continued to lobby Congress and generate voter support for enacting the Pendleton bill (Sageser 1935, 47–52).

Although political pressure was building for the adoption of some type of merit reform legislation, shifts in the political fortunes of the two parties help explain the exact timing of the passage of the Pendleton Act in 1883. Democrats took control of the House in March 1883, and Republicans began to fear that they would lose the 1884 presidential election and therefore lose control of the White House for the first time since the election of Lincoln. Federal patronage and assessments, especially by the Republican Congressional Committee, were central campaign issues in the fall 1882 congressional elections, and politicians were looking to introduce the kinds of reforms outlined in the Pendleton bill.[44] There was considerable political posturing occasioned by the bill. For Republicans, who stood to lose the 1884 presidential election, enactment of the law would mean that the Democrats would have fewer patronage positions from which to obtain political assessments.

The Pendleton bill also allowed for existing employees to be placed within the classified service. This facet of the bill did not go unnoticed by some Democrats. Senator Joseph Brown of Georgia suggested that the preamble of the bill state "a bill to perpetuate in office the Republicans who now control the patronage of the government" (*Congressional Record,* 47th Cong., 2d sess., p. 661). Many Democrats, however, were caught in a dilemma. Failure to vote for merit reform would cast them as being in favor of maintaining the system of spoils and allow Republicans the benefits of political assessments for the upcoming 1884 elections. Although assessments were becoming less important as a source of campaign revenues, Democrats also wanted to curtail Republican access to them. Nevertheless, they also sensed that victory and control of patronage were close at hand. These issues weighed in the voting decision faced by each member of Congress.

The debate in the Senate over the Pendleton Act occurred over the period from 12 December to 27 December 1882, when it was passed by the Senate; the House vote took place on 4 January 1883.[45] The bill was voted on during the lame-duck second session of the Forty-seventh Congress, which was controlled by the Republicans. It provoked considerable debate in the Senate. For example, Senator Warner Miller of New York argued, "No party can hope to manage the patronage of this government in its present magnitude and maintain itself before the people. The people demand efficiency in the officers. They only ask of the Post-Office Department that it shall take their mails and that it shall deliver them in the least possible time with the fewest possible mistakes" (*Congressional Record,* 47th Cong., 2d sess., p. 284).

One of the major objectives of the Pendleton bill was the separation of federal employees into two groups: classified (merit) and unclassified (patronage). As predicted, not all federal employees were placed within the merit service. When the law was implemented, 2,573 positions were placed in the classified customs service, 5,699 in the classified postal service, and 5,652 in the classified departmental service in Washington, D.C. (U.S. Civil Service Commission, *Annual Report,* 1889, 15). Senior officials, appointed by the president with the advice and consent of the Senate, were not covered by the act, nor were other positions not specifically designated by the law. Although the Pendleton Act affected only 13,924 positions out of a civilian labor force of some 131,860, it authorized the president to include additional positions through executive order (U.S. Civil Service Commission, *Annual Report,* 1889, 15). Unclassified positions remained to be filled via traditional patronage appointments.

Sections 1–3 of the Pendleton Act authorized the establishment of a Civil Service Commission of three persons, appointed by the president, to draw up rules for the administration and enforcement of a merit system. Competitive examinations were to be implemented for filling offices and for promotion within the classified service. Section 4 stated that the classified service was to include those clerks in customhouses employing fifty or more persons, clerks in post offices of fifty or more, and executive branch offices in Washington, D.C. (sec. 2) (47th Cong., 2d sess., 1883, chap. 27, p. 403). Additionally, the law called for the inclusion of the employees of any post office or customhouse once total employment reached fifty.

By construction, then, the Pendleton Act's provisions focused on large customhouses and post offices in the principal centers of business, commerce, and industry, where most federal services were directed. The cities affected were Albany, Baltimore, Boston, Brooklyn, Burlington, Buffalo, Chicago, Cincinnati, Cleveland, Detroit, Indianapolis, Kansas City, Louisville, Milwaukee, Newark, New Orleans, New York, Philadelphia, Pittsburgh, Port Huron, Michigan, Portland, Providence, Rochester, St. Louis, San Francisco, and Washington, D.C. (U.S. Civil Service Commission, *Annual Report,* 1884, 42–46). By targeting the largest customhouses and post offices, the Pendleton Act could place employees under a merit system to improve their performance and respond to the demands of business and reform groups (Hoogenboom 1968, 179–97; Skowronek 1982, 72).

The delivery of federal services through comparatively large facilities in major urban areas is reflected in postal and customs data. Postal workers accounted for 56 percent of all federal employees in 1881, and the cities covered by the Pendleton Act had 2,746 post carriers, 71 percent of all postal carriers in the postal service (U.S. Department of Commerce 1975, 1103; U.S. Post Office Department, *Annual Report,* 1884, 86). Per capita postal expenditures also tended to be highest in the most populous states. In New York, for example, per capita expenditure was $2.40 in 1900 (when data are available), almost six times that for South Carolina. In addition, the nine populous North Atlantic states had per capita expenditures of at least $1.40, while no rural South Central state had an expenditure greater than $0.73 (U.S. Post Office Department, *Annual Report,* 1900, 810). Similarly, of the eleven cities with customhouses covered by the Pendleton Act, all but three were among the twenty largest cities in the country in 1880, and they had 3,393 customs employees, 83 percent of all federal customs employees (U.S. Civil Service Commission, *Annual Report,* 1893–94, 132).

The clerical positions in Washington, D.C., placed under the departmental service affected more technical functions of government, such as surveys, where the use of examinations was more likely to result in the selection of higher-quality employees and promote the goal of achieving administrative efficiency.[46] Moreover, these positions were located in the nation's capital. Hence, it is unlikely that these employees were of much use as campaign workers for either members of Congress or local party officials. Appointments to the departmental service were to be apportioned among the citizens of the various states, according to population.

Besides addressing the concerns of voters in commercial centers about the efficiency of federal patronage workers in the post offices and customhouses, the act also took aim at reducing the potential for overt competition for control of classified federal workers by making them less attractive targets. The strongest language in the bill and its only explicit penalties were directed toward prohibiting the levying of political assessments. Moreover, threats of discharge were not to be used in soliciting funds.[47]

There is evidence that the reforms introduced by the Pendleton Act improved the performance of federal workers in the positions that were covered by the law. The merit exams called for by the Pendleton Act addressed issues necessary for performing particular tasks, and, importantly, not everyone passed. Applicants for most clerkships and nontechnical positions were tested for "common school" proficiency. Technical positions, such as engineers, architects, telegraphers, and accountants, required more specialized exams. Between July 1883 and January 1884, 3,542 applicants were examined by the commission, and 2,044, or 58 percent, received the required 65 percent passing rate (U.S. Civil Service Commission, *Annual Report,* 1884, 67). Between 1884 and 1885, 6,347 individuals were examined, and 4,141, or 65 percent passed (U.S. Civil Service Commission, *Annual Report,* 1885, 7). Data for assessing the productivity gains of testing under the merit system are limited to qualitative evidence, but they indicate a pattern of change. Although the Civil Service Commission that administered exams and employee hiring was not a disinterested party, it reported extensive productivity improvements after 1883. In its annual reports, testimonials were presented from postmasters and customs collectors regarding improvements in the functioning of their agencies with merit employees (U.S. Civil Service Commission, *Annual Reports,* 1884, 32–39, and 1885, 38). In its 1899 report (p. 17), the commission outlined increases in efficiency through extension of the classified service in the Treasury and Post Office Departments. In his analysis of the early years of the federal merit system, Carl Fish (1905, 232) estimated that $2 million was saved annually in the collection of customs.

In the Senate, the bill was passed by a vote of 38 to 5, with thirty-three members absent (*Congressional Record,* 47th Cong., 2d sess., p. 661). The yea votes were provided by twenty-three Republicans, fourteen Democrats, and one independent. All five of the nays came from Democrats, four of whom were from the South. In the House, the bill was approved with a vote of 155 to 47, with eighty-seven members not voting (*Congressional Record,* 47th Cong., 2d sess., p. 867). The votes in favor were cast by 102 Republicans, forty-nine Democrats, and four independents. Negative votes were cast by seven Republicans, thirty-nine Democrats, and one independent.[48]

Although the vote on the Pendleton Act reveals a break along party lines, our analysis suggests that there was more to the story than partisan politics. After all, Senator George Pendleton was a Democrat from Ohio, and a majority of the Democrats who voted on the bill supported it. Moreover, willingness to support reform was particularly strong among members who represented a locality with a large post office or customhouse in the vicinity. Indeed, of the thirty-six members of the House who had such a federal establishment in their district and who voted on the bill, thirty-five voted in favor. Of the thirty-six, twenty-one were Republicans and fifteen Democrats. The one negative vote in that group, however, was cast by a Democrat.

It is possible to examine more formally whether those members of the House of Representatives from major commercial centers were most likely to support the Pendleton Act as well as to examine the effects of party membership and other factors. Table 2.3 offers results obtained by applying a logit model to the votes registered in the House on the Pendleton Act. In addition to the official vote count reported above, we augmented the data set by including information on pairings and stated positions of seven additional representatives who did not formally vote.[49] Inclusion or exclusion of these seven additional votes does not alter our findings. Affirmative votes were set equal to unity and negative votes equal to zero. The explanatory variables are all qualitative. The first variable in the table accounts for the presence of a large post office or customhouse in the legislator's district or its immediate vicinity. As we noted earlier, the largest post offices and customhouses were in ares where complaints about the performance of the patronage system were the most intense. The next two variables identify the representative's party; the excluded category is Republican. The fourth variable is an interaction term and equals unity if the representative is both a Democrat and from the South. Our rationale here is that the South was largely rural at the time and that the provision of federal services was therefore relatively limited there.

The results of the logit analysis of the congressional vote on the Pendleton Act shown in equation (1) of table 2.3 indicate that the presence of a large post office or customhouse significantly (at the 5 percent level) increased the probability of voting in favor of the bill.[50] However, since most Republicans voted in favor of the act, the marginal effect of the presence of a large post office or customhouse on the probability of that group voting in favor is relatively small. Using the coefficients reported in equation (1), the marginal in-

Table 2.3   **Logit Analysis of the House of Representatives Vote on the Pendleton Act**

Variable	Eq. (1): Vote	Eq. (2): Vote	Eq. (3): Participation
Post office/customhouse	2.18	2.20	.38
	(2.04)	(2.05)	(.90)
Democrat	−1.53	−1.72	−.38
	(−2.77)	(−2.99)	(−1.05)
Independent	−1.14	−.93	−.67
	(−.96)	(−.77)	(−.94)
Southern Democrat	−1.84	−1.96	−.41
	(−3.59)	(−3.70)	(−1.03)
Lame duck	. . .	−.60	−.87
		(−1.29)	(−3.06)
Years in office	. . .	.05	.003
		(.82)	(.07)
Constant	2.52	2.65	1.67
	(6.42)	(4.82)	(4.86)
Log-likelihood function	−75.89	−74.77	−162.68
Number of observations	209	209	289
Likelihood ratio test:			
−2 × log-likelihood ratio	73.46	75.71	15.62
Degrees of freedom	4	6	6
Critical χ^2 value at the 5% level	9.49	12.59	12.59

Source: The vote is listed in the *Congressional Record,* 47th Cong., 2d sess., 1882, p. 867. Party affiliation and election data are from the *Congressional Quarterly's Guide to U.S. Elections* (1985) and the *Biographical Directory of the United States Congress: 1774–1989* (1989).

Note: For discussion of the variables, see the text. Asymptotic *t*-ratios are in parentheses.

crease in the probability for that group is only .06.[51] For Northern Democrats, the marginal increase is substantially greater, .23, and for Southern Democrats it is .51. This reinforces the argument regarding the importance of being from a district with a large federal installation in determining the position of a member of Congress on merit hiring, and it also shows that Southern Democrats, who represented mostly rural areas where there were no such facilities, were less likely to support the adoption of a merit system.

Equation (2) in table 2.3 examines a competing explanation for the shift to merit. A popular argument is that civil service reform came about only as those who favored spoils were driven from office.[52] If lame-duck representatives were mainly spoilsmen being driven from office, then we should expect them to have voted against the Pendleton Act. Hence, a fifth variable, set equal to unity if the representative either had lost or did not run for reelection in 1882, is included to test for any inordinate influence that may have been exerted by lame-duck representatives. In addition, if spoils were the currency of the "old guard," then it is plausible that members of Congress with longer periods of service would be more likely to oppose the act. Accordingly, a sixth variable measuring the number of years served in the House by each member was also included. The results reported in equation (2) of the table indicate that the votes of lame-duck representatives were not systematically different from those who had been successfully reelected to office. Nor is the coefficient for the time-in-office variable significantly different from zero. Accordingly, our results do not support the argument that reform came about as those who favored spoils were driven from office.[53]

Next, we consider whether absenteeism played a significant role in determining the pattern of votes cast on the Pendleton Act. In general, absenteeism was relatively high during the 1800s, and self-selection may have biased the results reported in equations (1) and (2). Equation (3) of the table examines congressional members' participation in the Pendleton Act vote using the same list of variables shown for equation (2). The dependent variable is assigned the value one if the member voted and zero otherwise. The results indicate that only the coefficient on the lame-duck variable is statistically significant at the 5 percent level. While this yields an interesting interpretation in that lame-duck status appears to induce shirking, the coefficient on that same variable was not statistically significant in equation (2).[54] Accordingly, the results reported in table 2.3 (eq. [1] and [2]) do not appear to be systematically biased because of absenteeism.[55]

2.6 Summary

In this chapter, we have argued that, within the context of changing economic and political conditions in the United States in the late nineteenth century, both the president and certain members of Congress had incentives to replace patronage with merit considerations for staffing federal positions. With the growth in the activities of the federal government in the post–Civil War period, its performance became of greater consequence for business profitability, and politicians came under pressure from business groups to provide government services more effectively than was possible under patronage. At the same time, it was becoming increasingly costly for federal politicians to control and benefit from a growing number of patronage employees. The problems of managing a growing federal labor force occurred within the context of a widening split between the local political party apparatus, which depended more on patronage, and national politicians, who faced broader interest-group demands for efficiency and who relied more on interest-group contributions to finance campaigns.

Our argument that the difficulties of administering a large patronage labor force were the major factors in the adoption of merit reform by the federal government is supported by similar efforts in certain states and cities. Indeed, the most populous states and cities with the largest government labor forces were the first to adopt merit employment rules. This pattern of civil service reform across jurisdictions with large numbers of patronage workers suggests that there were fundamental problems of labor management that required new institutional innovations at the federal, state, and local level. These issues have not been identified in the existing literature on the adoption of the merit system; hence, standard explanations miss the character of the real reforms that were made by federal politicians in 1883.

For example, the most common explanation is that moral outrage among civic-minded groups against the corruption and inefficiency inherent in patronage forced unwilling congressional politicians to replace patronage with merit hiring (Van Riper 1958; Hoogenboom 1968). Although there was concern in the country over the corruption and inefficiency of the patronage system, this interpretation focuses too much on external factors and neglects the incentives that vote-maximizing politicians had to replace a system of employment that we argue was increasingly costly and no longer capable of winning electoral support. But, even more important, the preoccupation with the actions of reform groups diverts attention from the underlying question of whether the patronage institution could serve politicians effectively when the government labor force became very large.

Another common explanation for the adoption of the merit system is that clever politicians devised the civil service system in order to "blanket in" or tenure their appointees and thus protect them from removal following adverse electoral results (U.S. House of Representatives 1976, 182). In this way, incumbent politicians could constrain their political competitors' access to patronage. This interpretation is a more cynical view of the shift to merit, suggesting that partisan motives remained dominant and that little real reform occurred in the organization and use of federal employees. We also find this explanation to be incomplete. First of all, it does not explain why civil service reform occurred when it did. Politicians would always have wanted to deny their competitors the benefits of the spoils. There is no obvious reason why this desire would have intensified in the late nineteenth century. Moreover, the notion that the merit service was established to protect incumbents does not fit the historical circumstances surrounding the enactment of the Pendleton Act. The Pendleton Act did *not* provide job tenure. As we discuss in chapter 3, provisions for substantial job security were added gradually over the late nineteenth and early twentieth centuries. After the Pendleton Act was passed, classified employees remained vulnerable to removal (and some were removed) as administrations changed. We examine the issue of tenure and additions to the merit system made by lame-duck politicians, those most likely to want to protect their appointees, in chapter 3. As a preview, we find that actions to place patronage workers into the merit service when their benefactors were leaving office accounted for much less of the growth of the civil service system than is argued in the historical literature.

There have been other explanations for the shift to merit employment that emphasize the concerns of vote-maximizing politicians, notably the work by Joe Reid and Michael Kurth (1988, 1989), Jack Knott and Gary Miller (1987), and Murray Horn (1988), but, by neglecting the patronage management problems that we stress, these analyses do not satisfactorily address the nature or timing of federal civil service reform. Reid and Kurth point to a decline in the derived demand for patronage workers as urban voters became more affluent and more homogeneous in the late nineteenth century. According to those authors, as this occurred, politicians shifted their demand from the particularistic government services provided through patronage to broader public goods better provided by merit employees. These demand shifts helped bring about a decline of the urban machine. Knott and Miller argue that reformers wanted efficiency and accountability for federal workers and that those demands led to conflict between reformers, who advocated the science of administration, and supporters of the local party machine. Horn places no emphasis on changing voter demands or desires for better performance; rather, he asserts that politicians desired a labor force that would be less vulnerable to political manipulation and legislative opportunism than were patronage workers. According to Horn, protection from removal and a rigid salary structure for bureaucrats were added to increase the durability of legislative agreements. With a civil service system, federal politicians would be less able to pressure federal workers to alter legislated policy in order to provide more favorable treatment to their constituents.

Two additional factors might be considered as contributing to the shift from patronage to merit. One, discussed by Charles Stewart (1989, 68–70), is a change in the fiscal position of the federal government. With an expanded role for the government in the late nineteenth century, expenditures grew, increasing the stringency of budget constraints. With the specter of federal deficits, reform movements from both within and outside government emerged to make it more efficient, and this process encouraged the professionalization of the bureaucracy under the merit system.[56] The other factor is an alleged rise in pork barrel exchanges, as an alternative mechanism to patronage, for fashioning agreements and coalitions between the president and the Congress. As pork barrel expenditures to specific districts grew (mostly river and harbor legislation and water projects), the reliance on patronage exchanges to forge congressional agreements may have declined. Hence, Congress would have become more willing to scrap patronage.[57]

We agree with the focus of the various studies summarized above, which is directed toward the rational decisions of politicians in weighing the relative benefits and costs of patronage and merit. Further, we are in agreement that the benefits of patronage were declining as compared to its costs for many federal politicians in the late nineteenth century. What is missing in these studies, however, is sufficient attention to the problems of control resulting from the growth in size of the federal labor force after the Civil War. Absent these management problems, shifts in demand for government services could have been handled by patronage appointees who passed proficiency tests, leaving no explanation for the creation of the merit system. Horn's discussion does not address the origins of the federal civil service system. As we point out, tenure and standard salary legislation came later; they were not part of the Pendleton Act. Moreover, his analysis does not address why political opportunism became a particular problem in 1883 and not earlier.

With regard to federal deficits, federal government receipts exceeded expenditures for twenty-seven years, from 1866 through 1893. Shortfalls occurred from 1894 through 1899, followed by surpluses through 1903 and then by short periods of deficit and surplus through 1917 and the start of World War I.[58] As noted by Stewart (1989, 70), concern over the better management of the federal budget led to the establishment of the Keep Committee by President Roosevelt in 1905 and the Taft Commission on Economy and Efficiency in 1912. But the rise of federal budget deficits and efforts to address them came much *later* than did the desire of the president and members of Congress to replace at least some of the spoils system with limited merit protections. The Jenckes bill proposing the establishment of a merit service was voted on in 1867 and again in 1870, and President Grant appointed the first Civil Service Commission in 1870 (U.S. House of Representatives 1976, 132–39). Civil service reform remained a perennial issue in political campaigns and in the federal government through 1883 and the Pendleton Act. All this activity, however, occurred during a period of unprecedented government surpluses, and even the enactment of the Pendleton Act predated by eleven years the rise of any federal budget deficits. Accordingly, federal deficits do not explain the initiation of the merit system.

Similarly, pork barrel exchanges may have become an alternative to patronage as a means of constructing political coalitions in Congress, but there is no clear pattern for explaining the shift from patronage to merit in the late nineteenth century. As described by Stewart (1989, 67), major pork barrel expenditures, such as river and harbor appropriations, did not grow as a share of the federal budget in the post–Civil War period, which was also a time of relatively stationary federal budgets (see also U.S. Department of Commerce 1975, 1104; Wilson 1986, 735).

By contrast, as we have documented in table 2.1, the federal government labor force grew by over 96 percent between 1871 and 1881 alone. Our emphasis on the growth of the federal labor force as a key element in the shift to merit highlights the labor management problems that arise when organization size increases. Moreover, this focus on the problems associated with the size of the patronage labor force offers an explanation for the timing of civil service reform, the identity of the constituent groups most interested in replacing patronage, the characteristics of the politicians most likely to be responsive to these concerns, and the specific attributes of the merit system created by the Pendleton Act.

The problems of administering an increasing number of patronage workers were clearly recognized by federal politicians. For example, the first page of the Senate report on the Pendleton Act contains the following passage:

In the beginning, even so late as 1801, there were 906 post-offices; now there are 44,848. Then there were 69 customs-houses; now there are 135. Then the revenues were less than $3,000,000; now they are $400,000,000. Then our ministers to foreign countries were 4; now they are 33. Then our consuls were 63; now they are 728. Then less than 1,000 men sufficed to administer the government; now more than 100,000 are needed. Then one man might personally know, appoint on their merits, supervise the performance of their duties, and for sufficient cause remove all the officers; now no single human being, however great his intelligence, discrimination, industry, endurance, devotion, even if relieved of every other duty, can possibly, unaided, select and retain in official station those best fitted to discharge the many and varied and delicate functions of the government. (U.S. Senate, "Report," 1882, I)

To conclude, we have argued that the president would take a leading role in promoting the adoption of merit employment and in constraining the growth of the patronage labor force. This is an issue that we examine in more detail in the following chapter. We analyze how competition among the president and members of Congress for control of the new merit labor force led to the adoption of additional refinements in the civil service system.

It is worthwhile noting at this point, however, that the Pendleton Act seems to have assisted the president in weakening the hold of the local machine on members of Congress and in strengthening national party unity. One measure of party cohesion is the proportion of roll-call votes decided along party lines, whereby the majority of Democratic members voted against a majority of the Republicans. This party-unity measure rose in the late nineteenth century with the rise of national party structures. For the Fiftieth Congress (1887–88), the party unity measure was 51.1 percent. It peaked during the Fifty-eighth Congress (1903–4) at 89.7 percent (Brady, Cooper, and Hurley 1979, 384). These figures suggest that constraining the volume of patronage, especially for low-level positions, not only reduced the influence of the local machine but likely increased the president's ability to discipline members of Congress to vote along party lines. By effectively controlling the quantity of patronage, the president would be able to increase the commitments (price) received in exchange from Congress. In essence, the Pendleton Act appears to have increased the president's ability to exercise market power.

Notes

1. Although there are restrictions, the U.S. Constitution (art. 2, sec. 2) vests the power to appoint officers in the president (see also Van Riper 1958, 13–16).

2. Although the Pendleton Act and various executive orders forbade certain political activities by federal employees, it is the 1939 Hatch Act (53 Stat. 1147) that is most noted for its restrictions on political activity. The granting of tenure to federal employ-

ees and how it relates to the concept of political neutrality are discussed in chap. 3 of this volume.

3. Two key works that adopt this view are Van Riper (1958) and Hoogenboom (1968).

4. We have only indirect evidence on the relative salary levels of federal patronage employees in the nineteenth century. As we discuss in chap. 4, there is considerable discussion about the deterioration in the real federal wage after 1883 and enactment of the Pendleton Act and a rise in voluntary separations (see Commons 1935, 70); Spero 1927, 33, 96; and Conyngton 1920). In chap. 4, we argue that, once politicians could no longer extract assessment payments, their interest in maintaining a relatively higher federal salary waned.

5. Fowler notes that the postmaster general was also involved in the collection of assessments from postal employees. For Andrew Johnson's election, the postmaster general stated, "They are going to tax the clerks in the New York post office on the 31st of this month for Political purposes, 1/2 per cent on salaries over $1,000 and 1 per cent on smaller Sums" (Fowler 1943, 140).

6. For discussions of patronage and its central role in American politics, particularly for the local party, see Fish (1905), Fowler (1943), Skowronek (1982), Hoogenboom (1968), and Van Riper (1958).

7. Wilson (1961) describes the role played by patronage in machine politics. His description applies equally well to federal patronage in the nineteenth century.

8. The use of patronage as a medium of negotiation between the president and members of Congress is noted by Cain, Ferejohn, and Fiorina (1987, 16).

9. Members of Congress were, of course, disgruntled by a president's refusal to allow them control over appointments in their own states. See, e.g., President Polk's comments on dealing with members of Congress (U.S. House of Representatives 1976, 90). Were members of Congress given the exclusive right to appoint even lower-level positions in their states or districts, the power of the president to use patronage in exchange for votes would be destroyed.

10. Customs duties were 95 percent of total government receipts in 1861 and 56 percent in 1891.

11. U.S. House of Representatives (1976, 156). This publication contains numerous complaints, especially those of presidents, about the time required of them for the allocation of patronage.

12. For discussion, see Skowronek (1982, 57–60).

13. Agency problems arose in a manner similar to that described in a firm context by Ross (1973), Jensen and Meckling (1976), and Williamson (1985).

14. Fowler (1943, 146). For discussion of the growing concern about the corruption and efficiency of patronage employees, see Greenstein (1964) and Griffith (1974a, 1974b).

15. For discussion of the first Civil Service Commission, see Van Riper (1958, 68–71); U.S. Civil Service Commission, *Annual Report* (1884, 13); and Sageser (1935, 24–30).

16. See Williamson (1967, 1970, and 1985). Issues of organization size and control are discussed by Ouchi (1977).

17. Council of State Governments (1942, 223–25); see also U.S. Department of Commerce (1975, 26–37). The most populous states that did not have civil service rules were Pennsylvania (second), Texas (sixth), and Missouri (tenth).

18. Other discussions of the pattern of adoption of civil service rules by states are in Faught (1915) and Tolbert and Zucker (1983, 28). Of the thirteen less populous states with civil service rules by 1941, ten adopted them between 1937 and 1941 in response to pressure from the federal government as a condition for receiving certain New Deal aid programs: Indiana, Tennessee, Alabama, Minnesota, Louisiana, Kansas, Connecti-

cut, Rhode Island, New Mexico, and Maine. States adopting civil service rules earlier were Wisconsin (1905), Maryland (1921), and Colorado (1907). Less populous states with no civil service regulations by 1941, ranked by 1940 population, included North Carolina, Georgia, Kentucky, Virginia, Iowa, Oklahoma, Mississippi, Arkansas, West Virginia, South Carolina, Florida, Washington, Nebraska, Oregon, South Dakota, North Dakota, Montana, Utah, Idaho, Arizona, New Hampshire, Vermont, Delaware, Wyoming, and Nevada.

19. Ridley and Nolting (1941, 128–52). This does not include Washington, D.C., which was governed differently—through federal legislation. The early adoption of merit rules by larger cities follows the pattern for state governments, with smaller cities adopting civil service later. Many smaller urban areas adopted merit reforms in response to New Deal requirements between 1930 and 1940. Also, the percentage of cities with no civil service system increases as size declines. Among the smaller cities in the size category 25,000–50,000, 37 percent had no merit system by 1941. In an examination of the characteristics of cities that adopted civil service coverage for their employees, using 1963 *Municipal Year Book* data, Wolfinger and Field (1966, 321–22) find a strong positive relation between a city's size and the likelihood that its municipal employees will be under civil service rules.

20. Wiebe (1967, 4–5) and Griffith (1974a, 15, 98, 269–70) argue that civil service reform spread from the federal government to the major cities, where patronage was associated with corruption and inefficiency. The call for greater efficiency was at the center of urban reform efforts between 1870 and 1900. Competition among cities required greater efficiency than that which could be provided through patronage—lower taxes, better services, professional police and fire protection, sanitation, and transit services. The efforts of early reformers to improve government efficiency through the removal of bosses, machines, and patronage is discussed by Greenstein (1964). Tolbert and Zucker (1983, 23) summarize other reasons for the adoption of civil service reforms.

21. There was well-developed trade among the regions, as described by North (1961). Nevertheless, the post–Civil War period was one of gradual integration of regional economies. For discussion, see Davis (1971) and Snowden (1990).

22. Kolbe (1985, 16) describes how local areas tended to be dominated by single parties, whose organization catered to the special interests of that region.

23. For discussion, see Higgs (1971), James (1983), and Atack (1985).

24. For discussion, see Libecap (1992) and Gilligan, Marshall, and Weingast (1989). Kolbe (1985, 44–56) claims that, prior to the Civil War, the dominant political class was made up of small, independent farmers, to whom the parties catered. After the Civil War, business entrepreneurs became the dominant class, and their interests controlled the Republican party and politics during the period 1864–96.

25. Shepsle and Weingast (1984) develop a model that emphasizes the geographic basis of political representation. From that they argue that the parochial interests of individual legislators will lead them to support policies that concentrate benefits in their districts and that make costs more general. This is the type of problem increasingly faced by the president and members of Congress as their interests began to diverge from those of the local party machine (see also McCubbins, Noll, and Weingast 1989).

26. For discussion of the shift to more national political parties in the late nineteenth century, see also Stewart (1989, 60).

27. See Alexander (1971), Overacker (1932), and Thayer (1973). Overacker (1932, 32, 71) provides a discussion of the rise in importance of alternative sources of campaign funds. Similarly, Alexander (1971, 3382–86) describes the cultivation and collection of funds from various business groups by the Finance Committees of the Democratic and Republican parties in the late nineteenth century.

28. Rusk (1974, 1029–35) discusses the adoption of the Australian ballot and regis-

tration reform. Prior to the secret ballot, parties printed ballots, distributed them to voters, and monitored the results. This allowed them to ensure that the party faithful voted as they were instructed. With the secret ballot, however, whereby neutral ballots were provided by the government and voting was private, parties could no longer police voting behavior as effectively. The urban states that were in the forefront of federal civil service reform were also the leaders in the adoption of the Australian ballot (see also Rusk 1970; and Walker 1969).

29. The growing pressure by interest groups on the federal government to provide services of various kinds is described by Becker (1982) and Kolko (1963). Skowronek (1982, 47) views civil service reform as a hallmark of the modern state, where government employees have tenure, are politically neutral, are hired on the basis of merit, and operate under uniform rules for promotion, discipline, and remuneration.

30. For discussion, see Van Riper (1958, 78–92).

31. Although some researchers have argued that ideology is a major factor in roll-call voting, Peltzman's (1984) results indicate that the characteristics of a legislator's constituents, plus campaign contributions, explain roll-call voting behavior. The link between constituent interests and roll-call voting is also made by Fiorina (1974, 1–43) and Cain, Ferejohn, and Fiorina (1987, 3).

32. See, e.g., Mayhew (1974a), Mueller (1989, 207), and Fiorina (1974, 35). Although reelection may not be the objective of every politician, as we show in the text, most members of the House in the late nineteenth century did seek reelection. The desire to obtain popular support or approval from their respective constituencies can induce elected officials to behave as if they were vote maximizers, seeking reelection. In support of this characterization of legislator and voter behavior, we note that there is empirical evidence indicating that, even in their last terms in office, members of Congress who have announced their pending retirement do not significantly alter their voting record (Lott and Bronars 1993).

33. For discussion of the professionalization of Congress, see Polsby (1968), who examines the rise of incumbency in the U.S. House of Representatives from 1789 to 1965, and Garand and Gross (1984), who extend the analysis through 1980. Mayhew (1974b), Fiorina (1977), Ferejohn (1977), and Hibbing (1991), among others, examine the rise in reelection rates in the twentieth century. Stewart (1989, 53–63) argues that reelection was a motivation for late nineteenth-century politicians.

34. The *Biographical Directory of the American Congress, 1774–1971* (1971, 218–22) lists those members of the House who were incumbents in December 1880, and the *Congressional Quarterly's Guide to U.S. Elections* (1985, 798–801) lists election results for 1880. It is possible to match those who ran in the election with their status in the House to determine who sought reelection. Of the 217 who sought reelection, 188 were reelected. Of the remaining 105 members, seventy-six did not run, and twenty-nine were defeated. With 293 members, the turnover rate was 35.84 percent. A similar procedure, using the *Biographical Directory of the United States Congress: 1774–1989* (1989, 215–22) and the *Guide to U.S. Elections* (1985, 802–5), indicates that 179 members sought reelection in 1882. This is 61 percent of the original 293 members of the House. (After the 1880 census, thirty-two seats were added for the incoming Forty-eighth Congress in 1883.) Of those 179, 135 were successful, and forty-four lost (114 did not seek reelection), giving a turnover rate for the original 293 seats of 53.9 percent.

35. Some senators, such as Roscoe Conkling of New York, were heavily dependent on the local party for support and were noted as spoilsmen (Van Riper 1958, 76). As we will show, others, like Senator Warren Miller, also of New York, recognized the problems of patronage for the electoral success of their party.

36. With the continued growth of the patronage pool, the president would eventually be faced with a problem similar to that portrayed by Coase (1972). In his example, a

monopolist is interested in finding a credible way to reduce the total stock of a durable good in order to assure that the quantity transacted maximizes total revenue. Coase assumes that a single individual owns a substantial block of land, e.g., all the land in the United States. Given a negatively sloped demand curve, the owner would maximize sales revenues where marginal revenue was equal to zero. But, if the stock of land exceeds the quantity at which marginal revenue was equal to zero, the owner would be confronted with the problem of trying to remove part of the stock from the marketplace, else the price will fall to the competitive level. Coase suggests that one possible way to accomplish this is for the owner to donate the "excess" land to the government, designating it for some restricted use. His basic message is that it is difficult to restrict the quantity sold, especially when one is dealing with a given stock. Where the monopolist has complete control over the output of a durable good, it is unlikely that the price will fall to the competitive level (see Bagnoli, Salant, and Swierzbinski 1989).

37. See, e.g., Van Riper's (1958, 232–33) account of President Wilson's efforts to manage patronage appointments in the postal service personally. Wilson quickly discovered the enormity of the task and ended up delegating the selection process.

38. U.S. House of Representatives (1976, 106) notes numerous complaints about the ineffectiveness of these earlier testing schemes.

39. The monitoring and performance problems associated with patronage were most severe in urban areas, which had the greatest concentrations of patronage employees and the most entrenched party machines. In those cities, the allegiance of patronage workers in the post offices and customhouses was most often with the local party boss. It is not surprising, then, that federal politicians from urban areas experienced the greatest loss of control over their appointees. Further, these were the same areas where constituents were demanding improvements in the quality of federal services. Hence, the very strength of the local urban machine provided the motivation for a vote-maximizing federal politician to break with the local party and support a reduction in patronage. This particular argument is presented more formally in app. A.

40. Hoogenboom (1968, 10). Senator Charles Sumner of Massachusetts introduced legislation for the establishment of a merit system in 1864, but it did not go far.

41. While there are differences in the way the British and U.S. civil service systems developed, there are also important similarities. Prior to 1850, patronage was the means for staffing the British bureaucracy. There were numerous disputes over the rights to appointments and mismanagement that attracted public attention. Reform occurred during the Victorian era, a time when the size of the British government was expanding. See, e.g., the account by Gladden (1967).

42. Dorman's *Civil Service* is discussed in Skowronek (1982, 48) and Van Riper (1958, 82–85).

43. For discussion of the actions of the first federal Civil Service Commission, see Van Riper (1958, 68–71).

44. For discussion of the political campaign, see Sageser (1935, 48–53) and Van Riper (1958, 89–94). In senate hearings, Pendleton stressed the costs of patronage and its impact on the functioning of government. He linked the growth of government to the downfall of patronage and went on to describe the effect on the president and the Congress. For example, he claimed that "the Executive Mansion is besieged, if not sacked, and its corridors and chambers are crowded each day with the ever-changing, but neverending, throng" (U.S. Senate, "Report," 1882, 2).

45. The final votes appear in the *Congressional Record,* 47th Cong., 2d sess., pp. 661 (Senate), 867 (House). Discussion is provided in Sageser (1935, 57–59).

46. For discussion of this point, see Skowronek (1982, 69).

47. Section 11 of the Pendleton Act prohibited any member of Congress, the judiciary, or the executive office from soliciting or receiving "any assessment, subscription,

or contribution for any political purpose whatever." Section 13 enjoined the use of threats of discharge, demotion, or, alternatively, promotion to solicit funds "or other valuable thing for any political purpose"; sec. 14 prohibited the granting of money or other services by federal employees for "the promotion of any political object"; and sec. 15 levied penalties for violation of these provisions of a $5,000 fine and/or imprisonment of three years.

48. Party affiliations were obtained by using the *Congressional Quarterly's Guide to U.S. Elections* (1985) and the *Biographical Directory of the United States Congress: 1774–1989* (1989).

49. Information on pairings and positions was obtained from the *Congressional Record,* 47th Cong., 2d sess., 1882, pp. 867–68.

50. Likelihood ratio tests of whether the contribution of the composite regression is significantly different from zero are also reported for each equation in table 2.3.

51. On the procedure for evaluating the derivatives of the probabilities in logit models, see Maddala (1983, 23).

52. Essentially, this is the hypothesis advanced by Van Riper (1958).

53. In explaining the shift to merit, we emphasize organizational size and the problems facing politicians of managing the patronage labor force as its numbers increased. This view is supported by the statistical results in table 2.3. The historical literature on civil service reform, however, focuses on exogenous factors, the role of reform groups in urban areas who pressured Congress to adopt merit. As a partial test of this competing hypothesis, we replaced the customhouse/post office variable in eqq (1) and (2) with an urbanization variable, which took the value of one if the representative's district was in one of the fifty largest cities in the United States. Urbanization increases the probability of voting in favor of the Pendleton Act, but comparisons of the log of the likelihood functions of the two specifications indicate that the presence of a customs or postal installation explicitly targeted by the Pendleton Act in a representative's district is a better predictor of voting than is the urbanization variable. It should also be noted that a number of large post offices and customhouses were not located within one of the fifty largest cities in 1880: Portland (Maine), Burlington (Vermont), Port Huron (Michigan), and Kansas City. For discussion, see Johnson and Libecap (1994).

54. This result is consistent with Lott and Bronars's (1993) analysis showing that members of Congress who have announced their pending retirement do not alter their votes from their historical voting patterns.

55. As an additional test of our key variable, post office/customhouse, we applied the same specification reported in table 2.3 to the House vote on the Jenckes bill. The results are as follows:

Variable		Variable	
Post office/customhouse	1.03	Lame duck	.13
	(2.07)		(.35)
Democrat	−.80	Years in office	.08
	(−1.62)		(1.00)
Other	−.52	Constant	−.38
	(−.85)		(−.91)
Southern Democrat	−.73	Log-likelihood function	−89.67
	(−.61)		

(*Source:* The vote is recorded in *Congressional Globe,* 39th Cong., 2d sess., 1867, pp. 1034–36. Other variables are taken from the *Congressional Quarterly's Guide to U.S. Elections* [1985] and the *Biographical Directory of the United States Congress: 1774–*

1989 [1989]. *Note:* Asymptotic *t*-ratios are in parentheses.) The vote on the Jenckes bill occurred in 1867, at a time when the House was dominated by Republicans. Thus, this can explain why party membership is not statistically significant in the above logit model. On the other hand, the coefficient on the post office/customhouse variable is positive and significantly different from zero. This result further supports our contention that organization size and problems of managing a growing patronage labor force were instrumental in fostering institutional change.

56. Stewart is interested, not specifically in patronage, but in broader budget and appropriations issues.

57. Wilson (1989) discusses pork barrel exchanges, but he is interested in the distribution of the pork to explain the broad coalitions that arose to support it. His tests support the notion of *universalism.* Stewart (1989, 89–98) also examines support for river and harbor legislation and water projects as part of his analysis of the budgeting process.

58. U.S. Department of Commerce (1975, 1104). Stewart (1989, 69) notes that there were "embarrassingly large surpluses" in the 1880s.

3 The Continuing Political Conflict over Control of Federal Employees and the Requirement for Further Institutional Change

3.1 Introduction

In 1884, slightly over 10 percent of the total federal civilian labor force of 131,208 were within the classified or competitive service (U.S. House of Representatives 1976, 305). By 1921, however, the federal labor force was much larger, with 562,252 employees, and 80 percent were in the classified civil service. In this chapter, we examine the extension of the merit service to most federal civilian employees, the granting of job tenure, and the adoption of requirements for political neutrality. We show that the expansion of the merit system was due principally to actions of the president, as authorized by the Pendleton Act (22 Stat. 403), although there was general support in Congress. The central role of the president is consistent with the arguments that we developed in chapter 2. Not only was the president the most national of all politicians and, thereby, the most likely to be identified by angry voters with patronage and poor performance by federal workers, but controlling the size of the patronage pool was necessary to allow the president to maximize the returns from trading patronage appointments with members of Congress for support on policy issues.

Additionally, we argue that provisions in the civil service system for job tenure and political neutrality, added gradually after the Pendleton Act was passed, were directed efforts by the president and the Congress to reduce costly competition over and manipulation of classified federal employees. Recall that, when the Pendleton Act was passed, the immediate concern of the president and the Congress was to weaken the authority of local party officials and to reduce the costs of ensuring that the growing federal labor force was responsive to the demands of influential constituents for government services. The structure of the new civil service that formally partitioned the labor force between patronage and merit employees responded to that initial concern. Once the civil service was established, however, problems arose because members of Congress sought control over federal employees. Demands were made on classified workers to engage in partisan activities under threat of dismissal. Additionally, pressures were placed on the president to declassify merit positions, returning them to the spoils system and direct use by politicians. In order to maintain the benefits of the new institutional structure put into place by the Pendleton Act, job-tenure guarantees and requirements for political neutrality were incorporated into civil service rules.

Through the process of extending the merit system to nonclassified employees and incremental adjustments in the civil service system, the move away from patronage was made more and more complete. While patronage employees were assets who facilitated political exchange, under the emerging civil service system federal workers were removed gradually from the competitive, political arena. By 1940, as a result of this process of incremental institution building, the federal civilian workforce could not be hired or fired at the will of politicians, nor could it be used explicitly to promote political campaigns. In fewer than sixty years, the conversion from the old patronage system to an insulated, ostensibly politically neutral civil service was achieved.

As we discussed in chapter 2, the notion that the inauguration and extension of the civil service system were in the interest of vote-maximizing federal politicians contrasts with more standard views of the origins of the classified service.[1] In addition to stressing the role of reformists, these views emphasize immediate political considerations—the desire of Republicans, first, to placate reformers and to deny Democrats access to the spoils after the election of 1884 and, second, to "blanket in" the party faithful in their federal jobs, following the defeat of the incumbent president.[2] If these purely partisan goals had been the primary forces behind the Pendleton Act, then nothing much would have come of it. Had the subsequent expansion of patronage been of significant value to the president or to a substantial majority of the members of Congress, then repeal of the Pendleton Act or a general declassification of merit positions would have been likely, whenever either political party dominated both the White House and the Congress. But this did not happen. Efforts to repeal the Pendleton Act, especially in 1886, met with bipartisan resistance. Instead, the merit system was expanded and its provisions broadened. Hence, there was more at stake for federal politicians in extending the merit system than merely limiting the access of their political competitors to the spoils.

The president, in particular, had an interest in controlling the size of the patronage workforce. Not only did he suffer because of a lack of performance by patronage workers, but, as shown in appendix B, he also had an incentive to manage the number of patronage workers in order to enhance their value. In general, Congress was supportive. Even so, the position of members of Congress on the issue was more complex than that of the president. The preferences of members of the Congress on the optimal number of appointees could be expected to vary, sometimes substantially. For example, preferences were likely to differ along party lines. The Constitution granted the president appointment power, and delegation of appointments by the president to members of Congress in exchange for support on legislation was usually restricted to members of the president's party. As Senator Pendleton stated during the debate over civil service reform, "The Republican party has at this time, in round numbers, 110,000 officers and employees under their control, and there are scarcely any Democrats. When I have presented at one of the Departments the name of a person from my State for appointment, the first question which I am most frequently met is, 'Is he a Democrat?' If so, that seals his fate of course" (*Congressional Record*, 47th Cong., 2d sess., 11 December 1882, p. 173).

Even as Congress in general desired limits on the growth of patronage after the Civil War, the phrase "to the victor go the spoils" suggests that support for restrictions on patronage at any point in time would vary between those whose party occupied the White House, the "ins," and those whose party did not, the "outs."[3] The House vote on the Pendleton Act, examined in chapter 2, shows the importance of the underlying pressures for civil service reform, with members whose districts had large customhouses or post offices voting in favor of the bill. Nevertheless, expecting to win congressional elections and the presidency in 1884, Democrats were more likely to have voted against the act than were Republicans.[4] After considering the effects of federal installations and other factors, it is likely that many Democrats did not want the limits on patronage authorized by the Pendleton Act until they had an opportunity to remove Republicans and to replace them with members of their own party. On the other hand, had Democrats not expected to win in the upcoming election, they might have desired even greater restrictions on patronage in order to limit the range of political appointments and assessments available to Republicans. Accordingly, controlling for expectations regarding success in future elections, it seems likely that congressional members from the president's party would be the demanders of patronage while those from the opposition would be more interested in restricting it. Moreover, within the president's party, it is likely that the majority of congressional members would prefer that a greater number of patronage positions be made available and the president fewer since he had to manage the overall patronage pool and therefore internalized more of the costs of patronage.

Although each member of Congress could be expected to compare the costs and benefits of expanding patronage, strict vote-maximizing behavior suggests that not all the costs of patronage would be internalized. Any scandal or inefficiency due to the actions of federal patronage workers would be more associated with the president than with individual members of Congress. As a consequence, we expect that the president would often be at odds with members of Congress from the same party over the size of the patronage pool and how coverage should be expanded in response to the growth of the federal labor force.

These issues were encountered as the president and the Congress grappled with patronage in the post–Civil War period. Clearly, the Pendleton Act of 1883 provided some relief, as it outlined a framework for improving the performance of federal employees and for making them less attractive targets for political manipulation. The act also established a bipartisan Civil Service Commission, its three commissioners (only two could be from the same party) appointed by the president with the consent of the Senate. The commission was authorized to select a chief examiner and establish local boards for drafting and administering exams for the classified service. The boards were to forward the names of those who passed with the highest scores to agencies for selection. Under the "Rule of Three," the three applicants who performed best were sent to the appointment officer for consideration.[5] The early exams tested basic practical knowledge, and 58 percent of those tested in 1884 achieved the required passing rate of 65 percent (U. S. Civil Service Commission, *Annual Report*, 1884, 67). With selection based more on merit than on base political considerations, members of the classified service could devote more time to providing government services than to performing duties for the party and political benefactors.

Despite these initial changes, the separation of classified employees from partisan activities was not complete. Classified employees remained free to participate in political campaigns and to make voluntary contributions. These employees were still of value to local politicians and members of Congress, and there remained ample ground for costly competition among politicians over their control and use. As before, those members of Congress who particularly valued the classified service could not withdraw unilaterally from the competition for federal workers. The positions would be secured by those who remained active in the spoils system, unless they were denied to all. In addition, as the size of the classified labor force grew relative to the number of patronage positions, the pressure on the president by party members to declassify merit employees increased. If the president had routinely caved in to such demands, the survival of the merit service would have been put into question. Moreover, the ability of the president to limit the number of patronage workers would have been weakened. To preserve the advantages offered by the merit service, both tenure provisions to reduce the use of threats of dismissal as a means of manipulation and requirements for political neutrality to reduce the value of federal employees for partisan purposes were gradually incorporated into civil service rules through actions of the president and the Congress.

Job tenure became a critical element for removing federal employees from the competitive political arena. Tenure had *not* been granted to members of the new classified service by the Pendleton Act: "This bill does not touch the questions of tenure of office, or removals from office, except that removals shall not be made for refusing to pay political assessments or to perform partisan service. It leaves both where it finds them" (U.S. Senate, "Report," 1882, ix). In part, the absence of tenure provisions in the law was due to a desire of members of Congress to avoid the formation of an "elite" civil service. Past government positions that had been filled through patronage had been temporary ones.[6] Hence, initially under the Pendleton Act, the employment of classified workers remained subject to the wishes of the president and their supervisors. An individual's position could be declassified, merit workers could be fired, and appeals were limited.

It soon became obvious to the president, however, that at least some tenure protections were necessary to reduce the pressures to expand patronage. Without provisions for limited job security, positions could be removed from the classified service by the president and returned to patronage. The ability to discharge employees so readily invited constant demands to declassify positions, especially following a change in the party controlling the White House. With newly acquired access to appointments, members of Congress with pent-up demand for patronage called for the removal of previous classified workers in order to respond to the claims of their constituents.

Congress also had another reason for providing some form of job security to classified employees. The president, cabinet members, and agency heads had more direct access to classified workers in the executive branch than did most members of Congress. As such, merit workers could be pressured by their supervisors to respond to the desires of the administration under penalty of removal, even if those actions were opposed by Congress. Hence, job security would also serve to limit manipulation of classified employees by the president. Once adopted, however, tenure provisions represented a marked change in the organization of the federal labor force from previous patronage practices.

An additional requirement for limiting costly competition over federal employees that represented another major change from patronage was political neutrality. To further reduce the incentive of politicians to compete for and manipulate classified federal workers and to allow them to focus on the provision of federal government services, political neutrality became a sought-after attribute for the civil service system. In 1907, civil service rules were explicitly expanded to prohibit classified employees from taking an active part in political campaigns.[7] With the passage of the first Hatch Act in 1939, this prohibition was extended to all rank-and-file federal workers, whether or not they were in the classified service. The broad coverage mandated by the Hatch Act was in response to problems that arose in controlling the political activities of patronage workers and their supervisors following a substantial expansion of patronage positions by the Roosevelt administration in the early 1930s. A directive that federal employees be neutral parties, impartial suppliers of federal services, and not directly involved in political campaigns was a notion that could not have been anticipated by Jacksonian politicians prior to the Civil War.

3.2   Efforts to Repeal the Pendleton Act

If short-term partisan considerations had been dominant in the enactment of the Pendleton Act, the law could have been repealed at any time, especially after a change in the party that controlled the presidency and the Congress, to allow for the expansion of patronage. When the Democrats won control of the House in 1886, there was considerable pressure on President Cleveland from party members to provide patronage jobs to reward their victory. As part of that movement, Senator Zebulon Vance, a Democrat from North Carolina, introduced a bill (S. 839) in January 1886 to repeal the Pendleton Act.[8] Vance charged that the Pendleton Act had been passed by Republicans to "perpetuate the official existence of [that party's] friends" in their government jobs (*Congressional Record,* 49th Cong., 1st sess., 31 March 1886, p. 2945). Vance argued that the law restricted the prerogatives of the new administration and that it weakened the party that was the vehicle for promoting the popular will. Every citizen was qualified, according to Vance, to hold any office: "There are one million American citizens competent to fill it [a vacant office]. Each has the right to apply for it equal in law to the right of any other man. Each has the right to go directly, without hindrance, to the appointing power. But the civil-service law says, not so: no one shall be appointed, no one's application shall be considered" (*Congressional Record,* 49th Cong., 1st sess., 31 March 1886, p. 2946).

Through repeal of the Pendleton Act, Vance wanted to return the federal civil service to patronage and hence open it to Democratic nominees. The repeal, however, was defeated on 18 June 1886 by a bipartisan vote of 33 to 6 (with thirty-seven abstentions) in the Senate. Thirty-one percent of the Democrats and 59 percent of the Republicans voted against the repeal; only 14 percent of the Republicans voted against the repeal; only 14 percent of the Democrats voted for it.[9] Even though Vance framed his bill as an effort to support Democrats in federal jobs, most of his Democratic colleagues failed to vote for the return of patronage. Republicans regained the White House and control of Congress in the elections of 1888, and the Democrats did so after the 1892 elections. Nevertheless, in these and other cases of one-party domination of both branches of government, when repeal of the Pendleton Act might have been possible, no serious efforts were initiated. While there were eight additional bills, sponsored by both Republicans and Democrats, introduced to repeal the Pendleton Act, none made it out of committee (Sageser 1935, 164). Most of the lingering opposition to the classified service came, not from federal politicians, but from low-level party officials, who were most affected by the loss of patronage (U.S. Civil Service Commission, *Annual Report,* 1886, 20, 60–61).

3.3 The President and the Extension of the Merit Service

3.3.1 Extension of the Classified Civil Service

The failure of efforts to repeal the Pendleton Act is important evidence because it shows that, collectively, members of Congress supported the concept of placing a segment of the federal workforce outside the patronage system and its narrow partisan uses. Yet, to varying degrees, each member had an incentive to continue to obtain and distribute patronage appointments while constraining similar actions by others. On the other hand, with the broadest national constituencies, with the most remote ties to local party machines, and as the most likely to be judged by voters for the overall performance of government, the president was in less of a position to free ride on the patronage system in the ways available to individual members of Congress. Accordingly, he should be the most avid supporter of the merit system and take a lead in extending it. The motives of the president in expanding the merit system to confine the size of the patronage pool are outlined in appendix B.

As a group, the Congress also had an incentive to expand the merit system in response to the growth of the federal labor force. For those who were members of the president's party, there was the continuing problem of managing the actions of patronage workers and local party officials in providing government services. Without at least a commensurate increase in the number of merit employees as the federal labor force grew, the patronage portion would have increased, intensifying the problems of control.

To extend the merit service, Congress would desire a relatively uncontroversial mechanism. One option was to grant the Civil Service Commission the authority to extend merit classifications to patronage positions. Another was to vote on the size of the merit service periodically. Neither of these options was adopted. Congress was reluctant to give the Civil Service Commission the authority to control the number of patronage positions. Disagreements between the commission and the Congress would have invited denials of funding and threatened the administration of the entire merit service. Periodic congressional votes on coverage had the risk of inviting pressure from local party officials to expand patronage. Moreover, if the opposition party controlled both houses of Congress, the outcome could have resulted in less patronage being made available than was desired by the president, inviting a veto. A third option, which avoided these conflicts, was to provide for the automatic expansion of the classified system as the federal labor force grew. Indeed, section 6 of the Pendleton Act required that positions in the customs and postal services be added to the classified service whenever a facility reached a staff size of fifty. In 1894, employees in customhouses and post offices with staffs of twenty or greater were added to the classified service, and the limit was further reduced to include customhouses with staffs of five in 1896 (U.S. Civil Service Commission, *Annual Reports,* 1894, 233, and 1897, 16–19).

Congress, however, through a provision of the Pendleton Act, relied on another method for extending the merit service. The primary solution adopted by Congress to the problem of determining the size of the patronage pool in the face of changing conditions was to assign authority to extend the merit system to the president.[10] Section 6 of the Pendleton Act gave the president the authority to classify positions within the executive department through executive orders and rules revisions drafted by department heads.

The granting of authority to expand the classified service to the president appears to have been a cost-effective measure. At any point in time, congressional action to extend merit classification to a particular class of positions was likely to have involved partisan debate and resistance. Although the merit system provided group benefits, individual members of Congress were under pressure to deliver patronage assignments to their supporters. Moreover, given expectations regarding winning the presidential election, some members of Congress would have incentives to resist new merit classifications in order to have access to patronage should their candidate be successful. Assigning authority to the president to extend the classified service avoided these contentious debates and allowed for controls on the number of patronage employees. Further, the delegation of classification authority served to preserve the implicit agreement in the Pendleton Act to limit congressional competition over obtaining patronage.[11] So long as the president's preferences were relatively close to that of the median member in Congress, the legislation would be preserved and conflict over the amount of patronage reduced.

The concern about potential congressional conflict over the expansion of merit classification was likely tied to the close balance that existed between the political parties at the time that the Pendleton Act was enacted in January 1883. The Senate was evenly divided between Republicans and Democrats, with the Republicans holding a slight advantage in the House.[12] Because of the results of the 1882 elections, it was known that the advantage in the House would shift to the Democrats in the next session of Congress and that the Republicans would have a two-seat advantage in the Senate. In the face of this balance in Congress and the uncertainty as to which party would occupy the White House after the elections of 1884, neither political party was interested in doing away with patronage entirely. After the presidential election, when it was clear as to who had won the White House, members of Congress from the in-coming president's party would most likely prefer an expansion of patronage. But the president, who had broader concerns, was likely to resist those demands.[13]

Once having given the president the authority to expand the merit system, members of Congress would be expected to act in their own self-interest and to seek selective increases in patronage. Because certain members of Congress benefited relatively more from patronage than did the president, the extension of the merit system through executive orders would not always go smoothly, and there would be demands on the president for declassification. Despite these pressures and the associated costs of bargaining with the Congress over the number of patronage workers, the president was motivated to take the lead in promoting the merit system and, thereby, limiting patronage. Indeed, it was not until 1935 that Congress passed legislation to add any significant number of positions to the classified service.[14] As shown in table 3.1, nearly 65 percent of the growth of the merit service between 1884 and 1903 was through executive orders by the president, with the remainder due to agency growth.[15]

In classifying positions, the president had to balance political benefits and costs. Patronage assignments, especially to the numerous fourth-class post-masterships (76,000 in 1896), remained valuable political assets (Skowronek 1982, 72). Fourth-class postmasterships were part-time positions in almost every town and village in the country, and giving them to political supporters throughout the politician's district was an effective way of rewarding those who had contributed to campaigns. Since the duties of fourth-class postmasters were limited, the risks of charges of scandal, ineptness, or lack of attention to which the postmasters' patrons would be exposed were slight. The control of these positions was therefore strongly desired by members of Congress.

The political pressures placed on each president by party officials for access to the spoils are illustrated by the experiences of the Cleveland, Harrison, Mc-Kinley, and Wilson administrations, which represented changes in the party controlling the White House. When Cleveland took office in 1885, it was the first time that the Democrats had captured the presidency in twenty-five years. With such a long dry spell, Democratic members of Congress and local party officials were naturally anxious to secure the patronage positions so long held by Republicans (Fowler 1943, 192). Since at that time the classified service was such a small portion of the overall federal labor force, it was little affected by the reallocation of the spoils. Nevertheless, Cleveland had to ward off demands from members of Congress to make some of the existing classifed positions, as well as patronage appointments, available to Democrats. There was a near revolt among the Democratic ranks at Cleveland's refusal to dump Republican officeholders and replace them with Democratic stalwarts (Sageser 1935, 114–15).

The time costs for the president in reviewing the hoards of office seekers were great: "Secretary of State Thomas F. Bayard reported on March 13, 1885, that the crowds of office-seekers were greater than in 1881. . . . No President since the Civil War had ever given such close personal attention to the applications for appointments" (Sageser 1935, 84). Cleveland found these pressures a burden and a diversion from public affairs that needed consideration. He also assured the National Civil Service Reform League that the Pendleton Act would be enforced, that Republicans in the classified service would not be removed, and that Democrats would not be added to the ranks purely for partisan reasons (Sageser 1935, 79–83).

During Cleveland's first administration, the size of the classified service more than doubled through executive orders and the growth of facilities already covered by provisions of the Pendleton Act. The largest addition was the classification of the Railway Mail Service by executive order, which added 5,320 positions to the classifed service. The Railway Mail Service was a hotbed of political scandal that embarrassed the president (Sageser 1935, 104–7). When the Republican Harrison took office in 1889, the party was ready to reassert control over appointments, but, as with Cleveland, Harrison resisted. He declared that he would review the recommendations and require that each office seeker demonstrate efficiency in the discharge of official duties. He also stressed that he would enforce the Pendleton Act and extend its coverage (Sageser 1935, 130–31).

The demands on Congress also were severe: "Hordes of men streamed to the capital, and, seeking out their Senators or Representatives, they pressed for rewards. . . . Local pressure was strong. . . . Cabinet offices were so crowded with Senators, congressmen, and their secretaries that it was impossible to get anybody's attention on a business matter" (Sageser 1935, 132–33). In response, Congress attempted to gain more control over the allocation of patronage by withholding appropriations for the Civil Service Commission from time to time. Even so, as indicated in table 3.1, the classified service grew by 39 percent during Harrison's administration, and 82 percent of the growth was through executive orders in agencies, such as the Indian Service, the Fish Commission, and Weather Bureau, and 548 free delivery post offices with 7,610 positions (Sageser 1935, 158–62; Skowronek 1982, 70–71).

Similar pressures were exerted on President Cleveland during his second term in office. In the Congress, the Democrats demanded that the White House remove additions to the classifed service made by the previous administration. Indeed, Cleveland commented that his party members were "heedless of the burdens and responsibilities of the incoming administration and of the duty our party owes to the people" (quoted in Sageser 1935, 185). Through executive orders between 1894 and 1896, Cleveland added 10,396 positions in the Indian Service, the Departments of Agriculture, the Interior, and the Post Office, the Internal Revenue Service, and the Government Printing Office as well as creating other merit positions. Moreover, through a revision of civil service rules approved by the president, 27,052 positions were added in the Treasury, Interior, and War Departments (Skowronek 1982, 70–71; Sageser 1935, 197–200). By the end of Cleveland's second administration, the classified service covered over 45 percent of all federal civilian positions, reducing the available patronage slots. This meant that, when McKinley took office, there was to be more serious pressure from Republican politicians for declassification, and McKinley did remove 9,185 of the positions added by Cleveland (Skowronek 1982, 71; Sageser 1935, 217–20). Despite this, the overall number of classified positions actually grew by 10,361 during McKinley's administration to 97,405, including 1,715 added through executive order. From McKinley's assassination in 1901 to the end of his second term in 1903, the presidency was assumed by Theodore Roosevelt, under whom 8,391 positions were added in the Rural Free Delivery Service and other departments through executive orders and rules revisions. By the end of 1903, the classified service included 108,000 positions, out of a total civilian federal labor force of 301,000 (See U. S. House of Representatives 1976, 305; and table 3.1).

When Woodrow Wilson assumed the presidency in 1913, the Democrats had been without access to the spoils since 1897. Although the number of classified positions had grown by 225 percent from 87,044 in 1897 to 282,597

Table 3.1   Sources of Growth of the Classified Service, 1884–1913

President	Classified Service	Federal Civilian Employment
Arthur (R), 1881–85:		
Pendleton Act	13,924	
Executive order	1,449	
Agency growth	200	
Total	15,573	131,208
Cleveland (D), 1885–89:		
Executive order	7,259	
Agency growth	4,498	
Total	27,330	159,936
Harrison (R), 1889–93:		
Executive order	8,690	
Agency growth	1,845	
Total	37,865	176,000
Cleveland (D), 1893–97:		
Executive order	42,511	
Agency growth	6,668	
Total	87,044	192,000
McKinley (R), 1897–1901:		
Executive order	1,715	
Agency growth	17,831	
Declassification	−9,185	
Total	97,405	256,000
Roosevelt (R), 1901–3:[a]		
Executive order	8,391	
Agency growth	538	
Congressional act	1,687	
Total	108,021	301,000
Roosevelt (R), 1903–9:		
Executive order	21,583	
Agency growth	105,336	
Total	234,940	376,794
Taft (R), 1909–13:		
Executive order	40,236	
Agency growth	7,421	
Total	282,597	469,879

Sources and notes: Classified Service data for the Arthur, Cleveland, McKinley, and first Roosevelt administrations are from Sageser (1935, 68, 107, 162, 199, 231) and Skowronek (1982, 70–71). For the second Roosevelt and Taft administrations, the data are from U.S. House of Representatives (1976, 207, 213). The data through the first Roosevelt administration represent the size of the classified service due to executive orders, agency growth, and congressional acts as of March 1885, 1889, 1893, 1897, 1901, and 1903. The totals are the sums from each of the categories. Since these totals represent March data for the last year that the president was in office, they differ slightly from those provided for the end of the year in U.S. House of Representatives (1976, 305), which are as follows: 1885, 15, 590; 1889, 29,650; 1897, 85,886; 1901, 106,205; and 1903, 135,453. March totals for the classified service and agency growth data are not available for the second Roosevelt administration or for McKinley. For those two administrations, the totals are for the end of the year as provided by U.S. House of Representatives (1976, 305): 1909, 234,940;

Table 3.1   (continued)

and 1913, 282,597. The contributions to the civil service due to agency growth were taken as the changes in the total classified service from 1903 and 1909 and from 1909 and 1913, less the additions due to executive orders, as documented in U.S. House of Representatives (1976, 207, 213). Agency growth includes the creation of some new agencies, such as the Food and Drug Administration. The additions to the classified service through executive orders include actions taken by department heads and civil service rules revisions to extend the classified service during the Arthur, Cleveland, and first Roosevelt administrations. These were initiated by the president. See, e.g., Sageser (1935, 62, 67, 103, 199) and U.S. House of Representatives (1976, 208–11). Total federal civilian employment is from U.S. House of Representatives (1976, 305) for 1884 (1885 is not available), 1897, 1901, 1903, 1909, 1913. Data for 1889 are from Sageser (1935, 107).
[a]The remainder of McKinley's term.

in 1913, the number of available patronage slots had grown by only 78 percent from 104,956 to 187,282.[16] Despite demands to reclassify some of the merit service to satisfy calls for patronage from Democrats, there were no major reclassifications of positions under Wilson, and the merit share of the federal labor force continued to increase. Wilson did, however, attempt tightly to control the assignment of the existing patronage slots by personally supervising the selection of applicants for each position. The task was too much, and Wilson was forced to delegate the responsibility of selecting and monitoring patronage assignments. This episode, like previous ones, illustrates the costs of managing an expanding patronage pool.[17]

Table 3.1 outlines the increase in the classified service by presidential administration between 1884 and 1913.[18] The table documents the important role of the president in expanding the size of the merit system after 1884. Figures 3.1 and 3.2 provide a longer-term perspective on the growth of the classified service. Figure 3.1 shows the expansion of the total federal labor force and patronage positions over the period 1884–1940. Notice that the absolute number of patronage employees (total civilian employment less merit employment) is relatively flat through 1917, suggesting that the president was comparatively successful in controlling the size of the patronage pool once the merit system was adopted. After the short blip that began in 1918, patronage levels remain steady and low through 1933, when they rise with the New Deal. Figure 3.2 describes the ratio of federal merit employment to total federal civilian employment from 1884 to 1940, and it reveals the incremental, although relatively steep, increase in the proportion of merit employment through 1921, where the proportion levels at approximately 80 percent. The proportion drops during the 1930s with the expansion of New Deal programs, which were often staffed by nonclassified employees. We consider this reversal when discussing the Hatch Act below.

3.3.2   Lame-Duck Additions and Party Dominance

Presidential executive orders to expand merit coverage could be used to accomplish a variety of objectives. The classification of positions in particular

Number of Employees (millions)

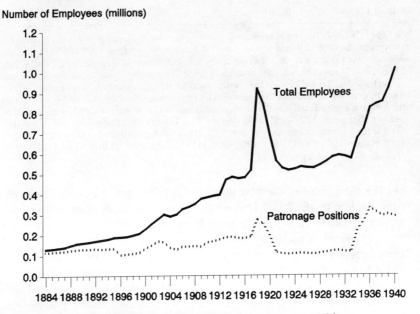

Fig. 3.1   Growth of total federal employment and patronage positions, 1884–1940.

Sources: The data on total federal civilian employment and the number of federal employees in the competitive service (classified) are from U.S. House of Representatives (1976, 305). However, data on total federal civilian employees for the years 1885–90, 1896, 1898, 1900, and 1902 were not reported. Estimates for these years were obtained using the *Annual Reports* of the U.S. Civil Service commission.

facilities or offices could improve productivity, and the qualitative evidence regarding the effects of the Pendleton Act presented in chapter 2 suggests that that was the case. Control of the number of patronage employees also gave the president greater power in negotiations with members of Congress over the exchange of appointments for support on policy issues.

A more commonly asserted goal of presidential extensions was to "blanket in" existing federal employees, not only to protect them under merit rules, but also to deny their patronage positions to political competitors.[19] Initially, this practice may have been relatively difficult because, under early Civil Service rules, incumbents in positions that had been recently classified could obtain merit status only if they passed a merit test and because promotion often required merit examinations.[20] President Cleveland, however, modified the rules in February 1888 to waive the requirement of merit testing of incumbents.[21] Accordingly, a president could classify positions in order to grant merit status to patronage appointees. Certainly, this procedure would allow a president to "blanket in" employees known to be loyal to the administration.

Although presidents did issue postelection executive orders to extend the classified service, we do not believe that this practice accounted for most of the growth of the merit system. Nor do we believe that blanketing in deserves as much emphasis as has been given to it in the historical literature. The focus on narrow partisan goals in extending the merit service diverts analysis from the fundamental problems facing the president in managing a large patronage labor force. There were a few dramatic cases of blanketing in, and these have received undue attention. We have stressed the incentives of politicians, especially those of the president, for limiting patronage. The analysis of voting on the Pendleton Act and the bipartisan rejection of efforts to repeal it indicate that the origins and extension of the merit service were due to factors beyond narrow, short-term partisan concerns with protecting party stalwarts. It is also important to note that, as discussed in more detail below, classified employees did not receive tenure under the terms of the Pendleton Act. Their positions could be declassifed, and they could be dismissed by the president. Substantial tenure protection did not come until after 1897. Hence, while postelection appointments might have provided some security to party workers, there was no long-term job guarantee once a new administration took office. At least at first, blanketing in certainly had the potential to be only temporary.

In addition, attempting to protect against future policy reversals by keeping the "right people" in the bureaucracy seemingly would have entailed merit protection from the president for high-level administrative positions. But merit status was not authorized by the Pendleton Act for the most senior officials in the bureaucracy. Finally, although the president was under intense pressure from party leaders to provide spoils, the White House typically resisted these

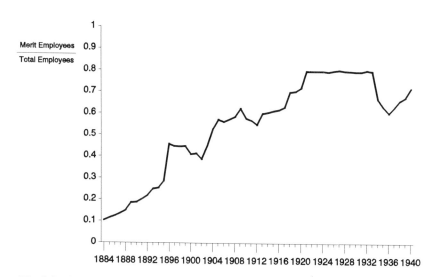

Fig. 3.2   **Proportion of merit to total federal civilian employees, 1884–1940.**
Sources: See fig. 3.1.

demands whenever possible and delayed in responding to them. The president did not want to lose control of the administrative framework of his administration to the spoils system. Indeed, a major aim of the president was to construct an executive-centered government, by controlling the number of patronage workers (Skowronek 1982, 180).

The actions of President Cleveland are good examples of presidential interests that were separate from those of party officials at the local level and of resistance to pressure brought to bear by members of Congress. On gaining office in 1885, Cleveland moved slowly in responding to the demands of Democratic party leaders to increase the availability of patronage appointments, preferring to meet and screen as many applicants as possible and thereby to maintain some control over the system. Further, his classification of 5,320 positions in the Railway Mail Service on 31 December, 1888, as he was leaving office, was as much in response to past embarrassment to the presidency from corruption and mismanagement in the service as to demands from the party. Indeed, there were other demands to save more Democrats, but Cleveland did not react to them. As with President Arthur before him, Cleveland did not want to jeopardize the merit system with extensive postelection expansions (U.S. House of Representatives 1976, 197). Moreover, with his administration on its way out of office, he could classify the Railway Mail Service and remove those positions from patronage access by local postmasters and other party officials, Democratic as well as Republican.[22] This action would ultimately strengthen the hand of the president by allowing him more control over federal workers and the administrative structure of the government.

Similarly, in December 1908, when Roosevelt hit at the heart of the remaining local patronage plums, fourth-class postmasterships, by placing them in the merit service, he did so in ways that added to presidential authority. He classifed 15,488 fourth-class postmasterships in fourteen states that had voted Republican in national contests in 1896, 1900, 1904, and 1908. These were in safe Republican areas, and their continuance as patronage served only to strengthen local party officials and the members of Congress tied to them. They did not serve the president, and they were removed from patronage. Postal patronage for the remaining fourth-class postmasterships in areas that could be successfully contested by Democrats were retained by Roosevelt for use by the incoming Republican president Taft. Taft classified 36,236 fourth-class postmasterships later in his administration (Skowronek 1982, 178–79; U.S. House of Representatives 1976, 207, 213).

Nevertheless, claims have been made that, during their last year in office, presidents responded to the demands of party leaders to classify the party faithful before the next administration took office and to reduce the ability of the incoming party to use those positions to generate political assessments (See Maranto and Schultz 1991, 62; Van Riper 1958, 117–20; U.S. House of Representatives 1976, 181–83). These have been referred to as "lame-duck" classifications.

Although postelection or lame-duck classifications were used from time to time in the first thirty years after the enactment of the Pendleton Act, the view that they were primarily a means by which presidents protected the party faithful ignores other, more critical factors in the growth of the merit system through executive orders. Generally, presidents appear to have used their authority to expand the classified service in order to enhance their authority and the effectiveness of the provision of government services to their national constituencies. In addition to being a response to more complex factors than is generally understood, lame-duck additions played a relatively smaller part in the overall development of the civil service system than is often believed. Consider the first thirty years of the merit service, when lame-duck classifications were most common. Table 3.2 describes the growth in the classifed service by presidential admistration from Arthur to Taft. As indicated in the table, lame-duck additions represented about 42 percent of all executive order classifications during the period, and they accounted for only about 20 percent of the total growth in the classified service. As the classifed service continued to grow in numbers and as a proportion of the total federal labor force, lame-duck additions played an even smaller role.

The conclusion that lame-duck additions did not play a dominant role in the expansion of the classifed service is further supported by regression analysis on the ratio of total classified to total federal civilian employees between 1884

Table 3.2   **Lame-Duck Additions to the Classified Service, 1884–1913**

President	Change in Total Classified Service	Additions Due to Executive Orders	Lame-Duck Additions
Arthur (R), 1881–85:	15,573	1,449	1,200
Cleveland (D), 1885–89:	11,757	7,259	5,320
Harrison (R), 1889–93:	10,535	8,690	7,924
Cleveland (D), 1893–97:	49,179	42,511	5,063
McKinley (R), 1897–1901:	10,361	1,715	. . .
Roosevelt (R), 1901–3:[a]	10,616	8,391	. . .
Roosevelt (R), 1903–9:	126,919	21,583	15,780
Taft (R), 1909–13:	47,657	40,236	20,000
Total	282,597	131,834	55,287

Sources and notes: Column 1 is the change in total classified service from one administration to the next, taken from table 3.1. Column 2 shows additions to the classified service through executive orders, taken from table 3.1. Column 3 shows lame-duck additions, which are those additions to the classified service made by the president from November of his last full year in office until the next March, when the new president assumed office. Lame-duck data are from Sageser (1935, 69, 106, 162, and 199) for the Arthur, Cleveland, and Harrison administrations. Lame-duck appointments for the Roosevelt and Taft administrations are from U.S. House of Representatives (1976, 207, 213, respectively). The 20,000 lame-duck additions shown for Taft were not additions to the total classified service since they had been given limited coverage earlier by Roosevelt. Taft placed them within the competitive, merit service (U.S. House of Representatives 1976, 213).
[a]The remainder of McKinley's term.

and 1940, when the modern civil service system was basically put in place. Because the problems of monitoring and controlling patronage workers are hypothesized to be linked to the size of the federal labor force, we expect that the ratio of merit to total employment will increase as the federal labor force expands (see app. B). Indeed, the classified service grew from 13,208 in 1883 to 726,827 in 1940, and, as shown in fig. 3.2 above, the proportion of classifed to total federal civilian employment increased rapidly. Table 3.3 describes regression results using the ratio of classified to total federal employees as the dependent variable. Since the ratio of merit to total employment cannot exceed unity, the specification is nonlinear, and we allow for a flexible functional form by including total employment, total employment squared, and total employment raised to the third power. The results reported for equation (1) reveal a close fit between the merit ratio and the total employment variables, with the merit proportion rising with increases in overall federal employment. While, given the plot in figure 3.2, this result is to be expected this specification makes it possible to do more to examine lame-duck appointments as an alternative explanation for the growth of the merit service.

Equations (2) and (3) in table 3.3 add variables to analyze the contribution of lame-duck additions to the growth of the classified service that are so emphasized in the literature. To test for the effects of these actions, we offer two additional specifications. In the first, three dummy variables that correspond to the first, second, and third years of each presidential term are included. The fourth year is the excluded category. If "blanketing-in frequently occurred near the end of an Administration" (U.S. House of Representatives 1976, 183), the three dummy variables should be significantly negative. The second specification focuses exclusively on the propensity of a lame-duck president about to be replaced by a member of the opposite party to blanket in patronage workers. Since presidential elections were held in the month of November and newly elected presidents took office the following year, a dummy variable was constructed that took the value of unity for both the year of the presidential election and the year immediately following a switch in the party controlling the White House. There were seven such switches in our data set.

Also included in these regression runs is a dummy variable to account for those situations when the majority party in the Senate and that in the House were the same as that of the president. If the shift to merit were strictly a partisan issue, as opposed to one involving the problems of labor management and control emphasized here, then, whenever a political party dominated both branches of government, there should be less incentive for the president and the Congress to give up patronage. This argument suggests that classifications would be more likely when political power was more evenly distributed or, alternatively, that when a party controlled both the presidency and the Congress, the use of patronage should increase.[23]

Table 3.3   **Extension of the Merit System, 1884–1940**

Variable	Eq. (1)	Eq. (2)	Eq. (3)
Total employment	.395E-05	.359E-05	.378E-05
	(7.05)	(6.00)	(6.61)
(Total employment)^2	−.434E-11	−.382E-11	−.409E-11
	(−5.50)	(−4.51)	(−5.11)
(Total employment)^3	.144E-23	.122E-23	.133E-23
	(4.03)	(3.18)	(3.69)
First year of	...	.002	...
presidential term		(.19)	
Second year of	...	−.014	...
presidential term		(−1.14)	
Third year of	...	−.008	...
presidential term		(−.88)	
Lame-duck president	...	...	.020
			(1.86)
Party dominance	...	.014	.010
		(.92)	(.86)
Constant	−.286	−.239	−.275
	(−2.85)	(−2.26)	(−2.69)
R^2	.9716	.9718	.9728
Log-likelihood function	107.94	110.34	110.30

Sources and notes: Data on total federal civilian employment and merit employment are taken from the sources listed for fig. 3.1. Party affiliation and election data are from U.S. Department of Commerce (1975, 1083). For discussion of the variables, see the text. The equations were estimated using a second-order autocorrelation error model and an iterative Cochrane-Orcutt procedure. Minus 2 times the log of the likelihood ratio for the restricted eq. (1) and the unrestricted eq. (2) is 4.79. With four restrictions, the critical value of the χ^2 distribution at the 90 percent level is 7.78. In contrast, minus 2 times the log of the likelihood ratio for eq. (1) and (3) is 4.72. With only two restrictions, the critical value of the χ^2 distribution is 4.6. *t*-ratios in parentheses.

The results reported for equation (2) of table 3.3 do not reveal any convincing evidence of a cycle in the growth of the ratio of merit to total employees. Moreover, the coefficient on the party dominance variable is not significantly different from zero. A likelihood ratio test, reported in the table, leads to a strong rejection of the hypothesis that these political variables are jointly significant and that they can explain the long-term shift to a merit system. The results reported for equation (3), however, suggest a tendency for lame-duck presidents to increase the proportion of merit to total federal employment following a victory by the opposing party. Although the coefficient on the variable representing the presence of a lame-duck president is statistically significant at the 10 percent level, the magnitude is relatively small, only .02. This coefficient can be interpreted as follows. Between 1884 and 1940, the ratio of merit to total federal employment went from .10 to .73. Assuming that blanketing in was permanent, then the seven incidents of lame-duck extensions accounted for no more than .14 (7 × .02) of the total increase in the ratio of .63, or about

22 percent of the growth of the merit portion of the labor force.[24] While lame-duck presidential appointments were made, the results presented here suggest that such actions played a smaller role in the shift from patronage to merit than has been emphasized in the historical literature. The lack of statistical significance for the party dominance variables in equations (2) and (3) also supports our general argument. The need to develop an institution to address the growing problems of controlling and managing the federal labor force, rather than short-term partisan interests, was the dominant force behind the adoption and extension of the merit service.

3.4   The Addition of Tenure Provisions

The Pendleton Act institutionalized the use of competitive examinations to improve the quality of the federal workforce in specific areas, and the gradual reduction in the relative number of patronage employees reduced the influence of local party officials over federal workers. Further, the exam requirement limited political discretion in placement, but the law did not provide for tenure for federal employees. The only explicit job-security protection granted classi-fed employees under the Pendleton Act was that "no person in the public ser-vice is for that reason under any obligations to contribute to any political fund, or to render any political service, and that he will not be removed or otherwise prejudiced for refusing to do so" (sec. 13). As Paul Van Riper pointed out, "Both the original civil service reformers and many subsequent American leg-islators have consistently fought against an overly absolute tenure as undesir-able and unnecessary for civil service reform" (1958, 101). Accordingly, the president's power to remove workers remained essentially intact for both the new classified service and the patronage positions.

Nevertheless, soon after the Pendleton Act was enacted, the president and the Congress, with a collective stake in the maintenance of the merit system, found that they could not just remove political considerations in hiring deci-sions but had to address removals as well. The political temptations would be great if the president could simply declassify positions, remove officeholders, and replace them with patronage employees. So long as it was easy to declas-sify positions, the president would be subject to demands from Congress and other party officials to expand patronage. The effectiveness of the merit service in limiting the number of patronage workers, then, depended on adjustments to the civil service system to provide protection against arbitrary removal.

3.4.1   McKinley's Executive Order

The first significant move toward tenure provisions was made by President McKinley in 1897. McKinley was under intense pressure from Republican party officials and some Republican members of Congress to reclassify the positions added by Democratic president Cleveland. Cleveland had added over 42,000 positions to the classifed service through executive orders. Had McKinley responded and declassified the positions, the merit system would have suffered a major setback, and efforts to control the number of patronage workers would have been compromised.

The merit system was especially valuable to the president, and wholesale declassifications of positions were resisted. Although McKinley did declassify approximately 9,000 positions in response to party demands, his action affected fewer than a fourth of Cleveland's additions to the classified service. Moreover, and more significant for the development of the federal civil service, McKinley issued an executive order on 27 July 1897, which became part of the Civil Service Rules, prohibiting removal from the classifed service except for just cause, with written notification and an opportunity to respond: "No removal shall be made from any position subject to competitive examination except for just cause and upon written charges filed with the head of the Department or other appointing officer, and of which the accused shall have full notice and an opportunity to make defense" (U.S. Civil Service Commission, *Annual Report*, 1897, 19).

Enforcement was left to the president, and this was the beginning of tenure provisions for federal employees. Under the new rule, the originating department was required to forward copies of the charges behind a planned dismissal along with the employee's response to the Civil Service Commission for review and recording. The Civil Service Commission called the requirement one of the most important rules ever issued relating to the classified service. Its restrictions on removal, including requirements that the reasons for dismissal be made public, were upheld early in the courts. The commission stated that the rule "lessens the temptation to make improper removals, and affords a just degree of protection to the faithful and efficient employees" (U.S. Civil Service Commission, *Annual Report*, 1897, 20).

3.4.2   The Lloyd-LaFollette Act

Once a merit system for classified employees was established, there remained the problem of whether the president or the Congress were to have direct control over these employees. With the decline in the number of patronage positions relative to total federal civilian employment, conflict between the president and the Congress over the federal workforce and the associated administration of government services shifted from patronage to the classified service. This became most apparent after Roosevelt replaced McKinley as president in 1901, when the classified service accounted for over 40 percent of the federal civilian labor force. Roosevelt sought to gain control of the merit civil service by attempting to sever ties between classified employees and officials outside the executive branch. In 1901, he ordered the Treasury Department to withhold the salary of any classified employee whose appointment violated civil service rules as a patronage assignment. Such assignments were most likely made by or on behalf of members of Congress (Skowronek 1982, 179). In addition, beginning in 1902, Roosevelt, and later Taft, issued so-called gag orders that forbade federal employees, "either directly or indirectly, individually or through association, to solicit an increase of pay or to influence in their own interest any other legislation whatever, either before Congress or its committees, or in any way save through the heads of the Departments in or under which they serve, on penalty of dismissal from the Government service" (Spero 1927, 96).

The enforcement of McKinley's earlier executive order regarding arbitrary dismissals rested with the president, so the threat to remove those employees who maintained direct ties to Congress rather than going through their department heads was a real one. Under the gag orders, federal employees were to convey their desires only through department officials, who had been appointed by the president. Although the immediate issue involved efforts by federal employees to form unions to lobby for pay increases, the concern in Congress went beyond unionization or salaries for government workers. Congress saw the gag orders as an assertion of presidential control over federal employees, with noncompliance penalized by dismissal. In response, in 1912 Congress passed the Lloyd-LaFollette Act (37 Stat. 555), which allowed federal employees to petition individually or collectively to join labor organizations that did not authorize the use of strikes. Importantly, the act strengthened McKinley's 1897 executive order by prohibiting the dismissal of classified employees for any reason, except efficiency, and by requiring that written notice of possible dismissal be issued and that the employee have the opportunity to respond (Spero 1927, 168).

3.4.3 Other Legislation Affecting Tenure

The Lloyd-LaFollette Act also demonstrates the rise of federal employees as an influential lobby group in molding civil service rules in their behalf through legislation. More ironclad tenure provisions were added in the Civil Service Retirement Act (41 Stat. 614) of 1920. Further tenure provisions, which raised the costs of dismissal by outlining elaborate grievance procedures, were added in the Classification Acts of 1923 and 1949 and the Civil Service Reform Act of 1978 (42 Stat. 1488, 63 Stat. 954, and 92 Stat. 1111, respectively).

Under current civil service provisions, career federal employees, particularly the rank and file, have tenured employment. Indeed, job tenure is a key characteristic of the federal civil service system. The degree of job tenure that now exists appears to go beyond that which would have been sought by the president and the Congress to maintain the integrity of the merit system. All that would have been necessary to reduce the temptation to fire and reclassify merit employees for patronage purposes was a provision to prevent arbitrary dismissal, along with a process for appeals and review. The tenure guarantees that exist, however, exceed these requirements. Under civil service rules, it is very costly for supervisors to remove employees, and even reductions in force (RIFs), such as those implemented in the early 1980s, do not lead to any significant numbers of involuntary separations from the federal service (Johnson and Libecap 1989b). To understand the degree of tenure guarantees that exist today requires consideration of the role of federal employee groups in influencing legislation regarding the civil service system. This important phenomenon in the process of institutional change is addressed in more detail in the following chapters.

3.5   Political Neutrality

Three fundamental characteristics of the federal civil service are that it covers most federal civilian employees, that classified employees essentially have job tenure, and that classified employees are restricted in the types of political activities in which they may engage. We have argued that extension of the classified service and tenure protections were the outcome of conscious efforts by the president, and to a lesser degree the Congress, to control the number of patronage appointments, to provide government services for influential constituents, and to limit opportunistic manipulation of federal employees. In this section, we argue that requirements for political neutrality were also necessary to reduce the value of federal workers as pure political assets for which local politicians, the president, and Congress could compete.

Merit achievement in testing for hiring and promotion, as required by the Pendleton Act, in itself implied some measure of political neutrality. Knowledge and skill were to replace political loyalty as conditions for employment and advancement. Additionally, the Pendleton Act's prohibition of political assessments and subsequent restrictions on arbitrary removal for purely partisan reasons, granted by McKinley's executive order and by the Lloyd-LaFollette Act, provided further distance between classified federal workers and party demands. But classified employees remained free to engage in political activities on their own accord. As long as government workers could participate in campaigns, they remained potentially valuable political assets, encouraging competition among the president and members of Congress for their control and partisan use. Both the president and the Congress could attempt to elicit campaign support from federal employees by promising them promotions and other benefits. Detecting this sort of quid pro quo behavior would be costly, and, if extensive, it posed a threat to the basic separation between the classified service and patronage.[25] Restricting the types of political activities in which federal workers could engage, however, could sufficiently reduce their value as political assets and, hence, reduce the incentives to compete for control over them.

As was the case with the extension of the merit system, the early moves toward requiring political neutrality came from the president.[26] In an executive order on 14 July 1888, President Cleveland prohibited the use of government offices for political purposes that interfered with public duties (Van Riper 1958, 187). Recall that Cleveland was under pressure, not only from Republicans in Congress, but also from members of his own party, who sought control over federal employees, merit and unclassified alike. Cleveland's executive order, however, could not be effectively enforced, in part because it made no distinction between the classified and the unclassified labor forces.

President Theodore Roosevelt again attempted to impose political neutrality on the federal labor force in his efforts to strengthen the president's authority relative to Congress. In 1902, he redefined political neutrality for unclassified employees by prohibiting the use of administrative offices for political purposes or to cause public scandal (Skowronek 1982, 179–80; Van Riper 1958, 187–203). Again, the president was concerned about the reputation of the administration. For classified employees, the neutrality requirement included the strict prohibition of all political activity. President Roosevelt's proscription against political activity became formally known as Civil Service Rule I and reads as follows:

> No person in the executive civil service shall use his official authority or influence for the purpose of interfering with an election or affecting the result thereof. Persons who by the provision of these rules are in the competitive classified service, while retaining the right to vote as they please and to express privately their opinions on all political subjects, shall take no active part in political management or in political campaigns. (U.S. Civil Service Commission, *Annual Report*, 1908, 104)

Although the president took the lead in advancing the merit system, the exchange of patronage employees with members of Congress remained a means of obtaining votes on various bills. The temptation to expand patronage appears to have been particularly strong during the administration of Franklin Roosevelt. Not only was there an extensive and often controversial New Deal legislative agenda that required congressional support, but the Depression was in full swing, bringing pressure from local constituents on members of Congress for government jobs.[27] A resurgence in the spoils system resulted in the early 1930s.

During the first Roosevelt administration, over sixty New Deal agencies were created and largely staffed outside the civil service system. Emphasis was placed on rapidly developing the agencies beyond the more cumbersome civil service procedures, and a premium was placed on obtaining employees who would be committed to the president's policy agenda. Many of the appointees were pure patronage workers, designed to build political support for the New Deal and the politicians who sponsored them. As figure 3.2 points out, during this time the proportion of merit workers within the overall federal civilian labor force declined from 80 percent in 1932 to a low of 60 percent in 1936. This change was the result of a 41 percent increase in total federal civilian employment, with only a modest increase in the number of employees within the classified service. By 1936, there were over 300,000 patronage positions available for distribution, more than at any other time in the nation's history (U.S. House of Representatives 1976, 305).

Congress was, at first, a willing partner in the expansion of patronage and by 1935 had exempted most New Deal agencies from merit system regulations (U.S. House of Representatives 1976, 254). With the expansion of patronage, however, came efforts by the president to distribute and use federal employees to defeat unsupportive congressional politicians and governors. In 1938, Roosevelt campaigned for Senator Alben Barkely of Kentucky against Governor A. B. Happy Chandler. Further, in 1938, Roosevelt attempted to purge members of Congress who did not support his programs (Van Riper 1958, 340). Patronage allotments were a major tool for rewarding and punishing candidates. These actions reduced congressional support for an expanded patronage labor force that was primarily available for political use by the president.

Both the president and the Congress, however, had another and more fundamental reason for being concerned about the actions of patronage workers during the New Deal. As had occurred previously, the large number of patronage positions presented the president and the Congress with the problem of managing their appointees. Patronage workers were often under the influence of local party or agency officials, whose actions were only loosely controlled by national politicians. This created an environment for potential embarrassment for the president and the Congress if their appointees were involved in scandals or used in ways that harmed influential constituents.

The experience at the Works Progress Administration (WPA) is a case in point. Most WPA officials at the field level were far removed from supervision by elected officials in Washington, D.C. WPA workers, dependent on federal employment during the Depression, were vulnerable to political assessments and other forms of extortion, and such actions appear to have been widespread (See *Congressional Record*, 76th Cong., 1st sess., 20 July 1939, pp. 9594–9640). Workers were required to make contributions to their project supervisor, and there was little accounting as to the end use of the funds. This form of political extortion of those who could least afford to pay generated a considerable amount of bad publicity for both the Congress and the president.[28] The sense that there was a problem controlling the vast number of patronage workers created by New Deal programs may well have induced the president, following the election of 1936, to move positions and agencies into the merit system. The proportion of federal employees covered under the classified system began to increase after 1936. Once classified, former patronage employees were less likely to be of value to local party officials, and there were explicit civil service rules prohibiting political assessments and threats of dismissal for failure to engage in campaign activities. Hence, classification reduced the chances for the types of scandals that occurred within the WPA. Nevertheless, the episode demonstrates the problems encountered in controlling a large patronage workforce and indicates that further constraints on the behavior of the president and the Congress would be required if costly competition over the control and use of federal employees were to be avoided.

The Hatch Acts of 1939 and 1940 (53 Stat. 1147 and 54 Stat. 767, respectively), which formalized the requirement for political neutrality, were the out-

come of these concerns. The Hatch Acts restricted federal workers (both classified and unclassified) and state and local employees funded by federal grants
from engaging in direct political activities.[29] Exemptions were made for persons paid from appropriations for the Office of the President and for those
appointed by the president with the consent of the Senate who were to be engaged in determining policy. All other government employees covered by the
sweeping provisions of the Hatch Acts were prohibited from taking an active
part in political management or political campaigns. Violation would bring
immediate dismissal. Previously, the Civil Service Commission had discretion
in determining punishment for the violation of civil service rules, such as Rule
I, which had restricted direct campaign efforts by classified employees. Under
the new laws, the discretion for punishing violations of prohibitions against
political activities was removed. The Hatch Acts represent the capstone in the
movement from open patronage conditions that existed in the 1880s to an insulated and, ostensibly, politically neutral civil service.

3.6 Summary

This chapter has outlined how the incentives of the president and the Congress to control federal employees after 1883 led to conscious efforts by both
parties to expand the merit system. Most of these extensions were through
executive orders issued by the president or the revision of civil service rules to
broaden coverage to new facilities. But extending the merit-testing framework
adopted in 1883 under the Pendleton Act was not enough; the original act did
not close important margins through which elected officials could still seek to
manipulate federal workers for narrow partisan purposes. So long as government employees remained vulnerable to the threat of removal for failure to
respond to these demands, and so long as classified positions could be declassified and returned to patronage, the merit system remained unstable. Under conditions of intense political pressure on the president from local party leaders
and certain members of Congress, the system could have unraveled. The president, the most national of all politicians and the one with the most to gain from
the retention of merit rules, was the first to act on the tenure issue. McKinley
issued his exective order in 1897 outlining tenure conditions and appeals processes. McKinley's actions were taken to head off demands from Congress for
greater partisan use of the growing classified service. Congress's turn on the
issue came fifteen years later with the Lloyd-LaFollette Act. In this case, the
Congress was responding to efforts by the president to obtain additional partisan control of the classified service. With job tenure and an elaborate appeals
process established over time, the threat of dismissal was no longer a credible
one to be used by politicians seeking to influence the behavior of federal employees.

Besides tenure, the requirement for political neutrality by federal employees
was necessary to reduce the incentive to compete for control of federal employ-

ees. As with tenure, it is hard to imagine a greater shift from old patronage practices than the notion of ordering political neutrality for government workers. Yet this was what was required to reduce the value of federal workers as partisan assets, subject to competitive control by the president and the Congress. Again, the president was the first to act on the issue. Cleveland attempted to instill political neutrality as a condition for all government employees, classified and patronage alike, in 1888. At that time, Cleveland was in a fervent battle with members of his party and with Republicans in Congress over federal workers. Theodore Roosevelt followed with another executive order for political neutrality for federal employees in 1902, when he outlined separate requirements for merit and unclassified employees. Congress completed the process by placing all rank-and-file federal workers outside direct political campaigns with the Hatch Acts of 1939 and 1940.

With the extension of the civil service system to include most federal civilian employees, and with the additions of rules providing for job tenure and compelling political neutrality, the fundamental characteristics of the modern civil service institution were put into place. We argue that this process of institutional change was the outcome of actions taken by vote-maximizing politicians, the president and the Congress, to place federal employees off limits to costly competition for control. Neither party could unilaterally withdraw from the competitive fray for patronage. Hence, rule changes taken at the behest of both parties were necessary to create an institutional structure that would allow the president and the Congress jointly to withdraw from contention over the federal labor force and to allow federal workers to focus on the delivery of government services.

Although the actions taken by the president and the Congress account for the origins and much of the basic structure of the federal civil service system, a third party, federal employees, became an important factor in the further development of the system. We argue that, through their efforts, additional provisions were placed into the civil service system that went beyond those that would be strictly desired by the president or the Congress. This phenomenon became more pronounced as the twentieth century progressed, and it is the subject of the following chapter.

Notes

1. Maranto and Schultz (1991, 44) make the argument that civil service reform had both a moral basis and an emphasis on short-term political gains (see also Van Riper 1958, 85).

2. The blanketing-in hypothesis continues to be advanced as the primary explanation for the growth of the civil service even in the more recent literature (see, e.g., Maranto and Schultz 1991, 51).

3. The traditional view is expressed by Hoogenboom: "Those who opposed spoils were usually out of power, but once these 'outs' were 'in' the evils of the system seemed to vanish" (1968, 7).

4. Recall that the coefficient on the variable Democrat shown in table 2.3 was negative and significant.

5. Sections 1, 2, and 3 of the Pendleton Act. Van Riper (1958, 104, 138) discusses the establishment of local boards, noting that, between 1884 and 1888, a "Rule of Four" was used.

6. See Van Riper (1958, 101). There was considerable discussion during the debate on the Pendleton Act in both the House and the Senate over whether the act would extend tenure to newly covered workers. This prompted Senator Pendleton to explain, "The bill does not touch the question of tenure of office or of removal from office. I see it stated by those who do not know that it provides for a seven years' tenure in office. There is noting like it in the bill. I see it stated that it provides for removals from office. There is nothing like it in the bill. Whether or not it would be advisable to limit removals are questions about which men will differ; but the bill as it is and as we invoke the judgement of the Senate upon it contains no provision either as to tenure of office or removals from office. It leaves these questions exactly as the law now finds them" (*Congressional Record*, 47th Cong. 2d sess., 12 December 1882, 207).

7. For a discussion of the development of these rules and how they relate to the Hatch Acts of 1939 and 1940, see Eccles (1981, 20–30).

8. For the debate on repeal, see *Congressional Record*, 49th Cong., 1st sess., pp. 401, 2287, 2945–52, and for the vote on S. 839, which called for a repeal of the Pendleton Act, see p. 5852.

9. *Congressional Record*, 49th Cong., 1st sess., p. 5852. In the Senate, 56 percent of the Democrats abstained from the vote.

10. Some constitutional issues were raised by these and other provisions of the Pendleton Act. Since the law authorized the Civil Service Commission to select employees on the basis of competitive exams, there was some question as to whether that was an unconstitutional invasion of the powers of the president and the Congress. See the discussion in Van Riper (1958, 105–8).

11. Goldstein and Weingast (1991) also argue that the delegation of policy-making authority to the president reflects a desire on the part of the Congress to guard against later reversals.

12. For the Forty-seventh Congress, Republicans held 147 seats and Democrats 135 in the House, and each party held thirty-seven seats in the Senate (U.S. Department of Commerce 1975, 1083).

13. There are other instances in which the existence of significant externalities has led the Congress to delegate authority to the president. See, e.g., Lohmann and O'Halloran's (1992) explanation for why Congress delegated trade policy-making authority to the president.

14. Congress did make minor additions to the classified service starting in 1903 (see Sageser 1935, 231; and U.S. House of Representatives 1976, 310). It was not until 1935 that congressional legislation regarding the Soil Conservation Service added a significant number of positions to the classified service.

15. Through the longer period 1884–1913, approximately 47 percent of the growth of the merit service was through executive orders.

16. U.S. House of Representatives (1976, 305). Patronage positions were calculated as the difference between total federal civilian employment and the classified labor force for 1897 and 1913 as listed in table 3.1.

17. For a discussion of Wilson's effort to monitor the assignment of patronage, see Van Riper (1958, 232–35).

18. As indicated in the note to table 3.1, the data are collected from a variety of sources. Most reflect revisions of Sageser's data by Skowronek. These sources were used to decompose the contributions of agency growth and executive orders to the overall growth of the classified service. In our figures and statistical work, where longer-term time series are involved, we have used the data in U.S. House of Representatives (1976, 305), which cover 1884–1975. These data do not identify the sources of the growth of the classified service. Although the data generally agree, there are small differences between some of the figures reported in table 3.1 and those in the U.S. House report.

19. For a discussion of the "blanketing-in" process, see U.S. House of Representatives (1976, 182–83) and Heclo (1977, 41).

20. For the variety of rules regarding merit status, examination, and promotion that existed in the early civil service, see U.S. Civil Service Commission, *Annual Report* (1888, 73–92). Gradually, these were standardized so that examinations were required for merit status and promotion.

21. U.S. House of Representatives (1976, 182). Later, the examination requirement for merit status was reinstated.

22. Harrison followed a similar practice in late 1892, when he extended classification to rural free delivery post offices. These positions had been bastions of patronage for local postmasters, and, once classified, they were no longer available for later patronage assignment.

23. This has been a popular argument. See, e.g., the analysis offered by Geddes (1991). In addition to the results reported here, we also constructed and tested other measures of party dominance. For example, two variables, one measuring the percentage of members of the Senate who were of the same party as the president and a similar measure for the House, were constructed. The results, however, were qualitatively the same as those reported in the text. Party dominance does not appear to have had a measurable effect on the development of the merit system. See also the discussion in Johnson and Libecap (1994).

24. Assuming that blanketing in was permanent suggests an alternative specification. For each of the seven incidents of a lame-duck president, a variable was constructed that was set equal to unity starting with the president's final year in office and remaining so until the end of the sample period, 1940. Although most of the coefficients on these seven variables were not significantly different from zero, the sum of their values was .12, supporting the result reported in the text. Moreover, the magnitude and level of significance of total federal employment variables remained essentially the same.

25. The problems of detection and policing that this posed for the president and members of Congress are similar to that of controlling cheating within a cartel.

26. President Theodore Roosevelt, in particular, appears to have been concerned with the political activity of federal workers (see Eccles 1981, 26).

27. Van Riper (1958, 320). Within the context of the model presented in app. B, these pressures would manifest themselves as increases in the demand for patronage.

28. Congressman Taylor of Tennessee reported that WPA workers had often been requested to contribute $5.00 per month when their entire monthly salary was only $30.00. This prompted the *Knoxville News-Sentinel* to state, "The political racket in Tennessee is enough to sicken any decent human being, and it is doubly sickening when worked on helpless relief clients" (*Congressional Record*, 76th Cong., 1st sess., 20 July 1939, p. 9598; see also Van Riper 1958, 340).

29. For discussion of the Hatch Acts, see Eccles (1981).

4   The Rise of Federal Employees as an Interest Group: The Early Years

4.1   Introduction

We are interested in the evolution of the civil service system as an institution for governing the employment and administration of the federal civilian labor force. In chapters 2 and 3, we emphasized the incentives that federal politicians had to change the process by which government employees were hired from purely patronage to a merit system. The process of institutional change, initiated by the president and the Congress in the creation of the classified service in 1883, however, changed relative prices in ways that affected the subsequent development of the civil service system.[1] In particular, the establishment of the merit service raised the benefits and lowered the costs to federal employees of organizing into labor unions. As such, federal employee unions and related lobby groups became a third party with an important stake in the further development of the civil service system. The classified service became a well-defined, distinct group among federal employees. These employees were hired and promoted on the basis of merit, and, as their positions became more permanent than they had been under patronage, they had a greater interest in organizing to ensure that the terms of the federal labor contract were to their benefit. Under the civil service system, it became easier for federal employees to organize. Where under patronage federal workers had identified with their political mentors and hence were fragmented, under the classified service they began to identify themselves as a distinct and more unified group. This facilitated the successful formation of federal employee unions, which could lobby Congress for legislative adjustments to the civil service system.

The rise of federal workers as a party interested in the institutional development of the civil service system suggests that the system would gradually assume attributes other than those strictly desired by the president and the Congress.[2] This element is overlooked in much of the current literature concerning the development of the civil service system. The role played by federal workers in the design of their own compensation systems and personnel rules is either ignored or, if acknowledged, portrayed as having had force only after President Kennedy signed Executive Order 10988 in 1962, which allowed unions limited collective-bargaining rights (see Levitan and Noden 1983; Freeman 1986). We believe, however, that federal employees were critical in the earlier development of the civil service system and that, without incorporating them as a third bargaining party in institutional change, the evolution of the system cannot adequately be explained. These issues are examined in this and the next chapter.

4.2   The Rise of Federal Employee Labor Unions

Prior to the 1880s, the federal labor movement was splintered and limited. With civilian employment based on patronage appointments, job tenure was short, and federal workers owed allegiance to their mentors. As a consequence, there was little shared sense of collective interests among federal workers. Under these conditions, there was no significant organized labor movement among the federal government's employees, and federal labor unions were virtually nonexistent (Nesbitt 1976, 3–80). Conditions began to change with the growth of the classified civil service after 1883. The growing interest among federal workers in forming labor unions after the Pendleton Act was passed was commented on by Sterling Spero, an early student of federal labor unions: "Gradually, as the patronage of these lower positions disappeared, Congressmen and politicians generally began to lose interest in the post office clerks and carriers, and these workers, thus thrown to their resources, soon found it necessary to unite among themselves in order to protect their interests and improve their lot. Besides, with their positions now made 'permanent', postal employees saw that they had a stake in the service and in good working conditions which they had not had before. Previously a man was in a government job one year and out of it the next, and it did not make very much difference if working conditions did leave much to be desired. But now these men began to feel that they were in the service to stay. . . . The organized movement among postal workers was the natural outcome of this changed situation" (1927, 61).

Indeed, one of the earliest efforts of organized civil service employees was to strengthen and expand their newly acquired independence through the merit system. The National Association of All Civil Service Employees was formed in 1896 to promote the extension of the classified service and additional civil service reform, such as the adoption of grievance procedures and the granting of greater job security (Spero 1927, 61).[3] At the association's first convention, a resolution was passed emphasizing that "the employees of the Classified Civil Service . . . do not . . . owe any duty to any political party, nor to any political leader. They are in no sense the private employees of any officer of the Government" (Spero 1948, 171). The association's lobbying efforts for additional changes in civil service rules after 1896 led to tension between the organization and the U.S. Civil Service Commission. The Civil Service Commission was appointed by the president under the provisions of the Pendleton Act to develop and administer civil service rules. The emerging differences between the commission and the association reflected the newly separate interests of the president and the Congress, on the one hand, who were responsible for the creation of the merit system, and the recently organized group of classified employees, on the other.

With the assistance of private-sector labor unions, such as the Knights of Labor in the late nineteenth century and the American Federation of Labor in the twentieth, classified employees began to form more traditional unions that also lobbied Congress for legislation regarding job classification and security, salaries, hours of work, workers' compensation, and retirement benefits. As the civil service share of federal employees grew and union membership expanded, federal unions, with the assistance of organized labor, became influential in obtaining new laws setting salaries and in designing administrative rules affecting working conditions.[4] Federal unions opened their headquarters in Washington, D.C.: they drafted laws for the classified service, carefully followed legislation that affected them, and appeared at committee hearings to advocate or oppose bills; they gave testimonial dinners for congressional supporters, issued honorary union memberships, and had influential members of Congress, especially the chair of the Civil Service Committee, address their national conventions. Federal unions also became active in political campaigns to promote their supporters and oppose their adversaries.

As the classified service grew in the twentieth century, the unions that formed were general ones, such as the National Federation of Federal Employees (NFFE), organized in 1917, and the American Federation of Government Employees (AFGE), organized in 1932, both affiliated with the American Federation of Labor (AFL). Most of the early unions, however, were more narrowly focused, involving postal workers, the largest group of federal employees. For example, in 1891, 63 percent of all executive branch civilian employees worked for the Post Office Department.[5] Local assemblies of letter carriers were established through the Knights of Labor in New York, Chicago, and other cities in the late 1880s. In 1890, the National Association of Letter Carriers and the National Association of Post Office Clerks were formed (Perlman and Taft 1935, 163–65). Railway postal clerks organized nationally in 1891 as the Railway Mail Association. Other federal unions included the National Federation of Post Office Clerks, organized and chartered by the AFL in 1906, and the more radical Brotherhood of Railway Postal Clerks that was formed in 1911. Union membership grew after 1912 and the enactment of the Lloyd-LaFollette Act, which removed potential penalties for belonging to labor unions. Spero (1927, 45) estimated that by 1920 there were some fifty federal employee unions affiliated with the AFL and that between 50 and 60 percent of the federal civilian labor force belonged to those unions.

The Lloyd-LaFollette Act (37 Stat. 539) was passed during conflict between the Post Office Department and federal postal unions over pay legislation that was under consideration in Congress. The conflict between the Post Office Department and the postal unions, as well as related efforts of the unions to influence other legislation in the early twentieth century, illustrates the growing role of federal employees in defining the structure of the civil service system.

After 1900, a variety of issues, ranging from salaries, hours of work, and pension provisions to actions for improving productivity, were raised by the postal unions and the Post Office Department. In general, the department was hostile to the new employee unions, and it often took a strong stand in opposing their lobbying efforts. The official view was that government workers were to be like soldiers and be independent of unions. As early as 1895, the Post Office Department attempted to limit the activities of postal employees to influence legislation. Postmaster General William L. Wilson issued the order "that here-after no Postmaster, Post-office Clerk, Letter Carrier, Railway Postal Clerk, or other postal employee, shall visit Washington, whether on leave with or without pay, for the purpose of influencing legislation before Congress" (quoted in Spero 1927, 85–86). The penalty for violation was dismissal.

By the turn of the century, postal salaries had declined in real terms, and various bills were under consideration in Congress for reclassifying positions and raising salaries. The legislation was, however, opposed by the Post Office Department and the chair of the House Post Office Committee, Representative Eugene Loud of California. Following intensive lobbying efforts by postal unions for the legislation, President Roosevelt issued the first of his gag orders on 31 January 1902, forbidding lobbying activity on pay or related issues, again with penalty of dismissal (Spero 1927, 97). The postal unions opposed the gag order, and the president's intervention offended Congress. Additionally, the unions organized an election campaign against Congressman Loud, whose committee position gave him virtual veto authority over any postal legislation. The postal unions, along with help from the AFL, were successful in contributing to Loud's defeat in the 1902 election (Spero 1927, 99). This demonstration of political muscle could not have been overlooked by other members of Congress. The role of federal employees in the election was investigated by the U.S. Civil Service Committee, which found that they had overstepped civil service rules, but no disciplinary action was taken (Spero 1927, 100).

The Post Office Department continued to resist the formation of postal unions and the influence that they attempted to exert on civil service work rules and salaries. In 1905, Postmaster General Cortelyou stated that labor organizations would have the sanction of the department only if they had as their object "improvements in the service or [were] of a purely fraternal or beneficial character. With any other purpose in view they are detrimental to the service, their members and the public" (quoted in Spero 1927, 110). Faced with opposition from the department and the president, the unions began to agitate against the gag orders to facilitate their access to Congress. President Roosevelt reacted by changing the tenure rule put into place by McKinley in 1897 in order to permit the removal of employees without notice. Under McKinley's earlier executive order, removals had required justification, notice, and an opportunity for employee response (U.S. Civil Service Commission, *Annual Report,* 1904, 69–70). President Roosevelt then reissued the gag order in January 1906 to reemphasize the restrictions on federal employee's access to members of Congress. Under the presidential directive, all communication with Congress was to be through executive branch department or agency heads.

With declining relative pay, labor turnover in the Post Office Department rose in 1906 and 1907. The department responded with a reclassification bill, creating six salary grades for clerks and carriers with automatic promotions within the lower grades to raise salaries (Spero 1927, 114–15).[6] The National Association of Letter Carriers demanded more, and the organization's president, James Holland, traveled to Washington, D.C., to convince Congress to amend the bill with more favorable promotion and pay provisions. The lobbying by the carriers' association was successful, and the Reclassification Act of 2 March 1907 (34 Stat. 1205) contained the promotion and salary schedule desired by the union. Nevertheless, for ignoring the gag order, Holland was fired by President Roosevelt as head of the Association of Letter Carriers (Spero 1927, 115).

Discontent with the gag orders and their restrictions on appeals to Congress continued to grow. On 26 November 1909, President Taft issued a new order as part of an efficiency and economy drive. The prohibition against responding to congressional requests for information was to be more strictly enforced, as evidenced by the dismissal of Chief Forester Gifford Pinchot for violation of the gag order. In 1911, the Brotherhood of Railway Postal Clerks was formed to carry the demands of postal workers to Congress more aggressively. As relations deteriorated between the department and its unions, members were demoted or dismissed. The AFL presented the legislation to Congress to limit the power of removal over civil service employees and to guarantee their right to organize labor unions that became the Lloyd-LaFollette Act (Spero 1927, 146, 158–68). President Taft and executive branch department heads intensely opposed the legislation, and Taft modified the gag orders to make them more palatable. Even so, Congress overwhelmingly passed the Lloyd-LaFollette bill as an amendment to the Post Office Appropriations Act on 24 August 1912. The law prohibited removal of civil service employees, except for efficiency reasons, and required written notices and an opportunity for rebuttal. Under the new law, membership in labor unions was not to be a reason for reduction in pay or removal.[7]

In 1913, the new postmaster general Albert S. Burleson continued to oppose unions and union interference in the administration of the Post Office Department. Cost-cutting measures were adopted, including a merit-demerit system, a reduction in the number of postal clerks, and adjustments in the way in which salaries were calculated, leading to some reductions. Burleson also unsuccessfully attempted to contract out the rural mail service, a move that he argued would save the government $13 million a year. Postal unions were quick to respond by lobbying Congress to thwart the measure (Spero 1927, 201). Additionally, when Postmaster General Burleson attempted to have the Lloyd-LaFollette Act repealed in 1917, intense lobbying efforts by federal unions and the AFL led to the defeat of the repeal effort (Spero 1927, 213–28).

Postal unions continued to pressure Congress for salary legislation despite opposition from the Post Office Department. The Postal Reclassification Act (41 Stat. 1045) was passed on 5 June 1920, and it defined a new series of salary grades (Spero 1927, 206–7).[8] Later in 1924, to show its gratitude to Senator LaFollette, the National Federation of Post Office Clerks vigorously supported his presidential candidacy (Spero 1948, 47). The political actions of federal unions in mobilizing their members and furthering their interests were exemplified by the letter sent by W. M. Collins, president of the Railway Mail Association, to association members in 1932. The letter described how candidates had voted on issues affecting postal clerks and declared that it was "entirely proper" that "you should remember your friends on election day" (Spero 1927, 47–48).

4.3 Changes in the Civil Service System in Response to Actions Taken by Federal Employee Groups

4.3.1 Salaries

As noted earlier, by 1900 federal employee salaries were declining in real terms relative to those earned by private-sector workers. Given the provisions of the Pendleton Act and the expanded coverage of federal workers under the merit system, this decline in salaries could be expected. Federal workers were becoming less valuable assets for members of Congress.

Patronage workers had been an important source of campaign contributions for members of Congress, and, even after the enactment of the Pendleton Act, they could still make voluntary contributions. That act, however, forbade the levying of assessments on classified federal employees by politicians, and the Civil Service Commission investigated allegations of extortion and enforced this provision of the law. Since classified workers could no longer effectively be coerced into paying assessments, both the president and members of Congress had little incentive to maintain the relatively high salaries that had previously compensated workers for making these contributions.

Under nineteenth-century compensation arrangements for federal employees, agency heads had considerable discretion in deciding where a particular worker would be placed.[9] The Pendleton Act did not distinguish between classified and unclassified employees in terms of pay, and the basic compensation schedules remained unaltered by the law. There is no evidence that patronage or merit workers in similar positions received different pay. Recall that entire facilities were made eligible for merit coverage whenever employment reached the prescribed limit (initially fifty, later twenty). This procedure meant that individuals in comparable jobs but at different size facilities would be under patronage in one case and merit in another. When the share of patronage workers (those available for direct partisan manipulation and assessments for campaign contributions) was large, Congress would desire to maintain relatively high pay for federal workers; hence, average salaries would be high. As the share of patronage employees dropped, however, the desire within Congress to maintain those salaries would dissipate. Accordingly, as the share of classified workers increased, relative pay for federal employees would be expected to fall.[10] In this section, we examine the available evidence regarding the pattern of federal salaries from the late nineteenth century through 1926. We also investigate attempts by federal employee unions to raise pay levels.

Available quantitative and qualitative evidence from various sources indicates that, from 1883 through 1917 and the advent of World War I, the relative salary level of federal employees fell. John R. Commons, (1935, 70) argued that the position of federal employees deteriorated in the late nineteenth and early twentieth centuries as nominal salaries remained generally constant but consumer prices rose, especially after 1910. He noted that nominal wages for postal employees were almost unchanged from 1895 to 1907 and that their purchasing power dropped by 26 percent during that period. Similarly, Spero (1927, 33, 96) discussed the lack of change in federal pay schedules and the fall in real incomes for postal employees after the turn of the century.[11]

It is possible to compare the patterns of federal and private pay, using data compiled by Paul Douglas (1930). Douglas provided average wages for various private-sector industries and the federal government as well as the relative weights used for computing an all-industry average wage that includes federal government wages.[12] Using these weights and individual industry data, we can calculate the average salaries for the private and government sectors. Table 4.1 provides the relevant average wage data for the private sector and the federal government from 1900 through 1926 and the ratios between the two.

The data in table 4.1 indicate that, between 1900 and 1917, nominal regular federal salaries rose by 25 percent, postal salaries by 30 percent, but private salaries by 63 percent. At the same time, however, the all-item CPI index rose by 54 percent (U.S. Department of Commerce, 1975, 211). Hence, government employees lost ground in real terms. The decline in their relative position is revealed by the ratios of federal to private pay. The comparatively better average weekly salary position of federal employees compared with those in manufacturing, coal mining, railroads, farming, and the building trades (the components of the private index) in 1900 is shown by the ratios of federal to private salaries in columns 4 and 5. Moving toward 1920, however, there is a noticeable fall in the size of the ratios. Federal employee salaries, in general, did not keep pace with increases in salaries elsewhere in the economy, particularly in the building trades, railways, coal mining, and manufacturing.[13] There was a

Table 4.1   Federal Government/Private-Sector Average Weekly Salaries,
                   1900–1926

Year	Federal ($)[a]		Private Sector ($)[a]	Ratio Federal to Private	
	Regular	Postal		Regular	Postal
1900	19.87	17.79	11.57	1.72	1.54
1901	20.13	18.00	11.75	1.71	1.54
1902	20.40	17.96	12.18	1.67	1.47
1903	20.52	17.85	12.66	1.62	1.41
1904	20.50	17.90	12.79	1.60	1.40
1905	20.62	17.98	12.97	1.59	1.39
1906	20.85	17.71	13.47	1.55	1.31
1907	21.04	18.15	13.89	1.51	1.31
1908	21.19	18.98	13.70	1.55	1.39
1909	21.27	19.63	13.88	1.53	1.41
1910	21.31	20.17	14.22	1.50	1.42
1911	21.46	20.60	14.39	1.49	1.43
1912	21.69	20.98	14.85	1.46	1.41
1913	21.85	21.62	15.21	1.44	1.42
1914	21.92	22.25	15.28	1.43	1.46
1915	22.15	22.35	15.39	1.44	1.45
1916	23.29	22.60	16.69	1.39	1.35
1917	24.90	23.21	18.91	1.32	1.23
1918	26.54	25.75	23.66	1.12	1.09
1919	29.23	31.12	26.94	1.08	1.16
1920	31.69	35.46	33.19	.95	1.07
1921	30.63	35.96	30.72	1.00	1.17
1922	31.25	35.46	29.40	1.06	1.21
1923	31.88	35.96	31.49	1.01	1.14
1924	32.85	37.19	32.75	1.00	1.14
1925	34.15	39.44	33.27	1.03	1.19
1926	34.79	40.92	33.88	1.03	1.21

Source: For the private industry salary averages, data were assembled from the "all manufacturing" data provided in Douglas (1930, 130); building trades (p. 137); coal mining (pp. 143, 162) (because combined anthracite and bituminous data begin with 1902, 1900 and 1901 include average wages from only bituminous coal mining); railway workers (p. 168); and farm labor (p. 186). The relative weights used to calculate the private-sector average are provided on p. 204.
[a]Current dollars.

rebound, beginning approximately in 1920, and postal employees did comparatively better than other federal employees. Federal postal unions organized earlier and were able to secure separate legislation for salaries and work rules as the twentieth century progressed.[14]

There are other indications of the deterioration in the salary position of federal employees. In 1916, the secretary of commerce reported a relative decline in the wages of government clerks that was making it increasingly difficult to fill government positions (see Johnson 1940, 25). Data compiled by Mary Conyngton on separation rates for federal workers reveal a similar pattern. Voluntary separation rates rose from 6.6 percent in 1909, to 12.5 percent in 1913, to 19.4 percent by 1917 (Conynton 1920, 15–20). Conyngton claimed that the documented rise in voluntary separations from the federal government labor force was due primarily to the deterioration in relative salaries of federal employees.

Given the comparative decline in federal salaries in the early twentieth century, federal unions had incentives to lobby for legislation to increase their salaries. The National Association of Letter Carriers, the National Federation of Federal Employees, and other federal unions actively promoted legislation, such as that in 1907, 1920, and 1923 for position reclassifications and opportunities for higher salaries.[15] These laws, especially the Classification Act of 1923, set the stage for gradual wage improvement, and by 1926, Spero could claim, most federal employees were paid more than their private-sector counterparts (Spero 1927, 31).

In lobbying for salary legislation, federal unions favored automatic salary increases and opposed efficiency ratings as a basis for pay adjustments. The president and the Congress, with interests in the effective provision of federal services, wanted salaries to reflect productivity, but such payment schemes could be divisive, and they relied on the discretionary actions of agency officials. As a result, federal employee unions had much less incentive to support those arrangements. Their generally successful efforts in opposing the widespread use of production ratings and supporting more automatic salary increases again reveal differences in the motivation of employee unions and that of the president and the Congress in the development of civil service rules.[16]

The Post Office Department, for example, attempted various standards of performance and demerit systems, beginning in 1910, which were opposed by federal unions. An example is one initiated in 1916: "Comparative ratings shall be given, on a scale of one hundred on the quantity of work the employees turn out. Such ratings shall be based on observations of the employee's work. . . . Clerks and carriers who set the standard for the office with relation to the work performed shall be rated one hundred. No employee shall be promoted to the $1,200 grade if his rating is less than 90 percent" (Spero 1927, 136–37, 190–91, 194). Similarly in 1914, the department attempted to drop the mileage basis for compensation for rural mail carriers and to replace it with a productivity measure that considered the number of pieces carried, the time required, and the weight of mail. The National Rural Letter Carriers' Association appealed to Congress with a bill defining mandatory salaries on twenty-four-mile routes (Spero 1927, 200–201). Across-the-board salary raises of $200 per grade were granted by Congress in 1918 (40 Stat. 742), with political pressure exerted by the postal unions to overcome opposition by Postmaster General Burleson (Spero 1927, 203).

In 1919, the Joint Commission on the Reclassification of Salaries was established to investigate possible salary structures and position classifications for the general classified service. One of the advisory groups consulted by the

Reclassified Commission was the National Federation of Federal Employees. The direct involvement of federal unions in setting federal employee salaries through legislation, as illustrated by the consultation with the NFFE, became an established part of the civil service system. The Reclassification Commission, with input from federal labor unions, issued its report in March 1920 (see U.S. House of Representatives 1920) calling for major reclassifications of all federal positions (Baruch 1941, 45–50). This report was criticized by the Bureau of Efficiency in the executive branch as an infringement on that agency's efforts to promote greater productivity and to lower costs in the federal government. The commission's recommendations were also opposed in the Senate for encouraging higher federal salaries (Spero 1927, 202–7; Spero 1948, 182–85; Van Riper 1958, 278–79, 296–97).[17]

The most important law regarding position classification and salaries for the general federal labor force was the Classification Act of 1923 (42 Stat. 1488).[18] The law created a Personnel Classification Board with three members, one each from the Civil Service Commission, the Bureau of Efficiency, and the Bureau of the Budget. This specific arrangement was opposed by the NFFE because it placed too much power in the hands of the Bureau of Efficiency and the Bureau of the Budget and assisted their efforts to reduce costs. Federal unions, however, endorsed the new classification of federal employee positions in Washington, D.C., as established by the law. These were gradually extended to the field service after 1923 (Baruch 1941, 58–59). The new position classifications included the professional and scientific service, the subprofessional service, the clerical, administrative, and fiscal service, and the custodial service. Each service was subdivided into between seven and fourteen grades, with a fixed salary range for each. The use of efficiency ratings was authorized by the law, but subject to review by the Personnel Classification Board. This was the first major legislation for uniform job positions, salaries, and promotions in the federal government, goals increasingly desired by federal unions because they reduced the discretion available to agency heads and supervisors.[19]

Prior to the passage of the 1923 law, many of the pay increases, especially for nonpostal positions, were under either lump-sums appropriations, where salary changes would be determined by department heads, or statutory appropriations, where Congress assigned salary levels to particular positions. But department heads determined the duties and qualifications for each position. Ismar Baruch notes, "Congress would appropriate a certain lump sum for a particular bureau or activity. The administrative official in charge of that bureau or activity could then create as many positions as he thought were necessary at the salaries he considered were necessary. . . . The salaries of positions paid from a lump-sum appropriation could be changed at the will of the executive" (1941, 34). Under the Classification Act of 1923, salaries were to be fixed by Congress according to uniform definitions of position duties and responsibilities as outlined by the Personnel Classification Board (Baruch 1941, 34).

With the uniform position structure defined by statute, unions could better lobby Congress for general salary increases that would apply broadly to federal employees without intervention by the agencies involved.

4.3.2   Hours of Work

Not only were federal employees able to raise their salaries by lobbying for pay legislation, but they were also able to obtain workplace benefits generally ahead of those in the private sector. Indeed, the federal government became a model for many of these benefits, and the precedents set at the federal level assisted in the spread of these benefits elsewhere in the economy. This joint effect explains the close collaboration between federal and private-sector unions in lobbying Congress for workplace benefits for federal workers. One benefit was the eight-hour day. A shorter workday was one of the initial demands of federal employee unions. Since in the late nineteenth century most federal employees were in the Post Office Department, and since postal unions were the first to organize, the earliest legislation regarding hours of work affected classified post office employees (Nesbitt 1976, 36–37).

Among postal workers, letter carriers were particularly well organized, and they lobbied Congress for maximum-hours legislation. Letter carriers were not covered by the 1868 federal law that limited hours of work for certain laborers, workmen, and mechanics, a law that also was not enforced. In their lobbying, the letter carriers turned to the Knights of Labor to assist them in pressuring Congress. A bill was drafted by the Knights of Labor for an eight-hour workday and sent to Congress in 1886. It was opposed by the Post Office Department, and, although it passed the Senate in June 1886, the bill was not voted on in the House (Spero 1927, 64–68). The letter carriers remained active in pushing for an eight-hour law, and one was reintroduced in Congress in 1888. Both the Knights of Labor and the newly organized National Association of Letter Carriers arranged demonstrations in support of the legislation outside the Capitol Building in Washington, D.C.

These lobbying efforts were successful. Two laws were passed, the first hours-of-work legislation enacted since 1868, one on 30 March 1888 for government printers (25 Stat. 57), the other on 24 May 1888 for the letter carriers (25 Stat. 157).[20] Once the legislation was enacted, the National Association of Letter Carriers monitored the actions of the Post Office Department in order to ensure its compliance. When the department attempted to evade the law, the union sued for overtime payment in an action that led to the Supreme Court ruling in 1893 in *United States v. Post* (148 U.S. 124) that overtime must be paid (Spero 1927, 73). These actions enhanced the prestige of the union and demonstrated to other federal employees the benefits of membership.

Congress enacted additional hours-of-work legislation for laborers and mechanics in the government service in 1892 (27 Stat. 340) and 1912 (37 Stat. 137).[21] Broader coverage and more complete restrictions on maximum hours for postal employees also were enacted in 1912 as the Reilly Eight-Hour-Day

Law (37 Stat. 539) for postal clerks and carriers.[22] The legislation was in section 5 of the post office appropriations bill for fiscal year 1913. The law was drafted by the National Association of Post Office Clerks and the National Carriers Association and opposed by the Post Office Department (Spero 1927, 84). Although the letter carriers had been covered by the 1888 eight-hour law, efforts of the Postal Department to evade the law led to action by the carriers' union to obtain clearer legislation that would also provide overtime pay and automatic promotions. The 1912 law, also for the first time, gave postal clerks, who organized unions later than the letter carriers, eight-hour-day benefits (Spero 1927, 177–80).

These 1912 laws covering federal employees played an important role in advancing the eight-hour-day movement elsewhere in the economy in a number of ways. First, the laws applied to men and were broader than state legislation, which tended to focus either on women and children or on men only in specific industries.[23] Early state laws, such as those passed in Colorado in 1899 or in Utah in 1895, for example, applied only to mines and smelters and were often declared unconstitutional by state courts.[24] State governments did not pass broad hours-of-work legislation for government employees until the 1930s, and general hours legislation from the federal government to cover most private employees did not come until the 1938 Fair Labor Standards Act.[25]

Second, federal legislation set precedents for the private sector and helped create a more favorable environment for hours-of-work restrictions, which were strongly opposed by the National Association of Manufacturers and other business groups.[26] Indeed, the AFL backed legislation for an eight-hour day for federal employees, even though it preferred to negotiate such benefits for its members in the private sector rather than relying on legislation. As noted by Commons, "Special protections for this group was sought, not because of any special hazard either for the public or for the workers involved, but because of the belief that where the government was the employer, its establishment of maximum hours would be more readily approved by the public and by the courts than would laws for other groups. These public works laws, it was believed, would then serve as an entering wedge for more legislation and as an example to private employers" (1935, 542).[27] For these two reasons, the eight-hour day for federal workers was a major aim of the AFL, and its Legislative Committee prepared bills and lobbied national political parties and candidates for it, beginning in 1902 (Perlman and Taft 1935, 152–57).

After the federal eight-hour laws were enacted in 1912, there were attempts to weaken their provisions. These efforts were strongly resisted by federal unions. The opposition of the National Federation of Federal Employees, the Stenographers and Typists Union, and other unions to amendments to appropriations bills to increase the minimum daily hours of work of government employees in Washington, D.C., sponsored by Representative Borland of Missouri between 1916 and 1918, illustrates the tactics taken by the unions. Borland argued that the amendments would "put government employees on the same workday basis as workers outside" (Spero 1948, 177). The amendments were successfully blocked in 1916 in committee after an "outpouring" of union opposition to the measures in Congress. The amendments were reintroduced in 1918 by Borland, who was running for reelection. Federal unions, assisted by the AFL, campaigned against Borland in his Kansas City district by sending members and funds to support his opponent. Borland lost, and "for years afterward, in the official magazine and in organizational leaflets, the union waved Borland's political scalp as its prize trophy" (Johnson 1940, 48).[28]

4.3.3   Workers' Compensation Provisions

Another benefit obtained by federal employees through active political lobbying of Congress for legislation was compulsory workers' compensation for injuries or death due to workplace accidents. As with the eight-hour day, federal workers' compensation provisions came earlier and were more generous than those authorized by state governments for their employees or those found in the private sector. Federal workers' compensation legislation also became a model for the states, most of which adopted such legislation after 1910 (see Lubove 1967, 263). By setting the precedent for compulsory compensation legislation, the federal government helped demonstrate that such laws were workable. This point was made during 1914 hearings in the House of Representatives: "There is no doubt but that the people of this country are completely converted to a belief in reasonable compensation legislation and look to the federal government to furnish a model system in its relations with its employees."[29]

Indeed, the link between the enactment of workers' compensation legislation by the federal government and its adoption in the private sector was seen as a direct one. President Theodore Roosevelt emphasized the leadership role of the federal government during congressional debate on the 1908 federal compensation law: "This same broad principle which should apply to the Government should ultimately be made applicable to all private employers (quoted in Nordlund 1991, 5). Further, as extensions to the 1908 law were being considered in 1912, Leonard Howland, member of Congress from Ohio, asserted that "the Federal Government should be willing to treat its own employees as well at least as it proposes to compel industrial enterprises to treat their employees" (U.S. House of Representatives 1912b, 10).

The key federal workers' compensation laws were enacted in 1908 and 1916. The 1908 federal law for compulsory compensation for injury or death, along with the 1916 extension for broader coverage, provided models for the states that enacted similar legislation between 1911 and 1930 (Paradis 1972, 212). The 1908 law (35 Stat. 556) provided compensation to artisans or laborers in manufacturing, arsenals, navy yards, rivers and arid lands construction projects, and employees of the Panama Canal Commission for injuries or death occurring in the course of employment. Under the law, an employee or his survivors received 100 percent of his salary for one year. The law was amended in 1912 (37 Stat. 74) to extend its provisions to any civilian employee in hazardous work in forestry and mines. The 1916 federal workers' compensation law—the Kern-McGillicuddy bill (39 Stat. 742)—applied to all civilian employees of the federal government, and it provided benefits for total disability of two-thirds salary, with no time limit, for a maximum of $66.67 per month and a minimum of $33.33 per month; for partial disability of two-thirds of the employee's loss in earning power due to an accident with no time limit on payments; and death benefits, depending on the number of beneficiaries, of up to two-thirds salary until the children reached age eighteen. Immediate medical assistance was also provided, and the waiting period to receive benefits was three days. A U.S. Employee's Compensation Commission was created to administer the law (see also Lubove 1967, 263).

These benefits were considerably more generous than those provided in state legislation. Roy Lubove (1967, 269–70) summarized state compensation laws and pointed out that they had limited benefits and low dollar payments to the injured or to their survivors. For example, the New Jersey workers' compensation statute of 1911 required a two-week waiting period, authorized a maximum payment for total disability of 50 percent of weekly wages up to $10.00 per week for 400 weeks, provided up to $10.00 per week for 300 weeks for partial disability, and outlined death benefits of 60 percent of wages up to $10.00 per week for 300 weeks.

Federal employee unions were active in lobbying Congress for workers' compensation legislation. An examination of the records of congressional hearings on proposed federal legislation between 1908 and 1916 reveals the role of federal unions and related groups, such as the National League of Employees of Navy Yards and Arsenals, the National Association of Letter Carriers, the Federal Civil Service Society, the National Association of Bureau of Animal Industry Employees, and others, in promoting the legislation.[30]

After enactment of federal legislation in 1908 and 1916, numerous state workers' compensation laws followed. In 1921, the U.S. Department of Labor described the adoption of workers' compensation laws and pointed out that the federal government led in the enactment of broad legislation. The first state law was adopted in Maryland in 1902, followed by one in Montana in 1909; but these laws were for mining only, and the Maryland law was declared unconstitutional.[31] Table 4.2 outlines the adoption of workers' compensation legislation between 1908 and 1919. It reveals that most of the state legislation came between 1911 and 1916, with only six states having no compensation law by 1921.

4.3.4   Pensions and Retirement Benefits

Another benefit obtained by federal employees generally in advance of their counterparts in the private sector and in state and local governments was pension coverage. Pensions for classified employees were provided by the retirement law of 22 May 1920, the Sterling-Lehlbach Act (41 Stat. 614). The law was enacted after considerable lobbying by federal unions and was considered model legislation for adoption by the states. Retirement provisions became an

Table 4.2   Enactment of General Workers' Compensation Legislation

Government Unit	Year	Government Unit	Year
Federal	1908	Maryland	1914
Washington	1911	Louisiana	1914
Kansas	1911	Wyoming	1915
Nevada	1911	Indiana	1915
New Jersey	1911	Montana	1915
California	1911	Oklahoma	1915
New Hampshire	1911	Vermont	1915
Wisconsin	1911	Maine	1915
Illinois	1911	Colorado	1915
Ohio	1911	Pennsylvania	1915
Massachusetts	1911	Federal	1916
Michigan	1912	Kentucky	1916
Rhode Island	1912	South Dakota	1917
Arizona	1912	New Mexico	1917
West Virginia	1913	Utah	1917
Oregon	1913	Idaho	1917
Texas	1913	Delaware	1917
Iowa	1913	Virginia	1918
Nebraska	1913	North Dakota	1919
Minnesota	1913	Tennessee	1919
Connecticut	1913	Missouri	1919
New York	1913	Alabama	1920

Source: U.S. Department of Commerce and Labor (1921, 13).

aim of federal employees after 1890, and, beginning in 1900, every session of Congress considered at least one bill to provide for pensions for the federal civilian labor force. Postal unions were active in campaigning for retirement provisions, and they periodically worked to defeat those members of Congress who opposed the legislation (Spero 1927, 270–83). Additionally, the U.S. Civil Service Retirement Association and the National Association of Civil Service Employees were formed, in part, to lobby for federal retirement legislation.[32] Congressional debate between 1900 and 1920 over federal pension provisions centered on the government's share of pension contributions and whether the federal government should assume new financial commitments of this scale.[33] Federal unions maintained pressure on Congress. By 1912, the Republican party platform endorsed pensions for civil service employees, and the Democratic party followed suit in its 1916 presidential platform (see U.S. Senate 1918, 5). The U.S. Civil Service Retirement Association, the National Association of Civil Service Employees, and the Letter Carriers Association joined forces to organize the Joint Conference on Retirement, which successfully lobbied Congress for passage of the 1920 retirement law. Other organizations supporting the legislation included the Railway Mail Association, the National Federation of Federal Employees, and the National Federation of Postal Employees.[34]

Part of the support of Congress for federal pension legislation was based on an efficiency drive following World War I. With tenure for civil servants, the federal government had accumulated a large number of older employees who were perceived to be less productive than younger workers. Pension benefits were viewed as a means of encouraging their retirement (see U.S. Senate 1918, 5; U.S. Senate 1919a, 3). Under the law, all classified civil service employees qualified for a pension after reaching age seventy and rendering at least fifteen years of service. Mechanics, letter carriers, and post office clerks (the most organized employees) were eligible for a pension after reaching age sixty-five, and railway mail clerks were eligible at age sixty-two. The ages at which employees qualified were also mandatory retirement ages, although an employee could be retained for two years beyond the mandatory age if the department head and the head of the Civil Service Commission approved. All eligible employees were required to contribute 2.5 percent of their salaries toward the payment of pensions. Pension benefits were determined by the number of years of service. Those who had served thirty or more years (class A employees) could receive 60 percent of their average annual salary during the last ten years of service. On the other hand, those who had more than fifteen years of service but fewer than eighteen years of service (class F employees) could receive 30 percent of their average annual salary during the last ten years of service.[35]

The 1920 Federal Retirement Act was considerably more generous than either state government or private pension provisions at the time. When the act was passed, only Massachusetts had a civil service retirement plan, which had been adopted in 1911.[36] The Massachusetts plan required all employees to contribute up to 5 percent of their salaries to a pension trust. Retirement was possible at age sixty and mandatory at age seventy. At retirement, the state purchased an annuity in the retiree's name equal to twice the value of the employee's accumulated contribution.[37] This amounted to 50 percent of each employee's pension. The federal government's contribution under the 1920 law, however, was approximately 67 percent.[38] Similarly, there were fewer than 300 nonfarm, private-sector pension plans in the United States in 1920. These plans covered around 10 percent of the civilian labor force, but the lack of funding and tight vesting restrictions meant that only a small portion of those workers ever received a retirement benefit.[39] Few private-sector plans matched the federal government's minimum pensions of from $180 (class F employees) to $360 (class A employees) for comparable years of service.[40]

4.4 Summary

In chapters 2 and 3, we emphasized the roles of the president and the Congress in the establishment and subsequent modification of the federal civil service system. Even so, there are other important attributes of the civil service system that are not so clearly in the interest of the president or the Congress. Relatively high salaries for lower-level employees, a compressed salary distribution compared with the private sector, near automatic promotions, and strict tenure rules are attributes of the current federal civil service system. Understanding why they were added requires going beyond the president and the Congress to an investigation of the role played by federal employee unions in lobbying for legislation in their interest. Indeed, automatic promotions, rather than those based on efficiency ratings, were at first opposed by the president and the Congress. As we point out early in this chapter, the creation of the merit system helped unite an otherwise fragmented federal civilian labor force. As the classified share of federal employees increased, more and more of these federal workers began to view themselves as distinct groups with a long-term interest in their jobs and labor contracts. The outcome was the rise of federal employee unions after 1883.

Federal employees became active in lobbying Congress for legislation recognizing the right to join unions and to lobby Congress without penalty of dismissal (Lloyd-LaFollette Act). They worked to raise their salaries, which had declined compared to those in the private sector after 1883. After 1920, the relative deterioration of federal salaries was reversed. Through other legislation, federal employees obtained additional workplace benefits before their private-sector counterparts, including the eight-hour day, comparatively liberal workers' compensation coverage, and more extensive pension provisions.

We have emphasized that, in their lobbying efforts, federal employee unions received important support, first, from the Knights of Labor and, later, from the AFL and other organized labor groups because the benefits received by federal workers could set useful precedents for other labor markets. Some federal unions were part of the AFL, such as the National Federation of Federal Employees and the National Federation of Post Office Clerks, so that coordination was natural. In addition, after 1905, the AFL began to look to legislation as a means, along with traditional contract negotiations, to advance the general goals of organized labor (Weinstein 1967, 159–65). Lobbying for legislation affecting federal employees became part of a broader legislative initiative of the AFL.

In the following chapters, we examine the further modification of the federal civil service system after 1930 by the president, the Congress, *and* federal unions. We conjecture as to why the lobbying efforts of federal employees appear to have been so successful, directing the development of the civil service system in ways beneficial to their interests.

Notes

1. Indeed, an understanding of the process of institutional change requires a recognition that, as relative prices change, new parties will be attracted to and seek to mold an institution to suit their needs. For an interesting study of how sugar import controls induced new interest groups (corn growers) and technology (corn sweeteners) with as

much at stake in the regulation as the original parties (domestic sugar growers and processors), see Krueger (1991).

2. The president and members of Congress, as well as some voters, may have foreseen the short-term effects of the civil service system as it was being assembled. But we are examining institutional development over a 100-year period, and politicians concerned with reelection necessarily focused their attention on short-term factors that affected critical constituents. These politicians had little incentive to follow the much longer-term development of the civil service system.

3. Johnson comments, "No motivation of civil service unions is stronger than the desire to maintain and extend the merit system. In some cases, where jobs are unstable and unclassified, union activity takes the form of maneuvering for new projects, transfers, or reemployment lists, all for the purpose of preserving employment. But in most cases union efforts are directed toward maintenance of the merit system where it now applies and extension of it to practically all exempted areas. . . . Relative to spoils, unorganized employees have to some extent taken over the watch-dog functions performed by the civil service reform groups" (1940, 38).

4. Johnson (1940, 23–26) argues that federal unions played a critical role in the development of civil service legislation and practices. In a more contemporary setting, Freeman (1986, 42) argues that public unions rely more on political influence than do private unions. They are both employees and voters and, hence, can influence the demand for government services.

5. U.S. Department of Commerce (1975, 1103). For discussion of the political activity of federal employee unions, see Johnson (1940, 27–37).

6. The salary grades were $600, $800, $900, $1,000, $1,100, and $1,200. Automatic promotions were authorized through $900 at second-class post offices and through $1,000 at first-class post offices.

7. During debate on the legislation in the second session of the Sixty-second Congress, the Senate did insert an antistrike provision because of its concern that union membership might lead to strikes by government employees.

8. Clerks and carriers were divided into five grades from $1,400 to $1,800 annually with $100 increments between them. This act is discussed in more detail later in the text.

9. For a detailed discussion of the pay schedules in effect during the period both before and after the passage of the Pendleton Act, see Baruch (1941).

10. An observed pattern of deterioration in the relative salary position of federal workers in the early period of the merit system is inconsistent with Horn's (1988) discussion of the motivation for civil service rules. Although Horn briefly examines the origins of the civil service system, he argues that the relatively high salaries and tenure protection currently observed for federal employees are reflections of an efficiency wage. According to Horn's agency explanation for civil service rules, Congress would provide high salaries in order to maintain and motivate the federal labor force. This, however, does not appear to have been the case during the initial forty years of the civil service system, when federal salaries seem to have declined compared to the private sector. Further, as we outline here and in subsequent chapters, the subsequent rise in federal salaries owes more to the lobbying activities of federal unions than to a desire of Congress to provide an efficiency wage.

11. For discussion of the decline in the relative wage of federal employees and associated problems of retention, see also Van Riper (1958, 243).

12. Unskilled labor is not included in the averages for either the private sector of the government. Although Douglas provides wage day information for unskilled workers in various industry groups, there are no comparable data for the federal government sector.

13. Only farm laborers did not outpace federal employees (see Douglas 1930, 130, 137, 162, 168, 186, 193).

14. Spero (1927) describes the actions of postal unions and specific classification and wage legislation obtained by them. Van Riper (1958, 273–74) points to the success of federal postal unions in obtaining special legislation to address their demands. On the other hand, general federal employee unions organized later and were not as aggressive.

15. For a summary of pay legislation, see U.S. House of Representatives (1931). Johnson (1940, 44) discusses the role of the NFFE in the enactment of the Classification Act of 1923. The actions of postal unions in particular are discussed in the text.

16. Van Riper (1958, 247) notes that the use of service ratings as a basis for promotion was very limited. He claims that this was because such ratings were difficult to implement and does not mention the opposition of federal unions to the use of efficiency ratings.

17. In the Senate, Senator Reed Smoot of Utah led the criticism of the Reclassification Committee's report. For discussion of the Bureau of Efficiency, see Baruch (1941, 38–44).

18. For discussion, see Baruch (1941, 50–59).

19. Already department heads were beginning to complain about their inability to implement new work rules and pay for productivity. See statements by James Davis, secretary of labor, and Attorney General Harry Daugherty in Davis, Daugherty, and Work (1923).

20. Dankert, Mann, and Northrup state that "agitatation for enforcement of legislation covering federal employees led to the 1888 eight-hour day law for workers in the Government Printing Office and the Post Office Department" (1965, 45).

21. The latter required that contracts between the U.S. government and laborers or mechanics be limited to eight hours. Penalties were outlined.

22. Section 5 provided that, after 4 March 1913, letter carriers in the city delivery service and clerks at first- and second-class post offices would work a maximum of eight hours a day.

23. In testimony regarding the proposed Fair Labor Standards Act, Lucy Mason, general secretary of National Consumers League, stated that only eleven states had eight-hour-day legislation and that most laws applied only to women (see U.S. Senate 1937, 403). Goldin (1988, 1990) argues that state legislation enacted after 1914 defining the maximum hours of work for women generally had a minimal effect on the actual hours worked and that it also tended to apply equally to men.

24. For a summary of state efforts prior to 1912, see U.S. House of Representatives (1912a, 8–10). Commons (1935, 542) ends a summary of state legislation with the conclusion that it was fragmentary and generally not effective.

25. Dankert, Mann, and Northrup (1965, 6) claim that hours of work per week in the private, nonagricultural sector did not decline to around forty hours until 1940. They also assert (p. 45) that there was little action by state governments to provide general hours legislation until 1933. For discussion of the lag by the states in passing hours limits for men in public works between 1914 and 1932, see also Commons (1935, 547, 558).

26. As evidence of a more favorable environment, state legislation setting hours of work was sustained by the Supreme Court in 1917 (243 U.S. 426, Bunting decision; Dankert, Mann, and Northrup 1965, 47). More boldly, Paradis (1972, 64) claims that the eight-hour day gathered momentum after the federal government's 1912 laws. For discussion of the important role of federal legislation in the hours-of-work movement, see also Cahill (1968, 82) and Commons and Andrews (1936, 119).

27. For similar comments, see Dankert, Mann, and Northrup (1965, 51).

28. For discussion, see Spero (1948, 176–81).

29. Testimony by Henry R. Seager, president of the American Association for Labor Legislation (see U.S. House of Representatives 1914, 10). Also, Lubove argues that

"considerable impetus to the compensation movement came from the enactment of the federal law in 1908, which had been strongly endorsed by President Theodore Roosevelt" (1967, 263). See also U.S. House of Representatives (1914, 10).

30. For example, during the 1914 hearings in the House of Representatives (U.S. House of Representatives 1914) on a workers' compensation bill, testimony was given by William E. Russell, president of the Federal Civil Service Society; S. J. Walkley, secretary of the National Association of Bureau of Animal Industry Employees; Edward J. Cantwell, national secretary of the National Association of Letter Carriers; Edward J. Gainer, president of the National Association of Letter Carriers; Frank J. Rogers, president of the United National Association of Post Office Clerks; and Arthur Holder, legislative committeeman of the AFL. All testified in favor of legislation to provide automatic compensation for civilian employees of the federal government for death or serious accident. This ultimately was provided in 1916. Additional discussion of the role that employee groups and unions played in the workers' compensation movement is provided in Weinstein (1967).

31. For additional discussion of early state legislation and the role played by federal laws, see Weinstein (1967), Lubove (1967), and Paradis (1972, 212).

32. One of the reasons that it took until 1920 for legislation to be passed was that the lobbyists promoted different kinds of retirement provisions. The U.S. Civil Service Retirement Association favored a contributory system, while the National Association of Civil Service Employees promoted pension legislation with more significant government contributions.

33. Numerous hearings were held between 1900 and 1920 on federal pensions (see, e.g., U.S. House of Representatives 1912c; and U.S. Senate 1919a).

34. For testimony, political support, and a history of federal retirement legislation, see U.S. Senate (1918, 1919a).

35. The coverage of the law, including payments by class of worker and contribution schemes, is outlined in U.S. Senate (1918, 1919a).

36. For a summary of city retirement plans in the United States, most of which were either disability plans or entirely funded by the workers, see "Civil Service Retirement" (1916).

37. The Massachusetts plan was considered by Congress for possible adoption in 1912 (see U.S. House of Representatives 1912c, 66–76).

38. This is estimated by Epstein (1928, 168).

39. For discussions of private-sector pension conditions, see Epstein (1928, 160), Epstein (1933, 148), and Craig (1992).

40. For a review of contemporary private-sector pension plans, see Conyngton (1926, 21–56). See also Brooks (1971, 305), who argues that pensions and vacations were established in government employment long before becoming commonplace in private employment.

5   The Maturation of Federal Employees as an Interest Group

5.1 Introduction

The legislative histories of major laws affecting the civil service system show that an active role in shaping them was played by early federal employee unions. The evidence offered in this chapter reveals that federal employee groups were able to utilize these earlier institutional changes to expand their influence and direct the subsequent course of the civil service system. Indeed, as an interest group, federal workers have done rather well. Even though federal workers do not have the right to strike, most of the evidence indicates that the compensation of federal employees generally exceeds the amount that they would earn either in the private sector or elsewhere in the public sector.

Federal unions have achieved this favorable outcome, at least in part, because they have been granted direct input into the design of the very institutions that determine their members' compensation. By law, federal wages must be comparable with those in the private sector. Yet federal employee unions have been able to influence the design of the surveys used to judge whether government salaries are equal to those in the private sector in ways that are favorable to federal workers. The influence that federal unions have had on salary legislation is also evident in the structure of salaries within the civil service. In lobbying for statutory wage increases, there has been considerable emphasis by the unions on an egalitarian pay schedule and on rewarding seniority within the bureaucracy. Through their efforts, federal unions have been able to secure a relatively high average wage, but there is considerable wage compression at upper-level positions. In addition, federal employees have extensive employment protection, and seniority, rather than merit, largely determines both individual salaries and employment security.

There are a number of reasons for the apparent emphasis by federal employee unions on an egalitarian pay schedule and seniority. In general, these have been goals of all labor unions (see Freeman and Medoff 1984). Trade unions have long pursued a policy of a "standard rate" of pay, partly because unions are political entities and must therefore remain responsive to the demands of the majority of their members. Indeed, a major determinant of the demand for union membership has been a desire to reduce perceived inequalities in compensation (see Farber and Saks 1980). Equalizing wages among workers contributes to solidarity in union establishments, without which "it is difficult to see how a union would be able to maintain its organizational strength" (Freeman and Medoff 1984, 80). Consistent with the notion that group solidarity is important for lowering the costs of collective action is union insistence on a wage rate, or range of rates, that is associated with particular jobs rather than with individuals. By deemphasizing the merits of individuals, unions seek to achieve a more cohesive organization.

Unions appear to have been successful in implementing egalitarian wage plans. A narrower range of wage dispersion is seen in the unionized, relative to the nonunionized, sectors of the U.S. economy (see Freeman 1980). Because unionized establishments have been induced to place less weight on the merits of individual workers, more weight is placed on other factors, such as seniority, for deciding promotion or job retention. While job protection based on seniority is also evident in nonunion establishments, the degree of seniority protection tends to be much greater for unionized ones (Freeman and Medoff 1984, 122–35).

More specifically for federal unions, the emphasis on egalitarian pay schedules helps promote solidarity among rank-and-file workers, who are members of different unions. Membership is spread across a number of unions, such as the American Federation of Government Employees (AFGE), the National Federation of Federal Employees (NFFE), the National Federation of Post Office Clerks, and the National Letter Carriers Association, and membership comes from clerical and lower-level management employees.[1] Individuals occupying more senior professional positions tend to belong to professional organizations, such as the American Bar Association, the American Federation of Technical Engineers, the American Optometric Association, and the National Society of Professional Engineers. In lobbying for salary legislation, and in commenting on the proposals of the president's pay agent, federal unions naturally have been more concerned about raising the salaries of their members than about raising the salaries of those employees in higher positions who are more likely to be members of professional groups.[2] Egalitarian objectives have helped solidify the different unions, at times to the disadvantage of higher-level federal employees.

The purpose of this chapter is to describe the structure of the federal pay system and to show how federal unions have influenced its design. Of course, unions have not received all that they have wanted. Nevertheless, their record, beginning with such early benefits legislation as the eight-hour day as well as with the classification and salary legislation examined in this chapter, indicates remarkable lobbying success. These findings bear directly on current debates over the direction of causality between rules (legislation and executive orders) and the growth of union influence. At issue is whether recent policy changes spurred the growth of federal unions, giving them greater bargaining power, or whether union political influence initiated the policy changes that brought further union growth and performance.[3] Federal unions and other employee groups grew out of the establishment of the merit system, which lowered the costs and raised the returns to membership. Federal unions then became active in securing favorable public policies regarding salaries, workplace benefits, and recognition.

We return to this issue in the conclusion to the chapter. In the chapter summary, we also consider some alternative explanations for the federal pay structure. We argue that, although the existing distribution of federal pay is inconsistent both with current notions of incentive wage structures and with merit principles, it is consistent with the common objectives of most labor unions.

5.2   Federal Pay Structures and Union Influence

5.2.1   Pay Structures

Federal civilian employees are currently covered by a number of different pay plans. The majority of these employees (see table 5.1) are under the General Schedule (GS) pay plan, which consists of eighteen grades.[4] This system is intended primarily for white-collar employees, and, in 1989, the General Schedule included approximately 53 percent of the federal civilian labor force. At least in principle, the grades are designed to reflect increasing degrees of difficulty and responsibility. Within grades GS-1–GS-15, there are ten scheduled steps for advancement within each grade. The General Schedule is a national pay system, and, until recently, it made no allowance for regional differences in the cost of living or local wage standards.[5] In addition, there is the Senior Executive Service, created by the 1978 Civil Service Reform Act (92 Stat. 1111), which covers a limited number of top officials who were previously

Table 5.1   **Civilian Employees in the Executive Branch of the Federal Government by Pay Group, 1949–89 (full-time employees)**

Year	General Schedule	Federal Wage System	Postal	Other System
1949	829,683	501,533	361,389	71,684
1969	1,273,695	592,218	654,477	119,145
1989	1,493,696	374,443	826,726	147,969

Sources and notes: U.S. Office of Personnel Management (1989). For 1949, employees classified under the Classification Act of 1923 are listed as General Schedule. The number of U.S. Postal Service employees in 1989 is from U.S. Post Office Department, *Annual Report of the Postmaster General, Fiscal Year 1989.*

in grades GS-16–GS-18 as well as other top managerial and policy positions that do not require Senate confirmation. Special pay plans also exist for members of the Foreign Service and certain occupations, such as physicians. The Federal Wage System (FWS) covers blue-collar employees—essentially trade, craft, and other labor occupations. Under the FWS, blue-collar workers are paid according to the prevailing rate for certain occupations in a designated geographic area. The other major pay system is that of postal workers. On 1 July 1971, the old post office ceased operating as a department of the federal government and began operating as the U.S. Postal Service, a public corporation.[6] In contrast to most GS and FWS employees, the wages and benefits of postal service workers are now set by collective bargaining.

The Classification Act of 4 March 1923 (42 Stat. 1488) established the basis for the current white-collar pay system of uniform position classification, promotions, and salaries.[7] Prior to the enactment of the 1923 law, departments were given lump-sum appropriations, and there were no rules that explicitly called for equal pay for equal work. Some salary rates were set by statute, and others were not. Hence, department heads had considerable authority in determining an employee's wage, and federal unions lobbied for legislation to reduce this discretion. The relative salary position of federal employees had been declining in the early twentieth century, and private-sector wage increases during World War I added to the sense within federal unions that they were losing ground. Lobbying efforts were mounted to raise the federal salary level and to change the federal salary structure. At the behest of the National Federation of Federal Employees (NFFE), one of the largest federal unions at that time, a commission was appointed to consider the establishment of a standardized pay plan that would set salary on the basis of the characteristics of the position, not of the individual holding the job (Nesbitt 1976, 62–66). There was considerable resistance to such a plan by members of Congress and bureau heads, who argued that determining pay was a prime management function, not the duty of a commission (U.S. House of Representatives 1920, 54).

Not only did the NFFE have to confront continuing opposition to pay increases and job standardization from such notables as Senator Reed Smoot, chair of the Appropriations Committee, and the Bureau of Efficiency, but the organization also ran into problems with federal workers who were skilled craftsmen. Congress had recognized the prevailing-rate principle for skilled workers in 1861, and this group of workers had little need for consistent position classification and salaries, especially since it might undermine wages earned in particular areas (Nesbitt 1976, 399). Although the NFFE and other federal unions finally prevailed in their efforts to obtain passage of the Classification Act of 1923, authorizing comparable pay for comparable work at the federal offices covered by the law, skilled employees were exempted from its provisions. These exemptions were maintained in the Classification Act of 1949 (63 Stat. 954), which formally extended the provisions of the 1923 law to the field service outside Washington, D.C. The distinction remains through the General Schedule with its national pay plan and the Federal Wage System with its prevailing-wage practices.

The Classification Act of 1923 applied immediately to only about 50,000 employees in the District of Columbia and was only slowly implemented for field service employees. One of the major decisions that had to be made in expanding the classification and pay system beyond the Washington, D.C., area was whether to allow geographic wage differentials (Feldman 1931, 41). With different position definitions and salaries between offices in Washington, D.C., and jobs in the field, the system became increasingly difficult to manage after 1923. Congress, however, was not willing to give up the micro management of federal wages until 1949. The dramatic expansion in federal employment between 1933 and 1940—the number of federal employees grew by 73 percent—and the creation of New Deal agencies in the 1930s raised the costs to Congress of managing federal salaries and provided the catalyst for the extension of position classification to the rest of the field services (U.S. Department of Commerce 1975, 1102). The Ramspeck Act of 1940, which extended the merit service to New Deal agencies, followed by the Hoover Commission report on personnel management practices, ultimately led to the passage of the Classification Act of 1949.[8] The law authorized the president to expand the functions of the Civil Service Commission and to develop a comprehensive national pay plan for GS workers.

Federal employee unions, such as the NFFE and the AFGE, were active supporters of the Classification Act of 1949, and they testified in favor of the bill during congressional hearings (U.S. Senate 1949). By extending the provisions of the Classification Act of 1923 to all merit employees, the 1949 law provided for uniform job classifications and salaries nationwide. As federal unions achieved their objective of "equal pay for equal work," supervisor discretion in individual salaries and promotions was reduced.[9] As we discuss later, Congress also supported the maintenance of uniform position classification and salary structures within the General Schedule because it offered a means to better monitor the personnel system.

5.2.2   Union Membership

The influence of federal unions in obtaining favorable public policies is illustrated by President Kennedy's 1962 Executive Order 10988. During the close 1960 presidential campaign, postal and other federal unions obtained a pledge from John Kennedy that, if elected, he would back collective-bargaining arrangements between federal workers and their agencies and departments (Nesbitt 1976, 19; Stern 1988, 55, 56). The support of federal workers and organized labor in general was essential for Kennedy's election. After Kennedy took office, organized labor continued the pressure. In September 1961, Andrew Biemiller, director of legislation for the AFL-CIO, urged the president to issue an executive order recognizing the right of federal employees to join labor unions and to engage in collective bargaining (see *New York*

Times, 14 September 1961, 14). In response to his earlier commitment, President Kennedy established a cabinet-level task force to explore federal employee-management relations, and, after receiving its recommendations, he announced in December 1961 that he would issue an executive order to give unions an enhanced status to help shape federal personnel policy (see *New York Times,* 5 December 1961, 27).

Executive Order 10988, issued in January 1962, established a labor-management program for federal executive branch employees. The order contained provisions for the formal recognition of unions, an official status previously denied in the federal service. Although the Lloyd-LaFollette Act of 1912 allowed federal employees to join unions without penalty of dismissal, it did not formally recognize labor units as bargaining units. With the 1962 executive order, federal unions were placed in a better position to represent their members' grievances over such issues as transfers, promotions, discharge, safety, and health. The order provided for a limited range of collective bargaining through the establishment of exclusive bargaining units to negotiate with agency and department heads, but it did not allow collective bargaining over wages.[10] Collective bargaining remained largely restricted to semiautonomous agencies such as the Tennessee Valley Authority. Moreover, the executive order reaffirmed the long-standing opposition by the federal government to strikes by federal workers.[11] Despite these provisions against collective bargaining over wages and the prohibition of strikes, Executive Order 10988 appears to have provided enough new benefits from union membership to contribute to the growth of federal unions after 1962 (table 5.2).

Table 5.2 describes union membership and employees in exclusive bargaining units for the executive branch and Post Office Department from 1958 through 1985 and shows the increase in membership following Executive Order 10988. Federal unions include formal organizations, such as the American Federation of Government Employees and, for the postal service, the American Postal Workers Union. There is a distinction between union membership and union representation in federal units. In some cases, nonmembers are included in union bargaining, with the result that the number of employees represented by the union exceeds union membership. In addition to formal unions, there can be other bargaining organizations that engage in collective bargaining. The table indicates that many executive branch employees in bargaining units are not union members. The percentage of union membership in the executive branch has declined since the peak in 1972, but membership in a bargaining unit has remained relatively stable. By law, collective bargaining cannot address salary or benefits issues, which are set by statute and executive order; hence, unions and other bargaining organizations must lobby Congress and the president for favorable actions regarding pay. Alternatively, membership in postal unions has remained more stable and includes a larger proportion of postal employment. Most bargaining units appear to be postal unions.[12]

Union membership among nonpostal employees has been greater for blue-

Table 5.2   Federal Employees' Membership in Unions and Bargaining Units

	Executive Branch			Post Office		
Year	Total Employment (thousands)	Union Membership (%)	Bargaining Units (%)	Total Employment (thousands)	Union Membership (%)	Bargaining Units (%)
1958	1,817	6.3	N.A.	538	73.1	N.A.
1960	1,808	6.2	N.A.	563	76.0	N.A.
1962	1,896	9.6	N.A.	588	76.0	N.A.
1964	1,884	12.2	12.2	585	84.8	85.3
1966	2,051	14.0	21.2	675	78.8	91.6
1968	2,289	16.8	34.9	731	86.1	84.7
1970	2,158	22.4	42.4	726	82.5	86.2
1972	2,073	26.4	52.2	697	88.4	86.8
1974	2,140	25.9	53.4	707	83.9	85.8
1976	2,126	20.7	56.0	676	94.9	85.7
1978	2,117	22.4	58.0	656	88.3	87.8
1980	2,109	21.2	59.3	660	88.4	88.8
1981	2,093	21.8	59.0	663	88.0	91.4
1983	2,120	20.9	58.2	663	87.1	92.2
1985	2,148	N.A.	57.9	717	N.A.	89.9

Source: Burton and Thomason (1988, 29).
Note: N.A. = not available.

collar (FWS) workers than for white-collar (GS) employees. This, in part, may be attributed to the manner in which wages have been determined in the federal sector. The principle of a prevailing rate of pay has long been the basis for determining wages for FWS employees, and local wage boards have existed to determine going rates in particular localities.[13] Although prior to Executive Order 10988 in 1962 there were no formal provisions for labor representation on local wage boards, federal unions representing FWS employees had been influential in board decisions. Further, since 1962, unions have been able to achieve even greater participation in the rate-fixing process because they are granted direct input into the design of wage-survey procedures. Formal representation allowed them to express their views with more force. As a consequence, in the 1960s, the Civil Service Commission was directed to develop a new federal wage system. The result was a major victory for those federal unions representing blue-collar employees. The new system not only maintained the basic concept of an "area prevailing wage" but also included automatic in-grade pay increases, based on longevity, that allowed federal wages to exceed private ones.[14] Despite claims that wage determination was strictly a management decision, through their unions FWS workers appear to have obtained considerable say in the outcome. Additionally, because decisions are made at the local level, individual FWS workers have had a stronger incentive to contribute to union activities than have GS workers, whose wages are determined by a national pay plan.

Another problem for widespread GS employee union membership is the large number of white-collar workers in the federal government. In 1983, for example, 444 different occupation codes were used to classify white-collar workers (U.S. Office of Personnel Management, *Federal Civilian Work Force Statistics: Monthly Release* [July 1984]). Many of those employees belonged to professional groups, such as the Society of Professional Engineers, which have historically opposed union membership. As Murray Nesbitt notes, "Thus, the unions which seek inclusive membership outside the Postal Service are faced with a dual problem of the skilled craft workers on the one hand and the professional, management, and supervisory employees on the other" (1976, 80). This dichotomy has resulted in the larger federal unions representing mainly the crafts, skilled and unskilled labor, postal workers, and clerical workers, while many professionals have abstained from union membership.[15]

Even so, federal unions and employee groups have achieved uncommon success in obtaining supportive legislation from Congress and executive orders from the president for GS employees. Before examining the actions of federal unions regarding pay, it is important briefly to address how well-organized postal unions have assisted other federal unions and employee groups in obtaining favorable salary legislation. As described in chapter 4, not only were postal unions, such as the National Association of Letter Carriers and the National Association of Post Office Clerks, the first federal labor organizations to form, but they were successful in obtaining early benefits, such as the eight-hour day. They also achieved relatively higher salaries before workers elsewhere in the federal government. As a result, postal unions became trendsetters that helped establish salary and benefit precedents for their colleagues in other parts of the federal government.

James Stern (1988, 55) notes that postal unions have long been among the most experienced and effective congressional lobbyists. As early as President Roosevelt's 1906 gag order, postal unions played a central role in labor-management negotiations in the federal government. Their lobbying of Congress to counter the gag order helped bring about the passage of the Lloyd-LaFollette Act (37 Stat. 539), protecting the rights of federal workers to organize to promote their own interests. Additionally, Richard Fenno describes the actions of postal employee unions in pressuring Congress for salary increases and how those efforts benefited other federal workers: "It is acknowledged by all participants that the postal workers 'carry the ball' and that all other federal employees 'ride on their backs' in getting pay raises" (1973, 247).[16] Because of the emphasis on equality of pay in the federal government, once postal workers obtained higher salaries, fairness issues were raised by other federal unions in calling on Congress to enact salary adjustment legislation. For example, in congressional hearings on federal salary legislation in 1970, representatives of the AFGE claimed that reforms were needed to give "classified and other statutory pay systems employees equal treatment with postal employees" (U.S. House of Representatives 1970, 91–92).

The role of federal unions and employee groups in influencing pay levels and the process by which they are determined is illustrated by the legislative histories of the Federal Salary Reform Act of 1962 (76 Stat. 841), the 1970 Federal Pay Comparability Act (84 Stat. 1946), and the Federal Employees Pay Comparability Act of 1990 (104 Stat. 1427). These are the key statutes that require that the wages of GS employees be comparable with those paid in the private sector. The laws outline how the private-sector comparisons are to be made, how they are to be translated into recommendations by the president to the Congress for statutory pay increases, and how federal unions and employee groups are to be involved in the process.[17] Not surprisingly, federal unions and employee groups have been active in lobbying for legislation that provides for significant union input into the survey and wage-increase process.

The 1962 Federal Salary Reform Act instituted annual private-sector surveys by the Bureau of Labor Statistics (BLS) for pay comparability. These surveys, known as the professional, administrative, technical, and clerical (PATC) surveys, became the basis for annual pay adjustments. Survey design included such matters as what industries to include, the minimum size of establishments in the survey, and what occupations to survey. In principle, the surveys were to provide information on private-sector earnings by occupation to the president's pay agent. The president could either accept the recommendations of the pay agent or propose a lower alternative to Congress by citing a national emergency or an economic condition affecting the general welfare. Although federal unions and employee groups, including the AFGE, the American Federation of Technical Engineers, and the National Association of Letter Carriers, testified in favor of the law, they soon became dissatisfied with the way in which it was implemented (U.S. Senate 1962). In testimony before Congress in 1970, representatives of the AFGE claimed that the president had failed to carry out the provisions of the Federal Salary Reform Act of 1962 and that comparability with the private sector had not been reached (U.S. House of Representatives 1970, 82–92). Accordingly, the AFGE and other unions lobbied for new legislation.

In 1970, two bills were under consideration for amending the 1962 Federal Salary Reform Act, H.R. 18403 and H.R. 18603. H.R. 18403 was introduced by Representative Morris Udall, who said that the AFGE has "been after me for many months to take actions on some kind of pay-setting reform legislation this year" (U.S. House of Representatives 1970, 81). The bill gave federal unions a more direct role in the salary comparability process by authorizing an Advisory Commission on Federal Pay of five members, of which one member was to come from the employee organization with the largest number of members in the General Schedule (in this case, the AFGE) and one from another organization of federal employees. The president was to appoint the other three members from among employees within the government. The advisory commission was to analyze the annual pay comparability survey conducted by the BLS and to recommend pay rates to the president. As such, it essentially took over the role of the president's pay agent (U.S. House of Representatives 1970, 6–8, 47–80). The president was to transmit the commission's report to Congress along with his recommendations for pay increases. The report was to be considered by the Congress in determining whether to accept or reject the president's recommendation.

H.R. 18603 was the administration bill, and it competed with the legislation favored by federal employee unions. The bill authorized a smaller committee with a less direct and more purely advisory role in the process of determining pay comparability. The bill called on the pay agent to consult with an Advisory Committee on Federal Salaries of three federal employees appointed by the president. There was no specific requirement that federal unions or employee groups be represented. The pay agent would then prepare a report comparing the rates of pay fixed by the agent, using surveys by the BLS, and those recommended by the advisory committee. The president would note any differences in submitting pay recommendations to the Congress (U.S. House of Representatives 1970, 40–45).

During congressional hearings in July 1970 on the competing bills, there were written statements and testimony from forty-two people, of whom thirty-seven were from federal unions or organizations of federal employees. Representatives of the AFGE asserted that the administration bill left management too much power over pay issues and made no specific provision for employee representation on the advisory committee. Representatives of the NFFE and the National Association of Government Employees (NAGE) also called for more direct involvement in the pay process (U.S. House of Representatives 1970, 111–23). Only smaller unions and associations, such as the National Association of Internal Revenue Employees, favored the administration bill—in order to avoid domination by the AFGE (U.S. House of Representatives 1970, 163).

Although the unions did not get H.R. 18403 passed, they did get modifications in the administration bill to increase their involvement in the salary determination process. The 1970 Federal Pay Comparability Act kept the pay agent but directed the agent to make recommendations based on input on survey design and interpretation of the results from two other bodies: an Advisory Committee on Federal Pay of three members appointed by the president and a Federal Employees Pay Council of five members, not employees of the government, but representatives of employee organizations from the three federal pay systems.[18] Up to three members could come from one organization, such as the AFGE. This committee was similar to that described in the Udall bill, and it was to consider the adequacy of the BLS survey, the process of pay comparability, and the proposed salary adjustments and give comments to the president. Its recommendations would also be considered by the Congress in reviewing the president's proposal. As such, the unions and employee groups achieved a committee with more independence and a greater role in the salary comparability process than was proscribed in the original administration bill.

Despite the changes authorized in the 1970 bill, dissatisfaction among federal unions and employee groups with the pay comparability process continued. Since its inception, the Federal Employees Pay Council was at odds with the recommendations of the pay agent and, in particular, with the final actions taken by the president. The view held by most members of the council was that the federal government had not honored its commitment to pay comparable wages. During 1986 congressional hearings to review the Federal Pay Comparability Act of 1970, there were complaints by both the advisory committee members and by members of the Federal Employees Pay Council that the president had not gone along with their recommendations (U.S. House of Representatives 1986, 3, 7, 13). It was noted that for eight years the president had proposed alternative pay rates to those recommended by the various advisory committees. Representatives of the AFGE and the NFFE, who were former members of the Federal Employees Pay Council, complained that the problem was in giving the president too much latitude in setting pay (U.S. House of Representatives 1986, 39–56). The Federal Employees Pay Council disbanded in protest in 1975.[19]

The continuing conflict over salary issues and efforts by federal unions to obtain greater influence over them brought a new round of legislation in 1990 with the Federal Employees Pay Comparability Act. In congressional hearings on the legislation, the president of the AFGE supported a particular version of the bill that would allow for annual salary adjustments based on an employment cost index (ECI) and that importantly replaced the president's pay agent with a thirteen-member body, the Federal Salary Council. The proposed Federal Salary Council was to be made up as follows: six seats to be held by labor representatives; three seats to be held by officials from the Office of Personnel Management, the Office of Management and Budget, and the Department of Labor, respectively; and four seats to be named by the president.[20] Not only were labor groups to receive a prominent position on the new pay council, but it was to have a more definitive role in implementing a new pay system. The president's discretion to defer recommended salary adjustments was to be restricted (U.S. House of Representatives 1990, 187).

The actual language of the 1990 Federal Employees Pay Comparability Act again did not give the employee groups all that they wanted, but they did achieve annual pay adjustments based on changes in the ECI, due in part to local conditions, and a majority of the membership on a new Federal Salary Council. The council was to have nine members—three impartial, six from employee organizations (with up to three from any one union or employee group). Unlike the 1970 law, the new legislation authorized only one advisory committee with a clearer mandate. The president's pay agent was retained but was to provide information to the council and to solicit its views and include them in the report to the president.

The record clearly documents the active role that federal unions played in shaping the federal compensation system. The unions have not been able to obtain a closed-shop designation, the explicit right to bargain over wages, or the right to strike, but they have been able to influence the legislation through which salary comparability is implemented. Although wage studies by economists examined in the next section, as well as time-series data, indicate a substantial wage advantage for most federal employees, relative to similar private-sector workers, the PATC surveys (designed with considerable union input), by contrast, suggest relatively lower wages for federal workers. Indeed, if one accepts the PATC survey results, federal salaries have fallen substantially behind those in the private sector, with the gap between the pay agent's recommendations and actual salary increases widening over time.[21] In 1979, for example, the president's pay agent reported, "After comparing Federal and private enterprise pay rates and considering the recommendations of employee organizations and unions, we have determined that the adjustment required would be a graduated increase ranging from a low of 8.80 percent at GS-6 to 15.43 percent at GS-15, and an indicated 23.64 percent at GS-18. The overall average percentage increase would be 10.41 percent" (President's Pay Agent 1980, 3). The actual increase that became effective on 1 October 1979 was an across-the-board salary adjustment equal to 7.0 percent.

There are reasons for questioning whether the PATC surveys really look at "comparable" situations in assessing private-sector wages. The surveys have been criticized for their geographic bias, emphasis on large private employers, and failure to include state and local employees when determining comparable wages.[22] Because smaller private establishments tend to pay lower salaries and are more likely to be located outside high-salary metropolitan areas, federal employee unions have been steadfastly against the inclusion of small establishments in the PATC surveys.[23] As we show in the next section, most federal workers tend to be paid more than state and local employees, a fact that explains why federal unions oppose having those workers included in the wage comparability surveys. Although with the passage of the Federal Employees Pay Comparability Act of 1990 Congress sought to correct some of these problems, the PATC surveys remain the primary basis for determining wage comparability with the private sector.

The decision in enacting the 1990 salary law to continue using the PATC surveys is, in itself, a reflection of the power of federal unions. In contrast to the survey results, standard human capital earnings regressions paint a very different picture, one that indicates that federal workers (except those in the most senior positions) are paid more than their private-sector counterparts. Yet this standard approach is not the official method for inferring the existence of a wage differential. Moreover, both the PATC surveys and human capital earnings regressions indicate considerable wage compression in the federal sector. Federal unions, like unions in the private sector, widely support egalitarian wage objectives.[24]

5.3   The Success of Federal Employees as an Interest Group

5.3.1   Relative Federal Salaries

In chapter 4, we argued that, with the gradual demise of patronage, congressional interest in maintaining comparatively high federal employee salaries in order to extract political assessments would diminish and, hence, that salaries would fall. The available evidence supports this prediction, with relative salaries declining from the 1880s through approximately 1920. After that time, however, following intense lobbying by unions, federal salaries began to rise relative to the private sector. National income and product account (NIPA) data (computer files, update 1991) reveal that the ratio of annual average salaries of federal civilian employees to private-sector workers was 1.36 in 1929, the first year these data were available. The relative advantage of federal salaries over those in the private sector has been maintained ever since, although there has been fluctuation in the size of the premium obtained by federal employees.

Figure 5.1 outlines the relative wage advantage between 1949 and 1990 of federal employees over both those in the private sector and state and local government employees. During the 1950s, the ratio of federal to private-sector wages remained fairly constant, but it grew in the 1960s and 1970s, a time when union representation in the federal sector was expanding. Over the period 1949–90, the ratio of federal to private-sector pay has averaged 1.31. For comparison, the ratio of federal to state and local government pay has averaged 1.35.

The data indicate that federal employees have done well compared to both groups in the postwar period. The NIPA data, however, do not control for job skills, education, or other factors that may account for higher relative federal pay. A more widely accepted procedure for comparing earnings across different groups of workers is to estimate a regression of the form

$$W_{ij} = X_{ij}\beta_j + \varepsilon_{ij},$$

where W is the wage rate for individual i in sector j, usually measured in logarithmic terms, so that the estimated coefficients measure approximately the percentage effect on wages due to changes in the right-hand-side variables. In the equation, X is a vector of measured characteristics of the individual worker, such as years of schooling, sex, race, location, and experience. The vector of regression coefficients, β, reflects the return or effect on wages due to a change in the corresponding element of the X vector for a member of group j.

Although there are a number of variants, comparisons between sectors can be obtained using the vector of estimated coefficients β_j and the characteristics

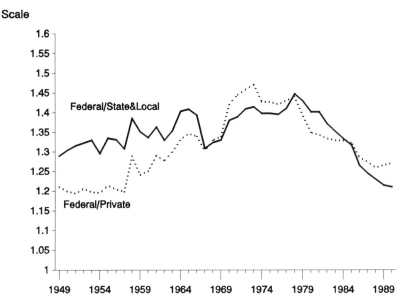

Fig. 5.1   **Relative federal wage advantage, 1949–90.**
Source: National income and product accounts.

of a representative individual employed in some other sector, k. This procedure
yields a prediction of what that same individual would earn if employed in
sector j. Subtracting this predicted value from the earnings estimate obtained
using the representative worker's own vector of coefficients, β_k, provides a
measure of the wage differential between sectors. Despite the potential problems with the use of relative federal wage ratios computed from NIPA data,
controlling for a host of socioeconomic characteristics does not alter the picture of a relative federal wage advangage shown in figure 5.1. Without exception, studies that have used Current Population Survey (CPS) data and standard
human capital earnings regressions reveal that most federal workers enjoy relatively higher wages than either their private- or their public-sector counterparts.[25]

One of the first comprehensive studies on relative federal sector pay that
attempted to control for variations in the attributes of workers was that of
Sharon Smith (1977). Her estimates were obtained using public use samples
of the census for the years 1960 and 1970 and CPS data files for 1973 and
1975. Smith estimated the basic human capital earnings equations described
above, with either individual hourly wage rates or annual earnings as the dependent variable. The controlling variables included measures of years of experience, education, race, sex, marital status, location, and major occupation.
Her results indicated not only that federal wages were above those for comparable workers in the private sector but also that there was considerable variation

in the size of the differential across groups.[26] In particular, the differential was greater for women, certain racial minorities, and federal employees stationed in rural areas. Her estimates for 1960, for example, indicated that the relative wage advantage was 8 percent for males and 13 percent for females (Smith 1977, 68).[27] According to Smith, the regional wage differentials reflected the use of a national pay scale for GS employees. The federal wage differential was lower in the Northeast and higher in the South. This is just the opposite of the pattern for private-sector wages, which have tended to be low in the South and high in the Northeast (Smith 1977, 91). Consistent with the NIPA data shown in figure 5.1, Smith (p. 63) also found that the wage differential between state and local workers and private-sector workers was, on average, close to zero in 1975.[28]

In addition to other studies, similar to Smith's, that have used CPS data and human capital earnings regressions, researchers have compared quit rates and job queues in the public and private sector. Unless the federal wage advantage reflects compensation for some negative, nonpecuniary condition associated with employment or location, quit rates should be lower and queues higher in the federal sector. This prediction is supported by the available research. Evidence from a variety of studies strongly indicates that quit rates are substantially lower in the federal sector.[29] Complementary evidence was presented by Alan Krueger (1988a, 1988b), who looked at application rates for federal and private-sector jobs. While Krueger cautioned that the comparisons may not reflect similar occupations, the data that he presented suggest that federal job openings attract more applicants than do positions in the private sector.[30] Thus, with the exception of the PATC surveys, which are influenced by federal unions and employee groups, the available evidence indicates that federal workers enjoy a relative wage advantage over workers elsewhere in the economy.

The NIPA data in figure 5.1 indicate that the federal wage advantage declined in the late 1970s. Although this decline may be a mere aberration in the general pattern of federal wages since the early 1920s, the effect on different groups of federal workers is revealing. Recent work by Larry Katz and Alan Krueger (1991, 1992) using CPS data and standard wage regressions, summarized in table 5.3, indicates that the relative decline in the federal wage since the late 1970s has been borne mostly by more highly educated employees.[31] In comparison, the pattern of wages in the private sector over the last decade has moved in the opposite direction. In the private sector, less-educated male workers have fared poorly, while more highly educated women have experienced significant increases in their real wages. A national federal pay structure that largely protects rank-and-file workers from the negative effects of changing patterns of pay in the private sector is, of course, consistent with the objectives of federal unions.

In recent years, increased attention has been focused on a so-called human resource crisis in the federal government that appears to be remedied only by increasing federal salaries (see, e.g., Hudson Institute 1988; Lane and Wolf

Table 5.3   **Federal/Private Percentage Wage Differentials, by Sex, Education, and Year**

	Male		Female	
	High School	College	High School	College
1960	8	. . .	13	. . .
1973/75	8	13	32	49
1979	2	7	22	16
1983	8	12	26	27
1988	5	1	25	21
1991	11	1	30	16

Source and notes: The reported differentials are log points. The 1960 figures are from Smith (1977, 68) and reflect the use of federal weights (sample mean values) to compare workers with the same characteristics. The mean educational level for federal workers in 1960 was twelve years for both males and females. The mean years of experience was approximately twenty-four years for both sexes (Smith 1977, 162–63). The source for all other years is Katz and Krueger (1992, table 1). Katz and Krueger report the expected wage for workers with the following characteristics: white, full-time employee, resident of an SMSA (standard metropolitan statistical area) with twenty-five years of experience.

Table 5.4   **Gini Coefficients for Pay Distribution in the Federal Government**

Year	Gini Coefficient	Year	Gini Coefficient
1928	.208	1969	.203
1949	.185	1979	.232
1960	.171	1989	.236

Sources and notes: The procedures for computing the Gini coefficients are described in Miller (1960). Data on federal pay distributions for 1928 are from Feldman (1931, app. D, p. 265). The source for all other years is Office of Personnel Management (1989).

1990; Levitan and Noden 1983; and Volcker 1988). There is little question that pay for top-level government executives is depressed and that higher-level positions are sometimes difficult to fill. But wage compression in the federal sector is hardly a new issue. Throughout much of the post–World War II period, either special pay ceilings or salary caps have been in effect for top-level GS positions (see Hartman 1980). While these ceilings are adjusted from time to time, maintaining a lid on the salaries of top officials has contributed to a federal pay structure that is far more egalitarian than that found for the U.S. labor force as a whole.

Table 5.4 presents Lorenz-Gini coefficients for the federal workforce for selected years starting in 1928. The Gini coefficient must lie between one and zero, with a value of zero implying no income inequality. In 1979, the Gini coefficient for the federal sector was .23. The private-sector coefficient for 1979 was approximately double that value, .45.[32] Although the Gini coefficients for the federal sector do not exhibit much variation between 1928 and 1989, there is some hint of an actual decrease in equality over time. Recent estimates for the entire U.S. labor market also indicate a decline in equality in the 1980s (see Levy and Murnane 1992). Nevertheless, the low Gini coefficients for the federal sector appear to be due mainly to an increase in the proportion of federal workers in higher GS level professional and managerial positions rather than to a managed response to changes in private-sector pay.[33] When compared to figures for the U.S. labor force as a whole, those presented in table 5.4 are not only consistent with the argument that the federal pay structure exhibits considerable compression but also indicate that this condition is not a new one. Federal employee unions have long sought to implement egalitarian pay systems.

In addition to relatively higher wages, federal workers also have health and retirement benefits that are considered superior to those provided in the private sector.[34] Figure 5.2 presents NIPA data on the ratio of total compensation of federal employees to that of private-sector and state and local employees. Including nonwage compensation increases slightly the federal relative advantage computed over the entire period 1949–90 shown in figure 5.1. It also negates much of the decline in the federal/private wage ratio exhibited since the late 1970s. Hence, taking the NIPA data with the numerous human capital earnings studies that control for a myriad of socioeconomic variables, the pic-

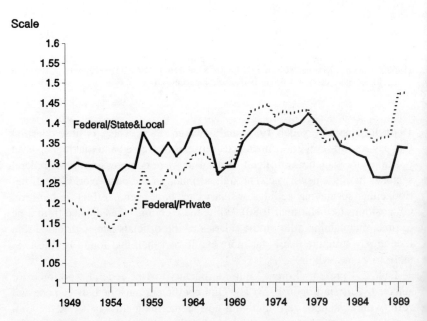

Fig. 5.2   Relative federal total compensation advantage, 1949–90.
Source: National income and product accounts.

ture that emerges is one of a federal labor force that is relatively well off. Contributing to that outcome is the influence that federal unions have had over the design and implementation of civil service rules governing promotions.

5.3.2   Promotion and the Returns to Tenure

The General Schedule provides GS grades that are linked to specific positions through the position classification process and uniform procedures for promotions. Subject to the approval of the Office of Personnel Management, supervisors in each agency define positions with regard to responsibilities and qualification requirements, and they coordinate with agency classifiers to select the appropriate occupation code and range of GS levels for positions. This process defines the immediate job ladder for each employee. Importantly, within grades GS-1–GS-15 there have historically been ten steps with pay increases of 3 percent each, thus providing a 30 percent salary range within each grade. A central responsibility for supervisors is the evaluation of subordinate performance. Typically, a five-point scale has been used, whereby 1 is unsatisfactory, 2 is minimally satisfactory, 3 is fully satisfactory, 4 exceeds fully satisfactory, and 5 is outstanding.[35] According to civil service rules, these ratings are to be used in managing and motivating subordinates for within-grade step salary increases and for promotion to higher GS grades. In practice, however, within-grade step salary increases have been largely automatic.

Under civil service rules there are significant costs and few benefits to supervisors who issue poor evaluations. The current rules require extensive documentation of poor performance, and the burden of proof lies with the supervisor. The supervisor must notify the subordinate ninety days in advance of his plan to assign a low rating to allow time for the subordinate to improve his performance and to develop a program of remedial training. Adverse ratings are subject to review by senior officials, and the employee can appeal through personnel channels within the agency and then to the Merit System Protection Board. Since the signing of Executive Order 10988, an employee within a unit represented by one of the federal unions may also use the union's negotiated grievance procedures. The unions have been aggressive in promoting the use of their grievance procedures and in their defense of employees (Nesbitt 1976, 235–67). Moreover, the unions and various employee groups have repeatedly lobbied Congress to reduce the discretionary authority of supervisors with regard to promotions and have fought attempts to use in-step promotions for performance incentives.

For example, with the Federal Salary Reform Act and the Postal Employees Salary Adjustment Act of 1962 (76 Stat. 850), the Congress added performance criteria for awarding within-grade step increases.[36] Under the law, the step increases would be granted after time requirements were met and after the employee's supervisor verified that the work was of an acceptable level of competence. This clause was designed to give supervisors discretion in awarding salary increases in an effort to improve the productivity of GS workers.

The provision for supervisory discretion, however, brought opposition from federal unions and related groups. During hearings before the House and Senate Post Office and Civil Service Committees, these groups sought to have the provision calling for an acceptable level of competence repealed. Among those testifying before the committees, only the Civil Service Commission and the Bureau of the Budget called for retention of a performance criteria. The director of the Civil Service Commission argued that under the 1962 law the step salary increase "was largely a matter for determination by those who have supervisory responsibility, that the increase was not an automatic right, and that it could and would be withheld if the performance was not up to standard." In opposition, the president of the AFGE emphasized to the committee members the political significance of federal white-collar employees: "There are 1.7 million persons looking to you, Mr. Chairman and members of this committee, to protect their interests." He went on, "We in the AFGE believe this provision should be repealed outright" (U.S. Senate 1965, 26, 129, 132). The members of the House and Senate committees appeared responsive to union demands. Although the performance criterion was not repealed, additional notification requirements were added.

There have been repeated efforts to tie in-step increases to performance, and, each time, federal unions have opposed the change. In 1975, the President's Panel on Federal Compensation noted that "most private employers and Federal agency managers who responded to the Federal Register notice on this issue favored changing the emphasis on within-grade advancement from longevity to merit. Federal employee unions expressed skepticism about management's ability to make necessary judgments about individual performance in a fair and objective manner, and favored retention of the present system" (U.S. Senate 1976, 467). The unwillingness on the part of the Congress clearly to mandate the use of merit performance ratings has not been lost on federal supervisors.

The documentation requirements and appeals processes raise the costs to supervisors who rate the performance of subordinates critically. Moreover, the reward system for supervisors does not appear to offer incentives that are sufficiently strong to overcome these costs. Although the Civil Service Reform Act of 1978 called for the use of merit-pay incentives for supervisors, the rewards have not been very high. In 1985, for example, the average award was around 2 percent, with a few individuals receiving as much as 10 percent.[37] While advancement to higher managerial positions or to the Senior Executive Service depends on the supervisor's performance, wage compression reduces the incentive to compete for those positions, especially via the costly route of negative subordinate evaluations. The costs and incentives facing supervisors appear to have contributed to the practice of granting high performance ratings within the federal civil service.

As the U.S. Classification Task Force noted, "Withholding an increase is difficult and requires extraordinary effort on the part of the supervisor to document. The path of least resistance is to grant the increase, and this is the path almost every supervisor chooses to follow" (1981, 87). The same point was made during hearings on the Civil Service Reform Act of 1978: "The prospect of successfully dealing with the appeals process, to ensure that the person is not returned to the rolls, causes managers to go through a long process of preparation that can take months or longer. Often the manager's conclusion is that the task is too formidable and he abandons the effort. At the least, the process is excessively delayed and far more time of the managers must be de-voted to the process than is justified" (United States Code 1978, 2762). In fiscal year 1986, over 98 percent of all GS-1–GS-12 employees received a fully satisfactory (3) rating or better. Only 1 percent were rated unsatisfactory (1).[38] This pattern of ratings appears to reflect a long-standing practice. The U.S. Classification Task Force (1981, 87) reported that typically less than 1 percent of those eligible are denied step salary increases. The effect of this policy is that subordinates who receive a fully satisfactory or higher rating are assured of receiving within-grade step salary increases.

Accordingly, step salary increases are virtually assured as soon as time requirements are fulfilled.[39] Similarly, promotion within the job ladder re-quires minimum time within a grade. There are over 400 occupation codes within the General Schedule, and each has a range of GS levels that can al-low for job ladder promotions. Promotion criteria are outlined in chapter 335 of the *Federal Personnel Manual* (U.S. Office of Personnel Management 1984), and time in grade is an important criterion. Hence, for the typical fed-eral employee, service time seems to be the primary factor for advancement. The earnings profiles for federal workers provide strong support for this argu-ment.

To examine earnings profiles of federal employees, we utilized the following human capital earnings regression:

$$\ln W_i = \beta_0 + \beta_1 E_i + \beta_2 E_i^2 + \beta_3 T_i + \beta_4 T_i^2 + \beta_5 E_i T_i + X_i d + \varepsilon_i.$$

Here, $\ln W_i$ is the log of the annual salary for individual i, E is total years of potential work experience (age minus years of schooling minus 6), T is tenure (time) with the current employer, ET is an interaction term, and X_i is a vector of socioeconomic variables. Squared terms are included to account for the usual concavity of earnings profiles. This particular specification was chosen be-cause it allows for the growth in earnings to be decomposed into two parts, experience and tenure.

Estimates of the parameters for the above equation for federal workers were obtained using a random sample of GS employees provided by the Office of Personnel Management. The estimation results are presented in detail in ap-pendix C.[40] The results show that both the total experience and the tenure vari-ables are statistically significant at better than the 1 percent level, and they exhibit the usual concave earnings profile.[41] Additionally, the coefficient on the interaction term, although small, is negative. This would seem to suggest that experience and tenure are not complements in the federal sector. Nevertheless, the earnings profile shows wages steadily increasing with job tenure.

Consider, for example, an individual with twenty years of tenure and no previous experience. Here, $E = T = 20$. Given the estimated coefficients, wages for this worker would increase 63 percent over the twenty-year period.[42] But, decomposing the total growth in earnings by subtracting the contribution of experience, the growth in earnings attributable solely to job tenure is 55 percent. Thus, tenure matters a great deal in the federal sector, and it appears to matter more than it does in the private sector.

While all the studies mentioned in the previous section that use CPS data to compare private and federal wages include a variable to account for total experience, none include a variable to account for tenure.[43] There are, however, other wage-regression studies of the private sector where the researchers have included job tenure as an explanatory variable. Masanori Hashimoto and John Raisian (1985), for example, provide estimates using the same specification as described above for private-sector employees in large firms, the size group that federal unions argue is the group that should be used for salary comparison purposes. As are the results reported in appendix C for federal workers, the estimates provided by Hashimoto and Raisian are statistically significant and exhibit a concave earnings profile.[44] Given their estimated coefficients, the earnings profile that emerges shows wages rising 103 percent over a twenty-year period. This is much higher than the increase for a federal worker over the same period of time and is consistent with our argument that there is wage compression in the federal sector. If wages are compressed in the federal sector relative to those in the private sector, we should expect the earnings profile for federal workers to be flatter. But there is more to the story. When the total growth in earnings is decomposed into its two parts, the percentage growth in earnings due to tenure in the private sector is only 36 percent. In addition, in Hashimoto and Raisian's regressions, the coefficient on the interaction term between experience and tenure, ET, is positive, suggesting that experience matters more in the private sector.

In addition to the study by Hashimoto and Raisian, who consider only male workers, there are a number of other studies that use CPS data and include job tenure in the regressions. Elaine Sorensen (1989) offers separate estimates for both males and females in nonmanufacturing jobs. Her results indicate that twenty years of job tenure will increase earnings by 43 percent for males and 48 percent for females.[45] Again, these returns are less than the 55 percent return found for federal workers.[46] These results suggest that tenure is more important for explaining earnings growth in the federal than in the private sector. Moreover, the returns to tenure in the private sector are often interpreted as reflecting investments in specific human capital.[47] In contrast, the arguments presented in this section suggest that the high returns to tenure in the federal government have much more to do with union influence on civil service rules and pay structures.

5.3.3   Removal Protection

Early in the development of the civil service system, both the president and the Congress found it necessary to grant federal workers protection from removals that were politically motivated. Contemporary protections against removals, however, appear to go well beyond what is required by federal politicians to reduce costly competition over the control of merit-system employees. Currently, individuals enter the federal labor force for a probationary period of one to two years. During that time, supervisors have much greater discretion in dismissing a subordinate for poor performance than they do once tenure has been granted. The extensive protection offered by the civil service system to tenured white-collar employees is demonstrated by the application of federal reduction-in-force (RIF) procedures. RIFs are the most drastic form of position reduction in the federal government. They can result in involuntary separations and the downgrading of employees to lower-ranked positions. Nevertheless, the procedural requirements are so designed to protect seniority that the permanent effect of RIFs on all but nontenured employees is limited.

RIF regulations, as defined in chapter 351 of the *Federal Personnel Manual* (U.S. Office of Personnel Management 1984), call for employees in the targeted positions to compete for remaining jobs. Besides tenure status, retention is based on seniority, veteran's status, and performance ratings, with seniority the most important factor. The emphasis on seniority once again reflects the ability of unions to prevail over traditional merit concepts, which emphasize performance ratings (Nesbitt 1976, 231). Under these criteria, temporary employees are the most vulnerable. Once a RIF extends to permanent employees, they can be transferred to positions in the agency not subject to RIFs, or they can bump lower-ranked employees. Any employee who is downgraded, however, retains his GS rank and salary for up to two years. Beyond that, salaries are adjusted until the downgraded employee's salary is commensurate with his or her new position. However, the adjustment period can be long since RIF procedures allow the individual to receive half of all authorized government salary increases until salaries are equalized.

In recent years, there has been much attention focused on the RIFs authorized by the Reagan administration (see, e.g., Levitan and Noden 1983). Between 1981 and 1983, over forty-two agencies were involved in reductions in force. Despite this, the numbers of workers who were affected involuntarily was small, demonstrating the limited effect that RIFs can have on permanent employees. Ninety percent of the workforce reduction was through voluntary attrition and early retirement that was costly to the government.[48] In 1981, only 2,629 personnel lost their jobs through RIFs, a figure that represents only 0.4 percent of total 1981 separations and only 0.09 percent of the average total civilian workforce for the year.[49] Further, a U.S. General Accounting Office (1985, 35–37) study of RIFs showed that, of the employees who were downgraded, many were quickly promoted. Of the 2,055 employees affected by the

RIFs, 744 were downgraded to lower GS level positions. In less than two years, however, nearly half were promoted to their pre-RIF positions.

5.3.4   A National Pay Plan

Since federal unions lack the right to bargain directly over wages, they must influence salaries in more indirect ways. One objective has been the adoption of a national pay plan for white-collar workers, an arrangement long opposed by federal managers and the President's Panel on Federal Compensation (U.S. Senate 1976, 466). Although national pay policies make civil service pay inflexible with respect to local conditions, these same inflexibilities and the problems they cause have been used by federal unions to justify across-the-board wage increases.

Recall that researchers, such as Smith (1977) and Katz and Krueger (1992), have found that the federal wage advantage varies across regions and is inversely related to local private-sector wages. They attribute this result to the existence of a national pay plan. Although GS salaries are not completely rigid, the wage regression results presented in appendix C indicate little regional variation in pay.[50] Federal GS salaries are somewhat lower in the Mountain and Southern states, reflecting private-sector pay patterns, but the difference is only around 2 percent. The coefficient on the Washington, D.C., dummy variable, however, reflects a rather larger differential, around 11 percent. Since Washington, D.C., is the "home office" and the final stage in the promotion process, this coefficient, in part, reflects competitive promotions for top management positions.[51] No doubt, there are localities, such as New York City and Washington, D.C., where the federal wage advantage for many occupations is smaller or may not exist. Hence, if pay comparability were the objective, salaries should be lowered in most localities and, perhaps, increased in a few. Historically, however, federal unions have opposed moving away from the national pay plan concept because wage compression and difficulties in hiring for certain special occupations can serve union objectives.

Having federal managers point out difficulties in hiring and retaining personnel in critical areas has induced prominent individuals, such as Paul Volcker (1988), to proclaim a "crisis" in public service. Wage compression and the inability to keep senior technicians and administrators have been used in congressional hearings as reasons to justify the enactment of new salary legislation.[52] For example, during hearings on the 1962 Federal Salary Reform Act, a representative of the Civil Service Commission emphasized salary compression as evidence of the need to reform and raise federal salaries. He stated that, owing to salary increases that focused on lower-level positions, the ratio of salaries between the lowest and the highest grades dropped from 8.8 in 1939 to 5.8 in 1962. The associated relative fall in senior-position salaries led to the loss of key upper-level personnel, a condition supported by representative testimonials given by individuals who allegedly left the federal government for more lucrative private-sector employment. Even so, union representatives called for across-the-board pay increases to raise wages for everyone (U.S. Senate 1962, 64–89). Congress responded to the calls for salary increases with an across-the-board raise, coupled with special advances for lower-level GS employees.

Wage compression has a long history in the federal government, but being able to illustrate problems in hiring has its benefits for federal unions. In contrast to blue-collar positions in the federal government, where occupations are few and relatively well defined, the General Schedule contains over 400 different occupation codes, some of which have no close counterpart in the private sector. The unions have argued that an adequate response to the problems of nonalignment between federal and market-determined wages for specific senior positions would require special adjustments within the system of position classification, opening the door to favoritism. The simple alternative that they have supported is to increase salaries across the board. In fact, between 1945 and the present, pay increases for GS workers have typically been across-the-board percentage increases.[53] This practice elevates all salaries, but the problem of wage compression remains. Wage compression seems to be a valuable tool for obtaining new wage increases.

Recent efforts to add flexibility to the federal pay structure again illustrate the influence of federal unions and professional organizations. The Federal Employees Pay Comparability Act of 1990 allows for increased pay flexibility by permitting region-specific wage differentials. However, federal wages can be adjusted only upward, not downward, assuring that these reforms are not likely to reduce the relative federal wage advantage for the typical worker.

5.4 Summary

At the end of chapter 3, we observed that one of the consequences of the creation of the classified (merit) service was that it encouraged federal employees to organize as an interest group with an important stake in the development of the civil service system. In chapter 4, we detailed the formation of early federal employee unions and their success in obtaining workplace benefits ahead of their private-sector counterparts as well as favorable salary increases. In this chapter, we have seen the process continue. Federal employee unions and related groups have become an integral part of the salary determination process, consulting on the design of comparability surveys and on the pay recommendations made to the president. Through their efforts they have achieved civil service rules that provide for unusual protections against involuntary removals, high returns to seniority (rather than merit), an egalitarian pay structure, and a salary-determination process that provides comparatively higher salaries than those for their counterparts in the private or other public sectors. These conditions are not new but have been in place for some time. Indeed, the federal wage advantage and tenure guarantees have existed since the 1920s.

Our emphasis on the role of federal unions and professional groups in influencing the development of the civil service system provides insight into the debate over the effect of public policy on the growth of unions. As outlined by John Burton and Terry Thomason (1988, 17–27) and Richard Freeman (1986, 45–48), there is a question of which came first, union strength or public policy promoting unions, such as Executive Order 10988? Freeman stresses the growth in public-sector unionism following 1962 as evidence of the importance of favorable public policies. For the federal government, however, the record seems clear that federal unions (especially postal unions) were active prior to the enactment of the Lloyd-LaFollette Act of 1912, that federal unions were extremely successful in obtaining favorable benefits and salary legislation prior to World War I and during the 1920s, and that Executive Order 10988 was itself a reflection of the political strength of federal employee unions. Union membership grew after 1962, and federal unions obtained critical roles in the salary comparability process. Nevertheless, this was a continuation of the longer-term process of institution development, where federal employee unions and groups have played a key and, perhaps, dominant role.

We argue that comparatively high salaries and returns to tenure for federal workers reflect the effectiveness of federal unions and professional groups as lobbyists. These attributes of the civil service system, however, may not have been due solely to the efforts of federal employees. It has, for example, been argued that the design of the federal wage structure instead reflects an attempt on the part of legislators to reduce shirking by providing federal workers with appropriate incentives.[54] Certainly, wage-incentive policies are prevalent in the private sector, and it is possible that they could be of even more value in the federal government. Although the federal pay structure does contain some incentives, closer inspection reveals major elements that are inconsistent with usual notions of incentive wages.

Consider, for example, Edward Lazear's (1981) point that, when it is costly to monitor the performance of workers, the firm may benefit by allowing wages to grow with tenure, even if productivity does not. In this case, earnings profiles increase with time because delaying payment until late in a worker's career reduces incentives to shirk. The worker is paid less than his or her marginal product initially and more later on, depending on a specified level of performance. If shirking is detected and results in dismissal, the worker will suffer a greater decline in the present value of future earnings than if payment had been tied to the value of marginal product in each time period. The steeper the earnings profile, the larger the penalty associated with shirking. Presumably, those firms faced with relatively higher costs of monitoring or where the costs of shirking are especially high will elect to have a steeper earnings profile.

The incentive to monitor workers can, of course, differ between the federal and the private sectors. As we have stressed, the federal government lacks a well-defined principal in charge of classified personnel. While the president is the most likely to be held accountable for the actions of federal employees, no federal politician occupies a position fully comparable to that of the residual claimant in the firm. As with other types of externalities problems, those affected have an incentive to develop contractual arrangements to help solve the problem. Rather than relying on their colleagues to monitor worker's performance, it is conceivable that federal politicians would be inclined to use payment schemes such as a steeper earnings profile to reduce shirking and to improve productivity.

Nevertheless, although federal politicians may desire these wage-incentive policies, the civil service system lacks the required structure. Except in cases of malfeasance, it is very costly to dismiss a federal employee, thus negating the use of a steep earnings profile as a device to reduce shirking. Moreover, except for the very top positions, promotions are routine through most job ladders. Even for top-level positions, it is not apparent how the federal wage structure alone would induce much in the way of greater effort. There is considerable wage compression, making it difficult to envision the federal pay structure as a good example of a "rank-order tournament" (see Lazear and Rosen 1981).

There remains, however, the problem of malfeasance and the use of higher salaries to prevent it. It may be that the typical clerical worker in the federal government is capable of causing more harm through maleficent behavior than is a private-sector worker. Even if that were true, it would seem that the relatively high retirement benefits that federal workers can expect, if they do not violate the law, would provide an adequate incentive device without also having to offer relatively higher salaries. Moreover, the dominant weight placed on service time in the determination of pay for all rank-and-file employees, regardless of whether their position presents a significant danger from maleficent behavior, works against an "efficiency-wage" explanation for the high level of federal salaries.

Perhaps, as Lazear has later suggested, pay compression can be efficient. If harmony is important, then equality of pay can be a means for achieving it. But Lazear's (1989) argument also implies that, if wage compression is a reaction to having a hawkish group of workers, the average wage in those firms will be lower. The wage regression evidence presented in this chapter, however, indicates that the average federal wage is above that in the private or other public sectors.

Accordingly, we conclude that the observed structure of civil service rules and the associated salary and benefits received by federal employees are not principally the result of efforts by politicians to improve efficiency in the delivery of government services. Although efficiency concerns were an early motivating device for the president and the Congress to begin the process of civil service reform, the dominant factor since perhaps the turn of the century is the active participation of federal unions and professional groups in the design of the institution in their behalf. In the next chapter, we address the nagging question of why federal workers have been so successful, especially compared to their counterparts at the state and local level.

Notes

1. For a discussion of federal unions and their membership, see Stern (1988). For the claim that at least half the members of the AFGE were wage board and low General Schedule employees, see Donoian (1967, 139).

2. As we describe later in the chapter, federal unions have taken a very active role in lobbying for salary legislation and in obtaining a position to influence the annual Bureau of Labor Statistics wage survey and the recommendations for salary increases made by the president's pay agent. Although professional associations are not passive, they are much less in evidence at congressional hearings, becoming more active periodically, lobbying for upper-end salary increases only after salary compression has been a factor for some time. For example, compare the list of groups providing testimony in U.S. House of Representatives (1970) for the Federal Salary Comparability Act of 1970 (84 Stat. 1946) and those in U.S. Senate (1962) for the 1962 Federal Salary Reform Act (76 Stat. 841, 1465). In the latter case, professional groups were especially concerned about the cumulative effects of wage compression and turned out in comparatively large numbers.

3. For a summary, see Burton and Thomason (1988, 17–27).

4. Annual data on employment levels and salaries of GS employees are available from U.S. Office of Personnel Management (1989).

5. This was changed under the Federal Pay Comparability Act of 1990 (104 Stat. 1427).

6. Authorization for this change came from the Postal Reorganization Act, 12 August 1970 (84 Stat. 719). For a historical analysis of the post office's change from a federal department to a government enterprise, see Adie (1977).

7. For a description of the circumstances leading to the adoption of position classification, see Feldman (1931, 17–22).

8. The report of the Hoover Commission in 1949 was instrumental in promoting the notion that position classification was essential for managing the federal bureaucracy.

9. Kappel Commission (1968, 1:121, 4:7, 65). Levitan and Noden (1983, 104) note that the AFGE was at one time especially determined to maintain a national pay plan for white-collar workers. Their position has softened in recent years as granting geographic wage differentials appears to be an effective way to increase general wages.

10. For discussions of the provisions of Executive Order 10988, see Howlett (1984) and Case (1986).

11. Federal law since the Lloyd-LaFollette Act has ruled out strikes. Section 305 of the Taft-Hartley Act of 1947 reads, "Any individual employed by the United States or any such agency who strikes shall be discharged immediately" (61 Stat. 136). While the federal government has at times wavered in its application of this provision, allowing certain types of work stoppages to occur, the firing of striking air traffic controllers by President Reagan illustrates the potential force of this law. For discussion, see Nesbitt (1976, 361–98) and Levitan and Noden (1983, 100–103).

12. For discussion of union membership and the distinctions among union membership, representation, and bargaining units, see Burton and Thomason (1988, 2–4, 30–31) and Levitan and Noden (1983, 4–9, 14–20).

13. For a discussion of how these boards functioned and the governance of federal wages in general, see Nesbitt (1976, 399–434).

14. Levitan and Noden (1983, 71) note that the new system for determining FWS wages has probably biased federal wages upward.

15. Levitan and Noden report that dues-paying membership in the AFGE, the largest of the federal unions, "is composed of clerical workers (45 percent), with blue collar workers accounting for 40 percent and professional for 15 percent" (1983, 20).

16. Even the Kappel Commission (1968, 1:25) noted that postal employee unions had been able to obtain salary levels higher than those in the general economy.

17. With the existence of geographic wage differences in the private sector, a federal wage set nationally is a contradiction in terms.

18. Under the Federal Pay Comparability Act of 1970, the size of the pay council was limited to five representatives. In 1975, e.g., the members of the Federal Employees Pay Council were the president of the National Treasury Employees Union, both the president and executive vice president of the AFGE, the president of the NFFE, and an economist from the Department of Research of the AFL-CIO (U.S. Senate 1976, 225). The Federal Pay Comparability Act of 1990 established a Federal Salary Council of nine members, six of whom are to be representatives of employee organizations that represent a substantial number of GS employees.

19. In 1978, e.g., all five members of the pay council resigned their positions. While that action attracted considerable attention, these former members continued to use the pay agent's annual report as a forum for expressing their displeasure at legislated pay increases. See President's Pay Agent (1980). See also the statement by Paul Volcker (U.S. House of Representatives 1989, 8).

20. The ECI was to consider private-sector wages and other locality-based comparability adjustments (U.S. House of Representatives 1990, 170–76).

21. U.S. Department of Labor (1981) provides a summary of the recommendations of the president's pay agent and actual increases for the 1970s. To achieve comparability in 1971, the pay agent recommended an increase of 6.5 percent. The actual increase was 5.5 percent. Throughout the 1970s, actual increases were below those recommended, and, by 1980, the pay agent was recommending an increase of 13.5 percent. The actual increase was 4.8 percent that year.

22. See, e.g., Smith (1977). A somewhat different point of view, one that attempts to rationalize the PATC surveys, is offered by Levitan and Noden (1983). See also Hartman (1983).

23. The existence of wage differentials based on firm size is well known in the literature on labor economics. Controlling for various employee characteristics, Katz and Krueger (1991) report differentials that range from approximately 8 to 25 percent higher in large firms.

24. See Freeman (1980). In 1975, federal unions opposed differential pay increases because, they claimed, such pay schemes are "inequitable" (U.S. Senate 1976, p. 237).

25. For a comprehensive survey of the studies completed prior to the mid-1980s, see Ehrenberg and Schwarz (1986).

26. Smith (1977) uses coefficients obtained via OLS estimation to calculate the wage differentials. More recent studies by Venti (1987) and Gyourko and Tracy (1988) show that correcting for the potential problem of selection bias does not alter the basic conclusion that there is a positive federal wage advantage.

27. The relative wage advantage figures were derived using federal weights to compare workers with the same characteristics. While women employed by the federal government have a relative wage advantage over their private-sector counterparts, within the federal government they earn less than males with similar education and experience (see app. C). The coefficient on Female is −.096, suggesting earnings that are 10 percent lower than those for male counterparts.

28. While most of the wage-regression studies referred to in the text seldom distinguish between union and nonunion workers, the available evidence indicates that federal workers continue to earn a wage premium even when the comparison made is to unionized private-sector workers. For example, Wachter and Perloff (1992, 29) report a wage premium for postal workers compared to private-sector workers of 21.3 percent. Comparing postal workers with private-sector unionized workers lowers the wage pre-

mium to 10.8 percent. Gyourko and Tracy (1988) find a wage differential of 14 percent in favor of unionized workers in the private sector, but they also find that federal workers enjoy a wage premium of 18 percent compared to all private-sector workers.

29. See Adie (1977), Long (1982), and Borjas (1982). Ippolito (1987) argues that low quit rates in the federal sector are due to the relatively higher pensions that federal workers can expect to receive if they remain on the job until retirement age. Federal workers do have excellent retirement benefits, and quit rates are undoubtedly affected by the fact that these benefits are lost if the worker quits before the specified retirement age. But Ippolito's argument that, "if the government wants the quit rate to be as high as the private sector, it can do this by raising the cash wage and lowering the pension amount" (p. 298) ignores the evidence provided by Smith (1977) and others using CPS data that federal wages exceed those in the private sector.

30. Given that there are queues for certain federal jobs, competition for these positions involves a cost that could lower the implied wage advantage (Bronars and Lott 1989).

31. Like Katz and Krueger, Freeman (1987) and Moulton (1990) use CPS data, but with different controlling variables. They also report finding a decline in the federal wage advantage.

32. The Gini coefficient for the entire U.S. labor force is based on various estimates reported by Levy and Murnane (1992, table 2, pt. 1). The figure refers to annual wages and salaries for all persons, sixteen years and older, with positive wage and salary incomes.

33. When the GS system was established in 1949, the average GS grade was 5.25. By 1989, the average had risen to 8.69 (U.S. Office of Personnel Management 1989).

34. For a comparison of retirement benefits, see Ippolito (1987). Using a 1980 survey conducted by the Office of Personnel Management, Levitan and Noden (1983, 83) suggest that expenditures on health benefits per employee are lower in the federal than in the private sector. Even if correct, this ignores the fact that large employers tend to receive substantial discounts on their health programs. Moreover, federal workers are in a better position to tailor their choice of health plans to their own specific circumstances.

35. See U.S. Merit System Protection Board (1987). The procedures that supervisors are to follow in evaluating subordinates are described in U.S. Office of Personnel Management (1984, chap. 430).

36. These two laws dealing with federal salary issues were part of a package of federal labor legislation.

37. The figures on the distribution of merit pay were supplied by the Office of Personnel Management.

38. Data on rating distributions for white-collar workers were provided by the Systems and Analysis Branch of the Office of Personnel Management.

39. There are also automatic step increases for FWS workers (see Levitan and Noden 1983, 73).

40. A more detailed analysis of these regression results is contained in Johnson and Libecap (1989a).

41. Given our large data set (16,616), the significance of a coefficient is not the main criterion. What matters is the size of the coefficients and the resulting earnings profile.

42. An estimate of the total percentage growth in earnings can be derived by setting E and T to predetermined values and substituting into $100[\exp(\beta_1 E + \beta_2 E^2 + \beta_3 T + \beta_4 T^2 + \beta_5 ET) - 1]$.

43. Venti (1987), e.g., used 1982 CPS data to compare federal and private-sector pay. He included years of potential experience and experience squared in his regressions,

but no measure of tenure. His results reveal little difference in the earnings profiles of private-sector and federal workers.

44. Hashimoto and Raisian (1985, 730) report the following results (the total number of observations was 3,750):

Variable	Coefficient	t-statistic
E	.0372	16.4
E^2	−.0007	−13.0
T	.0121	4.3
T^2	−.0003	−3.6
ET	.0003	2.3

45. For the estimated coefficients on the tenure variables, see Sorensen (1989, 68, app. D). Her finding that the returns to tenure in the private sector are somewhat higher for females than for males is consistent with other studies (see, e.g., Goldin 1990; and Hersch and Reagan 1993).

46. Since our estimation of the returns to tenure includes both males and females, it could be biased upward compared to an overall measure for the private sector if there were a greater proportion of females in the federal workforce. While it is correct that the proportion of females in state and local employment, including education, is higher than it is in the private sector, the proportion of females in the GS workforce in 1985, and in our sample data set, was .46. That figure is equivalent to the proportion of females employed in the private-sector workforce (see U.S. Department of Commerce 1991). Moreover, there is evidence that promotion probabilities in the federal government are very similar for men and women (Lewis 1986).

47. Because of the potential for bias when using cross-sectional data and OLS estimation procedures, there has been considerable debate over whether previous empirical results actually reflected a return to job tenure. Using longitudinal data on the private sector, Topel (1991) provides compelling evidence that job tenure does matter, lending support to the view that there are investments in specific human capital.

48. The effect of these RIFs is discussed in U.S. General Accounting Office (1985).

49. U.S. General Accounting Office (1985, 2) lists total number of employees involuntarily separated through RIFs. The 1981 figure was divided by the total federal separations and the average civilian workforce for that year, as provided in U.S. Office of Personnel Management, *Federal Civilian Work Force Statistics, Monthly Release* (December 1981, table 16).

50. Supervisors have exhibited a willingness to engage in discretionary actions to hire and retain individuals with desired skills (Johnson and Libecap, 1989b).

51. Johnson and Libecap (1989b) provide additional results suggesting that federal supervisors have also increased the salaries of clerical workers in the Washington, D.C., area. In part, this is due to difficulties experienced in hiring qualified workers in that area.

52. For a discussion of the problems in hiring scientists and engineers, see Campbell and Dix (1990).

53. For a chronology of federal pay legislation, see U.S. Office of Personnel Management (1989, table 19).

54. The notion that the federal employment contract mainly reflects an attempt by the Congress to reduce agency problems through performance incentives is advanced by Horn (1988).

6   Explaining the Success of Federal Employees as an Interest Group

6.1   Introduction

A major hypothesis advanced in this volume is that civil service reform allowed federal workers to become an entrenched special interest group of their own. The evidence presented in the previous two chapters suggests that they have been successful at increasing their compensation and job benefits relative to comparable private- and other public-sector workers, thus raising the question of how this record of successes was achieved. Clearly, there are fundamental differences in employer/employee bargaining in the federal sector compared to that in the private sector. Because negotiations over pay and civil service rules involve politicians and take place in the political arena, the observed differences between private and federal workers may be due to the voting power of the latter. The accomplishments of federal employees may also be due to the lobbying strength of federal unions in obtaining favorable statutes regarding the civil service system. In this chapter, we examine both the voting and the lobby lobbying influence of federal employees.

Voting power has received most of the attention. For example, Richard Freeman has noted, "Public sector unions, more so than private sector unions, can influence the employer's behavior through the political process. The principal reason for this is that public sector employees help elect both the executive and legislative branches of government" (1986, 42). Since public-sector employees help elect politicians, they are in a position to use their voting power to set the agenda at the bargaining table, and politicians have incentives to be responsive. In addition, there is an extensive literature that argues that public-sector employees are strongly motivated to use their voting power to elect candidates who support the expansion of government (see Downs 1967; Tullock 1974; Buchanan 1977; Bush and Denzau 1977; and Bennett and Orzechowski 1983).

The notion is that the salaries of these public-sector employees will increase with the growth of government.

With over 3 million full- and part-time federal civilian employees, federal workers clearly constitute a potentially powerful voting block. Nevertheless, we argue that there are a number of offsetting factors that limit the ability of federal workers to act as a cohesive voting force. First, with the exception of the Washington, D.C., metropolitan area, the federal labor force is geographically dispersed. Not only does this dispersion tend to dilute these workers' voting power, but it also increases the potential for free riding by raising the costs of collective action.[1] Second, because federal workers are highly protected by bureaucratic rules, they have less incentive to vote than if they were subject to political removals, as are patronage workers or other political appointees. Indeed, we show that the probability that a federal worker votes in a general election is no higher than that for a comparable private-sector worker. In contrast, the probability that a state or local government employee votes is significantly higher than that for a federal worker. Moreover, the number of employees in the state and local sector has grown far more rapidly over the past forty years than has federal employment. Even so, despite lower voter participation rates and slower growth, the empirical evidence indicates that the salary of a typical federal worker exceeds that of state and local employees by a substantial margin and that this wage advantage has persisted over time.[2]

These findings present a challenge to conventional arguments that stress the roles of voting power and the growth of government as central for understanding the relative successes of federal government employees. Although it is unlikely that the expansion of the federal sector would have had a negative effect on salaries, the evidence indicates that government growth is neither a necessary nor a sufficient condition for generating higher salaries for federal civilian employees. Instead of government expansion, the most important factor in explaining the comparative achievements of federal workers has been their ability to change civil service rules through statutes and (occasionally) executive orders to better reflect their interests. They have accomplished that objective through effective lobbying by federal employee unions.

In this regard, federal unions have acted much like other interest groups, promising votes and contributing money to campaigns. They too have benefited because they bargain at the national level, where the mobility of taxable resources is restricted relative to those of state and local entities. In bargaining with their employees over compensation plans, and in taking other actions that affect tax rates, state and local government officials must consider competing jurisdictions. High taxes in one region encourage firm migration to other regions. This is a less relevant concern for federal officials. Further, in their lobbying efforts, federal employee unions have been assisted by private-sector unions. Since resource mobility is of less concern to federal politicians, private-sector unions often have sought both national labor legislation that applies to most jurisdictions and legislation for federal employees because of the precedents that can be established for private workers. Accordingly, our explanation for the success of federal workers in obtaining attractive levels of compensation and workplace benefits emphasizes the attributes that have made them an effective interest group. Voting power is but one of those attributes, and the evidence presented in this chapter suggests that it has been overemphasized in the literature as an explanation for public-sector wage patterns.

6.2   The Voting Power of Federal Employees

One of the distinguishing features of the public choice paradigm is the assumption that individuals in the political arena, as in the marketplace, behave rationally and pursue their own self-interests. An excellent example of this approach is the hypothesis advanced by Anthony Downs that rational, utility-maximizing citizens would calculate relevant benefits and costs in deciding whether to vote. The fortunes of those in both the private and the public sectors are of course likely affected by who wins an election, but Downs argued that government employees had an especially strong incentive to vote because their incomes were closely tied to the outcome (Downs 1957, 254). As it has evolved, the hypothesis that government employees should have higher voter participation rates than the general population rests on the fundamental tenet that there is a positive relation between a public employee's income and the growth of the public sector. Because of that asserted relation, government workers are assumed to be more motivated than are their counterparts in the private sector to participate in political campaigns and to vote for those candidates who advocate an expansion of government services. Indeed, the idea that government workers would have higher voter participation rates, with an implied preference for government expansion, has been a major theme in much of the literature on the growth of government.[3]

In this section, we first review the evidence on public-sector voter participation rates. We then offer explanations for why federal workers are less likely to vote than are their state and local sector counterparts. As a result, we conclude that the voting power of federal workers cannot explain their wage advantage over state and local government employees and that we must look elsewhere to explain their political influence.

6.2.1   Public-Sector Voter Participation Rates

One of the earliest studies of voter behavior is Martin's (1933) analysis of local elections in Austin, Texas. His findings revealed a voter participation rate of 87 percent for public employees but only 58 percent for the general public. Although Martin's study was very limited in its scope, later studies have been supportive of his findings. James Bennett and William Orzechowski (1983), for example, presented empirical results, based on national elections, for the years 1964–78. Their study indicated that voter participation rates for all public employees—federal, state, and local—were approximately 18 percent higher than that for the general public. More recently, we used Current Population Survey (CPS) data tapes containing information on individual voter behavior for the 1984 and 1986 national elections to examine public-sector voting (Johnson and Libecap 1991). The calculated voter participation rates in 1984, measured as the number in a particular sample subgroup who stated that they had voted divided by the total population of the subgroup, were 77.1 percent for federal employees, 81.3 percent for state employees, 85.8 percent for local government employees, and 65.2 percent for private-sector employees. For the 1986 elections, the figures were 55.4 percent for federal workers, 69.1 percent for state employees, 72.4 percent for local government workers, and 46.7 percent for private-sector employees.

These results seem to indicate that public-sector employees have higher voter participation rates than do their counterparts in the private sector. If the federal relative wage advantage over state and local government workers is to be explained by voting power, it must follow that federal workers have higher voting participation rates than do their colleagues. The data, however, indicate just the opposite, that federal workers have lower, not higher, voter participation rates than other public-sector employees.

Although highly suggestive, the participation rates referred to above do not control for the various attributes of the voters. Within the context of Downs's model of voter participation, what matters is the marginal effect of a variable, ceteris paribus. That is, the correct test of the hypothesis posed by Downs requires an answer to the question, Do public-sector workers have an *added* incentive to vote? Accordingly, when testing the hypothesis, it is important to control for other differences in voter attributes that are likely to affect observed voter turnout. A number of studies have used estimating procedures that account for the effect of other variables besides occupation. One of the most noted studies is that of Raymond Wolfinger and S. J. Rosenstone (1980). In their extensive study of voting behavior, Wolfinger and Rosenstone use a probit model and CPS data to estimate the propensity of certain groups to vote. Included in their estimating equations are a broad array of individual socioeconomic characteristics, such as level of education. For the 1974 national elections, they find that the marginal increase in the probability of voting for teachers and federal employees, relative to private-sector employees, is only 5 percent. On the other hand, the marginal increases in voting for state and local employees, compared with private-sector employees, are 13 and 17 percent, respectively.

Wolfinger and Rosenstone's results suggest a smaller overall effect of government employment on the decision to vote than do the simple voter participation figures, but the pattern across political entities remains. Despite their grouping of federal employees and teachers, the probability of voting appears to be higher for state and local employees than for federal workers. Since many teachers are also local government employees, it is important to isolate the voting patterns of federal government workers.

Following Wolfinger and Rosenstone, we utilized a standard probit model and CPS data files for November 1984 and 1986 that contained special sub-sample surveys on whether individuals voted (Johnson and Libecap 1991). Included in the estimating equations were variables measuring each individual's education, age, marital status, sex, union membership, race, earnings, and occupation. The probit estimates of the coefficients for the local, state, and federal employee identifiers are reported in table 6.1. The results for all the included variables are shown in appendix D. The excluded category is private-sector employees. For both 1984 and 1986, the results indicate that federal employment does not significantly increase the probability of voting, relative to individuals employed in the private sector. The sign of the coefficient on the federal employment variable for 1986 actually is negative, although not statistically different from zero. In contrast, the coefficients on the state and local identifiers are significantly different from zero at the 5 percent level, one-tail test.

The marginal effects, obtained using the estimated parameters of the probit equation, are reported in table 6.2. These results indicate a much smaller effect of state and local government employment on the probability of voting than the corresponding figures of 13 and 17 percent reported by Wolfinger and Rosenstone (1980, 101). In addition, the results shown in table 6.2 indicate that federal workers are not compelled by some *added* incentive to vote more frequently than their counterparts in the private sector.[4] Thus, whether one considers the marginal effects or the basic statistics on voter participation rates, all the available evidence points in the same direction; namely, state and local employees are more likely to vote than are federal workers.

6.2.2   Comparing the Incentives of Public-Sector Employees to Vote

One possible explanation for why federal workers have lower voter participation rates than do state or local employees is the geographic distribution of

Table 6.1   **Probit Estimates of the Effect of Public-Sector Employment on Voting**

Variable	1984 Elections	1986 Elections
Federal	.058	−.032
	(.73)	(−.38)
State	.160	.282
	(1.88)	(3.74)
Local	.279	.312
	(4.32)	(4.85)

Source: Johnson and Libecap (1991).

Note: *t*-statistics are given in parentheses.

Table 6.2   Marginal Effects on Voting Participation by Level of Government

| | | Increase in the Probability of Voting Relative to Private-Sector Employees (in percentage terms) | | |
	Election	Federal	State	Local
	1984	1.59	3.96	6.21
	1986	−1.12	9.08	9.77

Source: Johnson and Libecap (1991).

the federal civilian workforce. If federal workers are to be an effective block, either in voting for president or in collectively determining a slate of favorable congressional candidates, they would have to overcome the tendency to free ride.[5] Peer-group pressure or explicit monitoring by federal unions and employee groups to limit shirking, however, are options, but they are unlikely to be effective because federal workers are so geographically dispersed. Although approximately 12 percent of all federal civilian employees work within the Washington, D.C., metropolitan area, most of the rest are located uniformly across the country. Figure 6.1 shows the distribution of federal employees by congressional district. Note that there are only ten districts, out of a total 435, with fewer than 3,000 federal employees and only nine districts with more than 24,000 federal employees in residence.[6]

With the exception of a few congressional districts, most of which are located close to the Washington, D.C., area, this dispersion means that federal employees are not a sufficiently large portion of the labor force to wield substantial voting power. Even in districts where their numbers are relatively large, federal employees may exert little influence in Congress. For example, the congressional delegate from the District of Columbia, where federal employees constituent almost 30 percent of the total workforce, is a nonvoting member of Congress. Moreover, to the extent that a federal worker did desire to vote for a congressional candidate who favored the expansion of his or her agency, there may be few opportunities to do so. Given their geographic dispersion, it is likely that only a small percentage of federal employees will reside in the district or state of those members of Congress who sit on important agency review committees. Given these conditions and the potential for free riding to occur, it is not surprising that the results in tables 6.1 and 6.2 indicate that the marginal effect of federal employment on the probability of voting is insignificant.

Besides group dispersion, there is another reason why federal workers would be less motivated to vote than are state and local employees. The former have been subject to much less patronage pressure than the latter. Although, as we discuss in chapter 8, recent Supreme Court rulings have greatly limited patronage practices, patronage remained a factor for state and local government employees long after it withered away at the federal level.[7] Under patron-

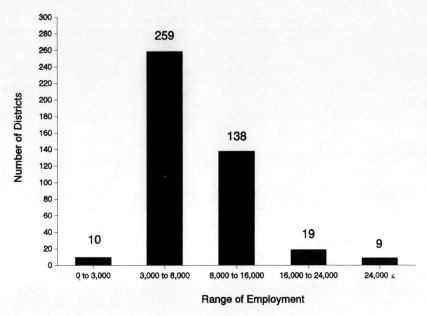

Fig. 6.1   Federal civilian employment by congressional district.
Source: U.S. Department of Commerce, (1983).

age, public-sector employees who owe their positions to political sponsors have a relatively greater stake in the outcome of an election than do those who have no such ties. In 1970, over 92 percent of all federal workers were within the classified or merit system (U.S. Department of Commerce 1975, 1102). As indicated in chapter 5, civil service rules protect federal employees from reductions in force and other adverse election outcomes. Of the remaining federal employees not covered by merit rules, most are in positions that are not considered political in nature and, hence, are unlikely to be affected by a change in administrations, at least, purely on the basis of party membership. To be sure, there are a limited number of federal political appointments at the senior level whose positions are temporary, lasting only as long as the administration. Presently, approximately 5,000 positions are available to the president for political appointments (see Pfiffner 1987).

Accordingly, should there be a change in the party controlling the White House, the vast majority of federal employees need not fear for their jobs. State and local government employees, however, have had much less protection. Rabin et al. (1985, 58) claim that only about 65 percent of state and local employees are covered under merit-system rules, and Glenn Stahl (1983, 47) notes that, at the state and local level, the mere presence of a merit-system law does not always provide security from changes in administration. In comparison to state and local government employees, then, federal employees have had less incentive to vote because of the widespread coverage of the civil service system and the comprehensive protections it provides.

So far, we have focused on the reasons why most rank-and-file federal employees would have less reason to vote in elections. It is time now to return to Downs's hypothesis to analyze the reasons underlying the prediction of greater voting participation by government employees. A basic tenet in much of the literature on bureaucratic behavior is that government workers are more motivated to vote than are private-sector workers because their career advancement and salaries depend on the growth of government.

There is support for this notion from the private sector. As described by Peter Doeringer and Michael Piore (1971), promotional opportunities are an integral part of internal labor markets, and advancement is often tied to the performance of the firm. There is also evidence indicating a positive relation between salary increases and organizational growth in large, private-sector firms (see Rosenbaum 1979). The pyramidal job structure described by Doeringer and Piore is assumed implicitly by those who assert significant positive relations among the growth of government, salaries, and the corresponding incentive for public-sector employees to vote. For example, Bennett and Orzechowski stated that, "as the firm (bureau) grows and new jobs are created, there is an increase in the likelihood of an employee (bureaucrat) rising to another position within the firm (bureau) where wages and productivity are higher." They emphasized that, "in the public sector, the effect is of greater importance because bureaucrats, as a voting block, can have an important influence on the outcome of elections" (1983, 272).

At first glance, the federal civil service system, especially for General Schedule (GS) employees, appears to be a classic internal labor market, with salaries a function of the position rather than of individual characteristics. Salaries increase as individuals move to higher positions within the hierarchy. We have examined the growth-salary relation in the federal government (Johnson and Libecap 1989a). A sample of 15,000 General Schedule employees in 1980 and in 1985 was used to test whether agency growth had a significant effect on salaries within the agency.[8] The data set and controlling variables used were similar to those described in appendix C. The research approach entailed pooling both data sets for 1980 and 1985 and introducing a set of dummy variables for the forty-five federal agencies within the sample. Since the dependent variable was the natural logarithm of individual wages, the inclusion of agency identifiers provided estimates of percentage changes in earnings associated with each agency over the five-year period.

Various estimating procedures were employed to examine the relation between changes in agency earnings and agency employment growth. In only one of the numerous tests performed did agency growth have a positive and statistically significant effect on salaries between 1980 and 1985. Even there, however, the effect was very small. On the basis of the estimated relation, an agency would have to double its size in order for salaries to increase by 4.4

percent, relative to an agency that did not grow. Moreover, when the Department of Defense was excluded from this particular sample, agency growth failed to have a statistically significant effect on salaries. Given the sensitivity of these results, it is difficult to conclude that a strong positive relation between agency growth and salaries exists.[9]

A principal weakness of the agency growth–salary hypothesis is that it fails to consider sufficiently the institutional environment. We point out two important examples. First, at least within the federal government, a pyramidal position structure, such as the General Schedule, does not imply pyramidal promotion opportunities. Under the civil service system, seniority within the federal government is so heavily weighted in promotion determination and salary-step increases that individuals who meet basic job qualification requirements will be advanced in many cases, regardless of what happens to agency size. Moreover, although in-grade step promotions are practically automatic, in other cases educational qualifications can impose severe restrictions on the upward mobility of federal workers. Finally, as outlined by civil service rules, ports of entry into the federal white-collar labor force exist throughout the range of GS grades, not just at that lower levels. Competition from new entrants could mitigate any positive effects that agency growth might otherwise have for the promotion of existing workers.

Second, under the civil service system, GS employees are paid according to a national pay plan, and government-employee salary increases typically have been in the form of across-the-board percentage adjustments. There is no specific link to agency characteristics in salary determination. Thus, any connection between government growth and salary increases would depend, instead, on the expansion of the total General Schedule labor force, not just on the growth of a particular agency.

It is conceivable that broad increases in the demand for government services could require higher salaries in order to staff new government positions. These conditions would force the president and the Congress to support new pay legislation. The size of the salary increase needed, of course, would depend on labor supply conditions.

We examine the relation between total federal employment growth and expansion of federal salaries. Table 6.3 reports regression results, where the dependent variable is the average annual, legislated percentage increase in pay for General Schedule employees from 1949 to 1990. These pay increases were regressed against the annual rate of inflation, the unemployment rate, and current and lagged annual rates of growth of total GS employment. Over the sample period, total GS employment expanded by 83 percent. Again, however, the evidence fails to support a positive relation between salary increases and staffing growth. None of the coefficients on the employment-growth variables is statistically significant from zero at the 5 percent level.

Certainly, there are some positions and special occupations for which the federal government has had difficulty in hiring and there is salary compres-

Table 6.3   General Schedule Pay Legislation and Employment Growth, 1949–90

	Eq. (1)	Eq. (2)
Constant term	3.33	4.78
	(2.40)	(3.06)
Inflation rate, t	.64	.63
	(3.91)	(4.07)
Unemployment rate, t	−.32	−.51
	(−1.27)	(−1.95)
GS employment growth, t	.04	.06
	(.25)	(.33)
GS employment growth, $t - 1$	. . .	−.12
		(−.97)
GS employment growth, $t - 2$	. . .	−.11
		(−.93)
$\bar{R}^2$	.19	.22

Sources and notes: The average annual GS legislated pay increase is from U.S. Office of Personnel Management (1989). The rate of inflation was calculated using the GNP deflator. The source for the GNP deflator and the unemployment rate is the *Economic Report of the President.* GS employment is from the U.S. Bureau of the Census. Both reported regressions were corrected for autocorrelation in the residuals. *t*-statistics are given in parentheses.

sion.[10] These conditions have helped federal labor unions in their efforts to secure legislated across-the-board pay increases that benefit their members. Further, if the federal government expanded into areas where federal pay was not competitive, there could be pressures on Congress to increase the salaries of all GS employees, but this seems unlikely to be a source of major change in wages for GS employees. Some blue-collar government workers may have more incentive to promote the advance of government into new areas because they are paid under the Federal Wage System with its concept of meeting locally prevailing rates. All in all, however, the growth of the federal government does not appear to be the key for explaining the continued existence of a federal wage advantage, relative to that of state and local employees.

There is additional evidence on this issue. Consider, for example, what has happened over time to federal, state, and local relative wages and employment growth. The ratio of federal to state and local government salaries can be computed using national income and product account (NIPA) data. While these measures do not control for changing characteristics of each sector's workforce, they offer a consistent times series of the ratio of federal (including postal) to state and local employee wages. The average value of the ratio for the period 1949–90 was 1.30. Between 1949 and 1990, total federal civilian employment, both full and part time, increased by 63 percent. In contrast, state and local government employment grew by 292 percent. Nevertheless, despite sharp differences in the employment growth experience by the two sectors, the wage ratio remained within the relatively narrow bounds of 1.22–1.39 throughout the period.[11] In addition, during the same time, the number of employees in the private sector increased 131 percent. Hence, not only did state and local employment grow much faster than did federal, but the slow growth of federal employment, relative to the private sector, implies that the voting power of federal workers most likely declined. Federal workers appear to have maintained their relative wage advantage independent of what was happening to their voting power or the expansion of government.[12]

Of course, it follows that, if the growth-salary linkage in the public sector is as weak as the evidence presented here suggests, public-sector voters would have little incentive to vote for the expansion of government, at least to facilitate advancement. They may, however, support the growth of government for other reasons. Although the evidence on the preferences of government workers for increases in the size of the public sector is limited, it does not indicate a strong desire for the expansion of government. For example, when Courant, Gramlich, and Rubinfeld (1980), examined a survey of Michigan voters regarding state and local government tax limitations, they found little difference between the preferences of state employees and those of the general electorate. Both groups preferred a reduction in state expenditures. State and local employees, however, desire a small increase in local government spending, while private-sector voters wanted a decrease. A much broader study is that of Blais, Blake, and Dion (1991), who examined voter preferences for the expansion of government in the United States and other countries. In their analysis for the United States, they assumed that Democratic party candidates were pro-growth and that voters who backed them were also pro-growth. The evidence that they mustered indicated that there was a tendency for public-sector employees to support Democratic candidates but that the link was modest at best.

When considered in its entirety, the evidence presented in this section does not support the hypothesis that public-sector employees have a strong incentive to use their voting power to promote the growth of government, with the objective of increasing their salaries. At least, this relation does not appear to be key for understanding the success of federal workers in obtaining comparatively high levels of compensation. Indeed, it is not at all clear why promoting public-sector growth would be the preferred route to higher salaries, rather than restricting the supply of government workers.[13] As both Tullock (1974) and Courant, Gramlich, and Rubinfeld (1980) have pointed out, there are likely to be limits to or an optimum size for the bureaucracy. If this limit were exceeded, a lower wage structure would result. Even in these models, however, the voting power of government workers is emphasized as a factor in determining the size of the bureaucracy. In contrast, we have shown that voting power alone cannot explain the success of federal workers. They appear, instead, to have relied more on lobbying to achieve their goals in the public arena.

6.3   Federal Workers: An Effective Interest Group

6.3.1   The Characteristics of Effective Interest Groups

In order to understand why federal employee unions seem to have been especially effective in the political arena, it is worthwhile reviewing some of the literature on interest groups. One common characteristic of successful interest groups is that they are small, relative to the group opposing them, and homogeneous. In setting regulation policy, and in other policy areas as well, small groups often seem capable of dominating larger ones. Sam Peltzman (1976) explains this phenomenon by showing that, in the political process, a small group with a large per capita stake in the outcome can outperform a much larger group, whose interests are diffused. Voting power matters in Peltzman's model, but voting is most often on a package of issues, and there are costs to being informed on each of them. Voters with a small per capita stake in the outcome are unlikely to expend substantial resources in becoming informed or in attempting to block the efforts of a group whose members have more at stake on a particular issue. Because of the free-rider problem, the small group will be relatively better at organizing its voters and in raising campaign funds to support selected officials. Vote-maximizing politicians can use these campaign resources to increase their probability of winning an election by attracting uninformed voters. Thus, campaign contributions and other political activities from small interest groups can make up for the lack of raw voting power.[14]

6.3.2   Federal Employees as an Interest Group and Their Political Environment

A large per capita stake in the outcome and organizational clout, generally enhanced by relatively small group size and homogeneity, are important characteristics of successful interest groups. As we will see, federal career employees, as a group, have some of these characteristics, but not all.

First, consider the constraints that they face. At over 3 million strong, they are not a small group. Furthermore, lobbying activities are carried out by federal employee unions, but, as we indicated in chapter 5, not all federal employees who are represented are union members. Although the proportion of federal workers represented by unions is high, especially when compared to the private sector, many of those who are in exclusive bargaining units are not actual dues-paying members.[15] While Congress has allowed the "union shop," it has not required nonmembers to pay monthly fees that are equal to union dues, as is practiced in the private sector. Federal unions also do not have at their disposal the same arsenal as private-sector unions. They cannot offer to engage in collective bargaining over salaries or benefits. Federal salaries instead are set by statute, and the unions are prohibited by law from striking.[16]

Moreover, until recently, federal unions were less able to use peer group pressure to raise campaign contributions.[17] Under the Hatch Act, federal workers were constrained in their political activities. They were free to vote, to express their political views as citizens, to attend political rallies (as spectators only), and to contribute money to partisan political campaigns, but they could not solicit campaign contributions that could be used by federal unions or employee groups in political action.

Despite these constraints, federal employee unions have developed as a formidable political force. As Gary Becker has pointed out, "The political effectiveness of a group is mainly determined not by its absolute efficiency . . . but by its efficiency relative to the efficiency of other groups" (1983, 380). Becker was referring to the relative ability of interest groups to control the free-rider problem and to the potential gains that they could capture relative to the costs (including the deadweight costs associated with the transfer) that they imposed on opposing parties. According to Becker, those interest groups that are better able to control free riding and increase the returns and reduce the costs of transfers will be more effective at exerting political influence.

Because federal unions are concerned with civil service rules and salaries and benefits for the general bureaucracy, their efforts generally do not antagonize any specific constituent group. That is, they are not seen as lobbying for specific benefits from particular agencies that might crowd out or otherwise harm competing special interests. Accordingly, the lobbying efforts of federal unions typically do not ignite opposition from well-organized interest groups.[18] The main group affected by the actions of federal employee unions in obtaining preferential pay, benefits, and work rules is general taxpayers. Compared with general taxpayers, federal workers as a group are small and much more homogeneous. Moreover, they have high per capita stakes in civil service and federal salary legislation, while the per capita costs to general taxpayers of any one bill are small. These conditions provide general taxpayers with little incentive to collect accurate information about the costs of federal salary statutes or civil service laws, and the individual costs of gaining such information are high.

Peltzman, Becker, and others have stressed that a lack of information and the incentive to collect it on the part of the general electorate is a key to understanding the success of special interest groups. This situation provides a partial explanation for the general salary advantage of federal rank-and-file employees over their counterparts in state and local governments. We expect citizen disinterest in legislation regarding bureaucratic rules and salaries to be greater at the federal level than at the state and local level.

There are far fewer federal employees than the aggregate state and local total, and, as we have indicated, they are fairly evenly spread across the country. Firsthand or direct knowledge by taxpayers of a significant federal wage advantage is unlikely.[19] Further, despite generally higher individual salaries, the federal wage bill is much less than the total for state and local government employees. In 1990, for example, total wages paid to state and local workers amounted to $355 billion, while total wages paid to federal civilian plus government enterprise workers were $101 billion (national income and product accounts, computer data files, updated 1991). Moreover, the federal wage bill is spread across all taxpayers, and it accounts for only a small part of total federal expenditures. In 1988, expenditures for wages and salaries at the federal level, including defense, were around 11 percent of total expenditures. The corresponding figure for state and local governments was around 35 percent (U.S. Department of Commerce 1988).

Accordingly, not only are the pay and performance of government workers more visible to state and local government taxpayers, but those taxpayers also have more reasons to be concerned and to collect information about them. This suggests that a state and local politician is more likely to be held directly accountable for increases in government wages than is a member of Congress. The latter is just one out of close to 500 elected federal officials, and, if the general electorate is disinterested in federal pay issues, so too will be elected officials.

Although direct evidence on just how disinterested federal officials are in civil service issues is difficult to come by, the lack of attention to these issues by most members of the Congress is apparent. Few members of the House seek assignment to the Committee on Post Office and Civil Service, and Congress as a whole appears to be largely unconcerned with pay and promotion issues. Consider, for example, the practice of grade inflation whereby supervisors routinely reclassify positions to higher GS grades than the position would otherwise warrant. Concern over grade inflation has been expressed in numerous federal studies by monitoring agencies. The U.S. Office of Personnel Management (1983, 4), for example, estimated that 14.3 percent of audited positions were overgraded. The U.S. Congressional Budget Office (1984, 9) charged that recent increases in the average GS grade were the result of supervisors responding to pressures to compensate workers for departures from pay comparability with the private sector, as mandated by the Federal Pay Comparability Act 1970. At least in part through grade inflation, the average GS grade has risen. For example, in only four years, the average GS grade rose from 8.16 in 1980 to 8.39 in 1984.[20] We compared the salaries of GS employees with identical characteristics in 1980 and again in 1985, using the same data set and variables described in appendix C (see also Johnson and Libecap 1989b). The results indicate that grade inflation contributed an additional 3 percent more to the salary of the typical GS employee than had been authorized by the Congress. Nevertheless, even though the existence of grade inflation has been reported to the Congress on numerous occasions, no real effort has been undertaken to curtail the practice, and it has continued. By 1989, for instance, the average GS grade had increased to 8.69 (U.S. Office of Personnel Management 1989, 10).

While federal taxpayers and their congressional representatives may be generally unconcerned about pay issues in the federal bureaucracy, federal employee unions are not. They work to develop close ties with specific members of Congress, especially those on the Postal and Civil Service Committees. Richard Fenno notes, "Congressmen who ask for membership on the Interior and Post Office Committees have the primary goal of helping their constituents and thereby insuring their reelection" (1973, 5). Although the committees dealing with civil service matters are not usually thought of as being the most preferred assignments, there is a tendency for members of Congress who have a relatively high proportion of federal workers residing in their districts to be members of those committees.[21] Moreover, because committee members are targeted by federal unions for special attention, having a major say over federal wage policy has its rewards.[22] As indicated by their presence in hearings on relevant legislation, federal unions closely monitor the actions of those members of Congress. In exchange for favorable legislation, federal unions offer political support in the form of articles and editorials in union newspapers and campaign activities by federal employees' spouses and friends who are not subject to Hatch Act constraints.[23] In addition, federal unions, just like the larger national labor unions, have their own political action committees (PACs), and these are not small.

Table 6.4 lists the top five federal employee PACs by the amount actually given to federal candidates. Although collectively the amounts given are large, it is the pattern of the campaign contributions that is most revealing. Data on the amount contributed by each of the five PACs listed in the table to individual members of the House and Senate are available from the Federal Elections Commission. If, as described above, these PACs focus their attention on members of the committees most directly concerned with civil service matters, then contributions to members of those committees should be higher than they are for nonmembers.

Consider first contributions to members of the House of Representatives. Since not all members received contributions, we utilize a tobit (censored regression) model to examine the relation between PAC contributions and membership on the House Committee on Post Office and Civil Service. Besides a qualitative variable for committee membership, the regression variables include a political party identifier (set equal to one if a Democrat) and a variable to account for the number of federal civilian employees residing in the member's district. The latter variable is included because interest groups supply both votes and money, which can be thought of as either substitutes or compliments.[24] Tables 6.5–6.7 report separate results of tobit regressions for each of the three election cycles (1985–86, 1987–88, and 1989–90, respectively) and for each individual PAC. The first dependent variable in all three tables is the sum of contributions from all five PACs. While the results indicate that being a member of the Democratic party clearly increases PAC contributions, committee membership also has a strong positive effect.[25] Indeed, the coefficient on the committee membership variable is positive and statistically significant

Table 6.4   Rank of Federal Union Political Action Committees in Terms of
                   Contributions to Federal Candidates

| | Election Cycle | | | | | |
| | 1985–86 | | 1987–88 | | 1989–90 | |
	Rank	Amount ($)	Rank	Amount ($)	Rank	Amount ($)
Letter Carriers Political Action Fund	3	1,491,875	4	1,732,482	4	1,731,050
Political Fund Committee of the American Postal Workers Union	18	724,145	14	898,075	12	964,828
National Rural Letter Carriers' Association Political Action Committee	22	504,455	26	398,280	24	430,875
American Federation of Government Employees Political Action Committee	34	268,585	35	211,515	46	161,774
National Treasury Employees' Union Political Action Committee	36	209,070	41	167,295	42	192,531

Source: Federal Election Commission, Washington, D.C.

Note: Rank is based on all labor PACs. In addition to the above, the National Association of Retired Federal Employees Political Action Committee is a major contributor: contributions were $1,493,395 in 1985–86, and the organization ranked fifth out of all contributors to federal candidates.

(at the 5 percent level) in all cases, strongly supporting the argument that federal labor unions focus attention on these particular members of Congress.

Table 6.8 presents the results of tobit regressions for PAC contributions to members of the Senate. Here, the relevant committee is the Subcommittee on Federal Services, Post Office and Civil Service of the Committee on Governmental Affairs. Because only one-third of the Senate is up for reelection in any given cycle, we combined all three election cycles (1985–86, 1987–88, and 1989–90), for a total of 300 observations.[26] Also, the federal employment variable is now measured as the ratio of total federal employment in the state to state total civilian employment. Because the Senate is substantially smaller than the House of Representatives, it is generally thought that the decision-making process there is less dependent on the committee structure.[27] Floor debate, for example, is more common in the Senate than in the House. As a consequence, we should not expect the results for the committee variable for the Senate to be as strong as it was for the House. Nevertheless, the results in table 6.8 indicate that federal employee PACs are more likely to contribute to

Table 6.5   **Tobit Estimates of PAC Contributions to Members of the House, 1985–86 Cycle**

Variable	Dependent Variable					
	SUM	PAC1	PAC2	PAC3	PAC4	PAC5
Member post office	9,653	5,204	3,315	1,752	1,830	1,908
and civil service	(7.57)	(6.05)	(8.12)	(4.78)	(8.22)	(5.98)
Democrat	8,487	6,443	3,614	1,668	1,078	2,297
	(13.16)	(12.57)	(13.10)	(8.96)	(3.71)	(7.63)
Federal employment	.089	.047	.017	−.006	.025	.055
	(2.26)	(1.54)	(1.26)	(−.49)	(2.64)	(5.06)
Constant	−4,419	−4,890	−2,864	−1,011	−2,365	−3,258
	(−7.15)	(−9.29)	(−10.03)	(−5.45)	(10.09)	(−10.02)
SEE	5,428	3,700	1,658	1,591	1,142	1,283
Log-likelihood function	−2,934	−2,251	−2,001	−1,019	−1,044	−1,019
Frequency of contributions > 0	.66	.52	.50	.54	.25	.25
Number of observations	433	433	433	433	433	433

Sources: Federal Elections Commission; *Congressional Quarterly Almanac* (1985–90); and U.S. Department of Commerce (1983).

Note: Reported regression coefficients were obtained by multiplying the normalized coefficients by the SEE. Asymptotic *t*-statistics are given in parentheses. SUM = total contributions from all five PACs; PAC1 = Letter Carriers Political Action Fund; PAC2 = Political Fund Committee of the American Postal Workers Union; PAC3 = National Rural Letter Carriers' Association; PAC4 = American Federation of Government Employees; PAC5 = National Treasury Employees.

committee members than to nonmembers. The coefficient on the committee membership variable is positive in all cases and is statistically significant (at the 10 percent level) for four out of the five PACs.

Focusing attention on committee members appears to have paid off for the federal unions. The legislative histories of recent and major civil service reform bills indicate how important committee support can be to federal employee unions. Final action on bills dealing with salary issues and civil service rules are often perfunctory, with little discussion on the floor of either chamber, and with bills passing by large margins. Debate and resolution are most generally carried out in the relevant committees.[28]

Federal employee unions have asserted that they could do more politically and, hence, be an even stronger lobbying group if the restrictive Hatch Act were repealed. In 1989, both the House and the Senate passed bills that would have permitted federal employees to raise money for and participate in political campaigns.[29] These measures would have allowed federal workers, while off duty, to distribute campaign literature, to solicit votes, to endorse candidates, and to raise funds for political action committees. Hearings on the Hatch Act Reform Amendments of 1989 revealed that federal employee unions strongly

Table 6.6   Tobit Estimates of PAC Contributions to Members of the House, 1987–88 Cycle

Variable	Dependent Variable					
	SUM	PAC1	PAC2	PAC3	PAC4	PAC5
Member post office and	12,093	5,657	4,756	1,680	1,673	2,073
civil service	(8.69)	(6.51)	(9.09)	(4.65)	(5.35)	(5.20)
Democrat	8,926	5,761	4,082	1,409	1,550	2,411
	(13.07)	(12.73)	(13.14)	(7.42)	(7.50)	(6.10)
Federal employment	.126	.012	.030	.034	.054	.068
	(2.92)	(.39)	(1.79)	(2.81)	(5.21)	(5.26)
Constant	−4,107	−2,719	−3,102	−1,533	−2,444	−4,062
	(−6.30)	(−6.10)	(−9.82)	(−8.07)	(−11.40)	(−9.53)
SEE	5,866	3,758	2,142	1,559	1,258	1,527
Log-likelihood function	−3,104	−2,674	−2,190	−1,838	−1,141	−770
Frequency of contributions > 0	.69	.62	.54	.43	.28	.18
Number of observations	432	432	432	432	432	

Sources: Federal Elections Commission; *Congressional Quarterly Almanac* (1987–88); and U.S. Department of Commerce (1983).

Note: Reported regression coefficients were obtained by multiplying the normalized coefficients by the SEE. Asymptotic *t*-statistics are given in parentheses. SUM = total contributions from all five PACs; PAC1 = Letter Carriers Political Action Fund; PAC2 = Political Fund Committee of the American Postal Workers Union; PAC3 = National Rural Letter Carriers' Association; PAC4 = American Federation of Government Employees; PAC5 = National Treasury Employees.

supported the repeal while President Bush adamantly rejected it.[30] Much of the testimony in support of the Hatch Act revisions emphasized that the law had a chilling effect on employee political participation. Although the evidence on voter participation rates presented in this chapter does not indicate that federal workers vote less than their counterparts in the private sector, the Hatch Act has restricted their active involvement in political campaigns.

Republicans in both the House and the Senate argued that the Hatch Act reform was based largely on the desire of Democrats to increase the contributions that they receive from federal employee PACs.[31] Nevertheless, both the House and the Senate versions passed their respective chambers by wide margins and included the yes votes of a number of Republicans.[32] President Bush, however, vetoed the bill, and the Senate, in a very close vote, failed to override it. But this defeat for the unions was short lived.

In 1993, both the House and the Senate again passed legislation that allowed greater political involvement by federal employees. (*Congressional Quarterly Weekly Report,* 25 September 1993, 2538). Under the compromise bill, however, federal workers would still be prohibited from running for partisan elective office, and supervisors would not be allowed to solicit funds from subordinates. In addition, restrictions were maintained for members of the Senior

Table 6.7   Tobit Estimates of PAC Contributions to Members of the House, 1989–90 Cycle

Variable	Dependent Variable					
	SUM	PAC1	PAC2	PAC3	PAC4	PAC5
Member post office and civil service	11,519	5,900	4,305	1,497	1,564	2,349
	(8.08)	(6.89)	(7.89)	(4.51)	(4.32)	(6.13)
Democrat	8,514	4,846	3,932	1,630	2,182	1,645
	(11.91)	(11.10)	(12.79)	(8.87)	(6.22)	(5.70)
Federal employment	.064	.001	.018	.022	.045	.050
	(1.37)	(.03)	(1.02)	(1.91)	(3.64)	(3.82)
Constant	−2,559	−1,425	−2,477	−1,435	−3,527	−3,207
	(−3.74)	(−3.29)	(−8.05)	(−7.77)	(−9.44)	(−10.69)
SEE	6,343	3,860	2,395	1,497	1,415	1,630
Log-likelihood function	−3,264	−2,917	−2,411	−2,002	−768	−851
Frequency of contributions > 0	.72	.67	.58	.50	.18	.20
Number of observations	433	433	433	433	433	433

Sources: Federal Elections Commission; Congressional Quarterly Almanac (1989–90); and U.S. Department of Commerce (1983).

Note: Reported regression coefficients were obtained by multiplying the normalized coefficients by the SEE. Asymptotic t-statistics are given in parentheses. SUM = total contributions from all five PACs; PAC1 = Letter Carriers Political Action Fund; PAC2 = Political Fund Committee of the American Postal Workers Union; PAC3 = National Rural Letter Carriers' Association; PAC4 = American Federation of Government Employees; PAC5 = National Treasury Employees.

Executive Service and other sensitive positions. Nevertheless, the bill granted federal workers considerable leeway to engage in political activities during their off-duty hours. President Clinton signed the bill on 6 October 1993.

The recent history of Hatch Act reform legislation illustrates the formidable political influence of federal employee unions. The efforts of the federal unions to repeal the legislative restrictions on the political activity of their members had wide support in the Congress. Although President Bush's veto was maintained in the Senate, the House voted to override by a margin of 327 to 93.[33]

Returning to table 6.4, it is clear from the figures presented there that the postal workers are the most active of federal unions and that they are major contributors to candidates for federal office. Postal workers were, as we have explained, one of the first groups to unionize after the passage of the Pendleton Act, and they have been active ever since, even engaging in a massive and illegal strike in New York in 1970 (Nesbitt 1976, 386–90). Unlike the GS pay plan, which has considerable variation in occupations, postal workers are a relatively homogeneous group, contributing to group solidarity. The campaign services that they have supplied to members of the Congress have apparently

Table 6.8 **Tobit Estimates of PAC Contributions to Members of the Senate**

Variable	Dependent Variable					
	SUM	PAC1	PAC2	PAC3	PAC4	PAC5
Member federal	8,752	2,039	2,622	3,724	2,017	2,457
services, post office	(2.05)	(1.00)	(1.65)	(2.63)	(1.76)	(1.80)
and civil service						
Democrat	13,579	6,495	5,540	3,248	3,575	3,494
	(6.36)	(6.35)	(6.59)	(4.33)	(5.31)	(4.49)
Federal employment/	17,045	18,471	18,151	5,974	14,432	17,081
state employment	(.42)	(.98)	(1.22)	(.42)	(1.32)	(1.29)
Constant	−11,993	−7,737	−6,858	−4,943	−6,154	−6,893
	(−4.94)	(−6.51)	(−7.08)	(−5.71)	(−7.96)	(−7.67)
SEE	15,227	6,630	5,303	4,992	3,558	4,346
Log-likelihood function	−1,538	−1,072	−1,027	−988	−622	−636
Frequency of	.43	.32	.31	.30	.19	.19
contributions > 0						
Number of observations	300	300	300	300	300	300

Sources: Federal Elections Commission; *Congressional Quarterly Almanac* (1985–90); and U.S. Bureau of the Census (1983).

Note: Reported regression coefficients were obtained by multiplying the normalized coefficients by the SEE. Asymptotic *t*-statistics are given in parentheses. SUM = total contributions from all five PACs; PAC1 = Letter Carriers Political Action Fund; PAC2 = Political Fund Committee of the American Postal Workers Union; PAC3 = National Rural Letter Carriers' Association; PAC4 = American Federation of Government Employees; PAC5 = National Treasury Employees.

paid off; postal employees' earnings are substantially higher than those of their private-sector counterparts (see Wachter and Perloff 1992).

In comparisons among federal workers, however, postal workers do not appear to receive a wage premium.[34] This outcome is consistent, at least over the long run, with the notion that the postal workers have been trendsetters, in terms of compensation, for all federal civilian workers. It also points out how important is the concept of wage comparability to federal workers and why they have fought for legislation that requires it. With mandated wage comparability, the success of one group is likely to benefit others. In the political arena, the concept of wage comparability with its connotation of equality is not a concept that can be easily attacked by most elected officials. The wage regression studies summarized in chapter 5 support this argument. Those studies indicate that the relative federal/private-sector wage advantage is greater for women and minorities than it is for white males, yielding greater equality of wages in the federal sector. It is also important to note that, in the public sector, the union/nonunion wage gap is less than the wage gap found in the private sector.[35] One possible explanation for this is that spillover effects are greater in the public sector because elected officials are more easily pressured into concessions that tend to equalize pay than private-sector employers.

In their lobbying efforts, federal unions also receive important support from organized labor. Indeed, there is a sort of symbiotic relation among labor unions, and most federal unions are closely aligned with larger private-sector unions.[36] In the private sector, unions have supported one another through sympathy strikes, work slowdowns, and company boycotts. Such actions appear costly, compared to the support that private-sector and federal unions can provide one another in the political arena. Given restrictions on strikes and collective bargaining in the federal sector, the focus is on legislation. In the political arena, votes and campaign contributions are what count, and both federal and private unions have become adept in political maneuvering.

An example of collaborative union action is Executive Order 10988, issued by President Kennedy in 1962 to recognize federal unions. As we pointed out in chapter 5, organized labor played a key role in securing presidential candidate Kennedy's support for federal union recognition, by offering votes in exchange for his promise to act on the issue. Organized labor also monitors the roll-call voting behavior of members of Congress on issues related to labor in general and reports the findings to their rank-and-file members. Similarly, federal unions rank politicians, not only on their support for issues directly affecting federal workers, but also on issues affecting organized labor in general.[37] Private-sector unions make substantial campaign contributions to many federal politicians, and how these elected officials vote on issues related to federal workers can be taken as a sign of their support or opposition to organized labor more generally.

State and local government workers benefit much less from this sort of collaboration. Organized labor is not as active in state and local governments. Although labor issues are not unimportant at the state and local level, organized labor especially has sought favorable legislation from the federal government. With many jurisdictions, an organized lobbying effort across most of the states, for example, would be very costly. More important, federal actions set precedents that state laws do not, and resources are more mobile across state lines than they are across international boundaries, suggesting that federal politicians would be less concerned about the cost effects of labor legislation than would be state politicians. For these reasons, focus on the federal government is the more effective choice. This focus, in turn, implies that organized labor will spend more effort on scrutinizing and promoting federal politicians than on state and local politicians. The attention given to federal politicians by organized labor benefits federal workers by increasing their ability to exert political pressure. In contrast, the comparatively lower interest of organized labor in state and local governments means that the opportunities to join forces with local government workers are fewer, reducing their relative effectiveness as political lobbyists.

The issue of limited factor mobility at the federal level has other implications and deserves more discussion. Courant, Gramlich, and Rubinfeld (1979) have argued that increases in public-sector wages are constrained by the mobility of private employers, who are the taxed group. Clearly, the potential for the exit of residents and businesses (the Tiebout adjustment) to discipline elected officials seems greater at the state and local level. Not only is there considerable tax competition across states and localities, but the negative effects of state and local taxes on capital formation and personal income are substantially greater when expenditures are used for the explicit purpose of transferring income.[38] Wage premiums in the public sector would appear to fit that category. Moreover, the pressures on elected officials to curtail expenditures are far more apparent at the state and local level than at the federal. Tax-limitation legislation, such as California's Proposition 13, has proliferated across the country since the late 1970s. The implications of this discussion are clear. Because factor mobility is less at the federal level, the derived demand for the services of federal workers is also likely to be less elastic, and this condition gives federal unions greater power.[39]

There have been numerous studies that have estimated the elasticity of demand for public-sector workers at the state and local level (see Ehrenberg and Schwarz 1986). All these studies report well-behaved demand functions, with negative wage elasticities. In contrast, the number of published studies that report estimates of demand elasticities for federal workers is extremely rare. Indeed, Freeman, who reports estimated demand functions for state and local employment using NIPA data, notes that the regressions for the federal sector yield "quite different results" (1987, 202). Our own efforts at estimating federal employment demand, using variables similar to those used by Freeman for his state and local equations (total budget expenditures, the unemployment rate, and the rate of inflation), produced a positive, but not statistically significant, coefficient on the federal wage variable. The analysis and data presented by Larry Katz and Alan Krueger (1991, 1992) also reveal substantial differences between the two jurisdictions. Although Katz and Krueger do not estimate employment demand functions, the comparisons that they make show that federal wages are far less responsive to economic conditions and changes in private-sector wages than are state and local wages. Thus, the available empirical evidence supports the argument that employment demand at the federal level is less elastic than for state and local employees, and this condition contributes to the relative effectiveness of federal workers as an interest group.

Finally, it is important to note that the desires of federal unions in lobbying for civil service and related pay legislation often coincide with the interests of the Congress and the president, but for different reasons. As we have suggested, the president and the Congress compete for control of the federal bureaucracy, particularly senior career officials, who are in a position potentially to mold and direct policy. To limit the opportunistic manipulation of senior members of the bureaucracy, the president and the Congress have supported legislation that limits their ability to access and pressure bureaucrats. As we explain in chapter 7 they have an incentive to support tenure guarantees against arbitrary removal and salary caps to limit the rewards that might be offered to senior officials in exchange for certain administrative actions. Federal unions, whose membership is drawn largely from the rank and file, not from the senior levels, however, favor similar legislative provisions. They have sought tenure guarantees for their members, even though the rank and file are much less likely to be the targets of presidential and congressional competition. Moreover, salary caps for senior officials have served to assist unions in achieving a more egalitarian wage structure within the bureaucracy. Additionally, as the salary caps have contributed to an inability of the federal government to keep or hire senior officials, the popular solution has been to raise all salaries through across-the-board percentage increases.[40] Hence, the salary caps have provided a convenient mechanism for federal unions to focus the attention of Congress on wage increases for their members.

6.3.3 Summary

The evidence presented in this chapter indicates that relative interest group effectiveness, not voting power or the growth of government, explains the higher salaries achieved by federal workers compared to those paid to state and local employees. A major reason why federal unions are so effective is that they face relatively low costs in exerting political influence. Federal workers are a less conspicuous group to the general electorate, both in terms of their numbers and as a percentage of total budget expenditures, than are state and local government employees, and factor resources are less mobile at the federal level. In addition, both the president and the Congress appear receptive to legislation that can serve to demonstrate political support for benefits that are popular among the broader workforce. How well federal workers are treated provides a signal to organized labor that supplies both votes and funds to federal politicians. All these factors contribute to making the employment demand function at the federal level less elastic than it is at the state and local level. Federal workers have been organized to lobby Congress since the turn of the century, and they have been able to take advantage of these conditions to pressure for higher wages and other workplace benefits under the civil service system.

Notes

1. We use the term *voting power* loosely and measure it as a simple ratio, such as the ratio of public-sector workers to the total labor force. A more precise measure would adjust for voter participation rates, family ties, and other factors and include the entire voting population. See, e.g., the voting power index suggested by Bush and Denzau (1977). Given the vast differences in the numbers of federal workers relative to the entire workforce or in relation to state and local employment, there is little to be gained for our purposes by such refinements.

2. Most studies that compare federal government salaries with state and local gov-

ernment salaries use CPS data and log-linear earnings regressions with demographic, occupational, and other controls. The studies summarized by Ehrenberg and Schwarz (1986, 1249) indicate that the federal/private wage differential is around 15 percent for males and 24 percent for females. The state/private wage differentials are negative for males and around 10 percent for females. At the local government level, the wage differentials are negative for males and close to zero for females. Similar findings are reported by Freeman (1987, 192). The following percentage wage differentials for federal/private-sector employees are based on his table 8.5B:

Type	1972	1977	1982
Federal public administration	31	26	20
State public administration	5	7	6
Local public administration	−5	6	10
Teacher	−1	−7	−11
Postal	25	32	35

This table indicates a substantial advantage for all types of federal civilian employees relative to state and local workers. See also the more recent estimates offered by Katz and Krueger (1991, 1992). While Katz and Krueger do not report an aggregate comparison such as Freeman's, their findings listed by gender, education, and experience reveal a federal wage advantage in all categories.

3. This argument has a long history, but its current prominence can largely be attributed to a collection of papers in a volume edited by Thomas Borcherding (1977). The lead paper in that volume is that of James Buchanan (1977, 14), who argues, "Bureaucrats are no different from other persons, and, like others, they will rationally vote to further their own interests as producers when given the opportunity. Clearly their interests lie in an expanding governmental sector, and especially in one that expands the number of employees. Salaries can be increased much more rapidly in an expanding agency than in a declining or stagnant one." For a brief survey of the literature on bureaucracy and the growth of government, see Mueller (1989, 337–42).

4. The major reason for the difference between the simple measures of voter participation rates, which show federal workers voting at a higher rate than private-sector workers, and the probit estimates is that the latter control for the level of education and federal workers tend to be more highly educated than are private-sector voters. The level of education has a very strong positive effect on the probability of voting. See the probit results reported in app. D.

5. Moreover, shirking is usually thought to be greater in larger groups than in smaller ones. See, e.g., the discussion by Olson (1965) and empirical evidence indicating that group size negatively affects voter turnout in Hansen, Palfrey, and Rosenthal (1987). In 1980, there were approximately 3 million full- and part-time federal civilian, 4 million state, and 10 million local government employees. Comparisons of federal, state, and local employment are from U.S. Bureau of the Census figures as reported in data files of the national income and product accounts. If we consider the entire nation as the relevant political jurisdiction for federal workers, then there is no other political jurisdiction, state or local, with anywhere near the same number of public employees. The closest is the state of California, with 380,000 state employees. Thus, it is also plausible that federal workers are less likely to vote because of their larger group size.

6. Employment figures are based on the 1980 census and are reported in U.S. Department of Commerce (1983), by state and congressional district.

7. See Wolfinger (1972). Although patronage creates an added incentive for public

employees to vote, the potential for free riding remains. However like politicians at the federal level in the nineteenth century, state and local politicians have an incentive to monitor the voting behavior of employees, and the failure of an employee to vote is taken as a sign of disloyalty. As Wolfinger and Rosenstone note, "Political machines often coerce their members to vote and keep records of their performance" (1980, 96).

8. Young (1991) provides a comprehensive survey of studies dealing with the relation between public-sector growth and salaries. In addition to our work, there is a study by Grandjean (1981), who analyzed a longitudinal sample of federal white-collar employees. While Grandjean reports results for only a few major agencies, his findings suggest that agency earnings differentials have little to do with fluctuations in agency size.

9. While there is evidence indicating that the size of a political entity, in terms of its budget, has a positive effect on salaries (Freeman 1987), there is no direct evidence supporting a positive growth-salary relation at the state or local level. It has, however, been suggested in the labor literature that public-sector unions are capable of influencing not only the supply of labor but its demand as well. Supposedly, increasing the demand for labor can lead to an increase in employment and wages simultaneously. There is some evidence indicating that unions at the municipal level have increased employment (Zax and Ichniowski 1988), leading some to argue that public-sector unions both desire to increase employment and have the political clout to do so. More recent evidence, however, questions those results and indicates that the observed effect may be largely due to endogenous choice, whereby unionization is more likely to occur in larger municipalities (Trejo 1991).

10. On problems in hiring and retaining scientists and engineers, see Campbell and Dix (1990). Also, this is a long-standing problem. Many senior management and professional groups have testified about the problems due to salary compression (U.S. Senate 1949). And salary is an often-stated reason for leaving the Senior Executive Service (SES) and other higher-ranking positions (U.S. Merit Systems Protection Board 1989, 1990).

11. The federal relative wage advantage did, however, decline in the 1980s. This decline is also consistent with the results reported by Katz and Krueger (1992), who used CPS data and earnings regressions to compare federal salaries with those of state and local employees. Nevertheless, this decline does not appear to be related to an increase in the rate of employment growth at the state and local level. The most rapid period of expansion for state and local employment was in the 1960s and the early 1970s. This was also the time when the federal wage advantage was the greatest.

12. Despite substantial differences in rates of employment growth, changes in the relative size of these two public groups had no effect on their relative wages. Regressing Y_t, the ratio of the federal wage to state and local wages, on X_t, the ratio of federal employment to state and local, yielded the following results (t-statistics are given in parentheses):

$$Y_t = 1.33 - 0.13X_t.$$
$$(22.5)\ (-0.9)$$

13. The available evidence suggests that private-sector unions do not contract for added employment (Wessels 1991).

14. Becker also has a model of competition among pressure groups for political favors that emphasizes small group size and large campaign contributions as a major determinant. Indeed, he does not consider the constraint of majority voting important because "voter preferences are frequently not a crucial *independent* force in political behavior. These preferences can be manipulated and created through the information and misinformation provided by interested pressure groups" (1983, 392).

15. See Freeman (1986). For example, the number of employees represented by the American Federation of Government Employees is around 700,000. The number of active dues-paying members, however, is much smaller, 210,000 (AFGE 1988).

16. The right of state and local employee unions to strike is also greatly limited (see Freeman 1986).

17. Removal of the constraint on soliciting funds has been the major motive behind recent attempts to amend the Hatch Act. The reform amendments are discussed later in the chapter.

18. A reading of the congressional hearings for federal pay or civil service legislation reveals relatively little organized opposition from other interest groups. Federal unions and professional groups, as well as private-sector unions, dominate the testimony. Opposition has generally come only from the Civil Service Commission (now, the Office of Personnel Management) and the Bureau of the Budget (see, e.g., U.S. Senate 1962; and U.S. House 1970). We realize that, in the aggregate, the lobbying actions of federal unions do raise costs for other special interests because they affect the performance of government. Each statute regarding civil service rules or federal pay applies governmentwide, with only an incremental effect on particular agencies or interests. Most special interests have direct competitors and must focus on them.

19. Moreover, federal unions actively disseminate information that suggests that federal employees are underpaid, relative to their private-sector counterparts, and that disputes studies made by economists. Federal unions can point to wage disparities at the senior level, where wage compression has led to lower federal salaries. Senior career officials tend not to be union members, and caps on their salaries reflect (as we argue) a desire of the president and the Congress to control the opportunistic manipulation of senior administrators. Nevertheless, since the unions have an interest in providing information to taxpayers that indicates a salary discrepancy, more taxpayers are likely to believe that federal employees are underpaid rather than overpaid. For related discussion, see Lane and Wolf (1990) and Levitan and Noden (1983).

20. While some of this increase could be attributed to the hiring of more highly skilled professional employees, much of it appears to be due to grade inflation, as the results from Johnson and Libecap (1989b) indicate.

21. For example, we examined membership on the House Post Office and Civil Service Committee for the Eighty-sixth Congress (1960) through the 101st Congress (1988) to see whether representatives from the three districts surrounding Washington, D.C., were more likely to be on the committee. The test utilized compared the mean number of Congresses in which the three Washington, D.C.-area districts were represented on the committee with the mean for other congressional districts that were represented at least once on the committee. This provides for a somewhat stronger test than simply looking at all districts. The mean for the three Washington, D.C., districts was 6.67 (standard deviation, 0.71) Congresses, while the mean for the other 130 districts represented at least once on the committee was 3.09 (standard deviation, 2.83). A t-test indicates that these means are significantly different at the 1 percent level. The data utilized are from the U.S. Bureau of the Census, congressional district data for the various congresses.

22. Fenno (1973, 42) points out that lobbyists for the postal service unions spend much of their time with members of Congress, who are on the committees most important to their members and arrange testimonial dinners and other activities to raise funds and deliver votes.

23. For a discussion of postal unions' methods for influencing Congress, see Kappel Commission (1968, 4:7.60–7.64).

24. See the discussion offered by Stratmann (1992). His empirical evidence, which relates to agricultural PACs, indicates that campaign contributions at first increase with

the voting power of these interest groups but after a point decline with further increases in voting power. In addition to the results reported in tables 6.5–6.8 below, we also utilized a quadratic functional form for the federal employment variable. In none of the cases did the quadratic specification provide a better fit.

25. That labor PACs contribute more to Democrats than to Republicans is well known in the literature (see e.g., Peltzman 1984).

26. Contributions were deflated using the CPI.

27. Fenno notes, "The root institutional differences between the Senate and the House are those of size, procedure, constituency, and tenure. They, in turn, combine to produce very different decisionmaking structures in the two chambers. The smaller size of the Senate makes it possible for each individual Senator to have more of an impact on chamber decision making than the individual House member—both as a matter of proportional weight and as a matter of procedural opportunity" (1973, 145–46).

28. The legislative history of the Civil Service Reform Act of 1978 is illustrative. Lengthy hearings were held by the various committees, during which federal labor unions were given ample time to express their views (*Congressional Quarterly Almanac* 1978, 818–35). The Senate approved the conference agreement on a voice vote, while the House passed it by a vote of 365 to 8. Action on the 1990 federal pay reform bill was similar (*Congressional Quarterly Almanac* 1990, 406–7).

29. The House bill was H.R. 20 and the Senate version S. 135. For a brief history of this legislation, see *Congressional Quarterly Almanac* (1990, 408–11).

30. Hearings on S. 135 contain testimony by the major federal employee unions listing support, while the Department of Justice, the Federal Election Commission, and other federal agencies stated their opposition (see U.S. Senate 1989). Joining in support of the measure was the American Civil Liberties Union (ACLU), which argued that the Hatch Act effectively denied federal employees the guarantee of freedom of speech under the First Amendment to the Constitution.

31. See *Congressional Quarterly Almanac* (1990, 411) and U.S. Senate (1989). The results offered in tables 6.5–6.8 clearly support the view that federal labor unions contribute more to Democrats.

32. The House passed without amendment or conference the Senate version of H.R. 20 by a vote of 334 to 87. There were ninety Republicans voting in favor (*Congressional Quarterly Almanac* 1990, 410).

33. On the Republican side, there were eighty-four votes in favor of the override, while ninety voted against the measure (*Congressional Quarterly Almanac* 1990, 64-H). In the Senate, the override vote failed to obtain the two-thirds majority needed. The final vote was 65 to 35, with ten Republicans voting for an override and thirty-five against.

34. Borjas (1980) uses central personnel data files obtained from the U.S. Office of Personnel Management and estimates agency earnings differentials across the federal government. His results do not indicate a major difference between the postal service and other federal agencies. The results reported by Freeman (1987), who used CPS data, also show little or no difference between postal and other federal employees.

35. See, e.g., the discussion of these sector differences in Freeman (1986). Lewis (1990), however, points out that, while the gaps are smaller in the public sector, there are important exceptions.

36. For example, the American Federation of Government Employees is affiliated with the AFL-CIO.

37. Consider, e.g., the following ten issues voted on by the Senate in 1991 that the AFGE used for the purpose of ranking the members of that body: (1) Davis Bacon Act (amendments to); (2) Mexico Free Trade–Fast Track; (3) Gag Rule (prohibited funding

to clinics whose medical staff counseled on abortion; (4) Motor Voter Registration Act; (5) Unemployment Benefits Extension; (6) Capital Gains Tax Reduction; (7) Family and Medical Leave Act; (8) Family and Medical Leave–Substitute Amendment; (9) Supreme Court Nomination–Clarence Thomas; and (10) Unemployment Benefits Extension–Veto Override. Some of the issues used to rank members of the House of Representatives were somewhat more germane to federal workers as they dealt with working conditions and use of drug testing by federal agencies. Nevertheless, the above list shows that the rankings given to federal politicians depend on a broad array of issues. The source for the above list is the "1991 AFGE Voting Record—First Session—102nd Congress," available from the AFGE, Washington, D.C.

38. See, e.g., Newman (1983), Helms (1985), and Benson and Johnson (1986). These studies suggest that the magnitude of the effect of taxes on economic growth depends on what the tax revenue is being used for. Pure transfers have a substantial negative effect. Since merely increasing the salaries of state and local workers would effectively amount to a transfer of income, the negative effects are likely to be greater than for other forms of expenditures.

39. Becker's (1983) point that successful interest groups will be relatively more efficient (have lower costs) is applicable here as well. Because the demand function is less elastic at the federal level, the deadweight costs that result from the distorting effects of taxes used to pay for higher wages are likely to be less. Hence, redistribution through higher wages is less costly at the federal level.

40. As Congress considers pay legislation, for the reasons we have described in this chapter, it is politically difficult to enact salary increases just for the limited numbers of the most senior members of the bureaucracy.

7   The Implications of a Protected Bureaucracy

7.1   Introduction

The "problem of bureaucracy" is a lack of productivity and accountability within the federal workforce. It is not new. Indeed, throughout the post–World War II period, politicians have run campaigns denouncing the bureaucracy as being bound in red tape and unresponsive to private citizens. Further, blue-ribbon task forces have been set up to devise ways to improve the performance of the federal labor force, and legislation to implement the recommendations has been enacted.[1] Among the most recent legislation to be considered is the Government Performance and Results Act of 1993, with the goal of improving "the efficiency and effectiveness of Federal programs by establishing a system to set goals for program performance and to measure results" (U.S. Senate 1993, 2). But the problem of bureaucracy remains. It is the result of an environment where neither the president nor the Congress has well-defined property rights over the federal bureaucracy. The current civil service system is, itself, an imperfect institutional response to these conditions.

Over a 100-year period, a civil service system has been put into place that makes it difficult for the president, senior agency officials, or members of Congress to motivate workers to be productive through the use of basic instruments, such as merit promotions, or to remove those employees who do not perform adequately in their jobs. Rather, under civil service rules, pay and promotion are based on time on the job, not productivity; salaries are set within a national pay plan and statutory salary adjustments that generally involve across-the-board percentage increases; and job-tenure guarantees are granted to virtually all career civil service employees. Within this structure, federal supervisors are constrained severely in their ability to reward or to punish their subordinates according to job performance.

In pondering the problem of bureaucracy, the literature has viewed it as a single entity. This is a mistake that obscures satisfactory analysis of the issue. The federal civilian labor force, however, is a mixture of both political appointees and career civil servants. Three categories of federal civilian employees now exist: presidential appointees at the cabinet and agency head level, who generally set administration policies and are accountable to (and can be removed by) the president; senior career officials, who also are part of agency management and policy administration but who are not strictly answerable to the president and are protected by civil service tenure guarantees; and rank-and-file career employees, who perform agency functions and have day-to-day contact with constituents. This last group also has tenure protections and is paid according to civil service guidelines. Hence, each of these three groups operates under different constraints with separate motives, and any discussion of bureaucratic behavior must consider the implications of these distinctions.

We have emphasized the influence of federal employee unions in explaining the development of the federal civil service system in the twentieth century. Certainly, the lobbying efforts of these unions have resulted in many of the familiar attributes of the current institution—uniform position definition, a national pay plan, across-the-board salary increases, and strict tenure guarantees for rank-and-file employees. Union actions alone, however, do not explain why the president and the Congress would be generally responsive to union lobbying pressure or why more concerted efforts to address the problem of bureaucracy apparently are not undertaken. It would seem that there would be high political returns to those politicians who successfully responded to long-standing voter complaints about the performance of the bureaucracy.

To understand the relative lack of progress in reforming the civil service, despite all the rhetoric, one must take into account the lack of clear political property rights to the federal bureaucracy.[2] The confusion over who controls the bureaucracy, the president or the Congress, that exists in the Constitution reduces the incentives of politicians to engage in long-term, meaningful reform. Moreover, in order to mitigate the costs of political competition over the bureaucracy, the president and members of Congress have agreed to civil service rules that inhibit their influence over career federal employees. The rules that have been adopted to shield federal career employees from political manipulation, however, have insulated the bureaucracy from more legitimate political control, contributing directly to voter complaints about responsiveness and productivity. Measures to ensure political neutrality have also created opportunities for federal unions to emerge as a third party in the design of civil service rules. Hence, the absence of a clear principal who would benefit from reform of the bureaucracy seriously complicates any efforts to change the system.

7.2   The Debates over Political Autonomy, Neutrality, and the Extent of Bureaucratic Discretion

Perhaps it is not surprising that the literature on bureaucracy mirrors the confusion surrounding political jurisdiction over federal career employees. There are conflicting views as to the importance of political autonomy and as to whether bureaucratic behavior matters at all in the design and implementation of government policy. For these reasons, no satisfactory explanations for the persistence of the problems of bureaucracy have been offered. Unresolved is the issue of whether the bureaucracy should be accountable to politicians. In early discussions of civil service reform by Woodrow Wilson (1887) and others, there was a sense that a dichotomy between politics and administration was not only desirable but achievable as well. In more recent work by political scientists and economists, it is generally accepted that politics and administration are inseparable (see, e.g., Moe 1989, 1991). Even so, among many historians and students of public administration, the notion remains that effective administration requires protecting bureaucrats from the intervention of politicians so that they can perform their duties in a neutral, technical, and professional manner.[3]

For example, analyses of New Deal regulatory policies point to a goal of creating independent and insulated regulatory agencies. The objective was to allow administrative officials to serve as self-starting, technically expert agents of change. The belief was that the fundamental changes in the economy and society envisioned by the Roosevelt administration could be achieved only through a separation of politics from administration. As Cass Sunstein points out, "the enduring legacy of the period is the insulated administrator, immersed in a particular area of expertise, equipped with broad discretion, and expected to carry out a set of traditionally separated functions" (1987, 441). The emphasis on creating an independent bureaucracy affected the design of regulatory agencies, raising the costs for politicians of subsequently controlling them and contributing to current controversies over the behavior of regulatory bodies.

The view that bureaucrats not only could be but should be apolitical, professional civil servants also muddles reform efforts to achieve greater bureaucratic accountability. The National Federation of Federal Employees (NFFE), for instance, warned that the professional competence of its members was placed at risk by proposals in the Civil Service Reform Act of 1978 to give supervisors greater authority in awarding performance pay. Union representative Sam Silverman expressed the union's "strong and determined opposition to the Carter proposal for Civil Service 'Reform,' HR 11280, S 2640. . . . The bill would lead also to a hierarchization of the civil service, in the sense that the employee's emphasis would now be on currying favor with his superior, rather than on solving problems" (U.S. Senate 1978, 407).

Although bureaucratic autonomy has been viewed as a laudable goal by some, others have viewed it more cynically. Public choice writers, such as Gordon Tullock (1965) and William Niskanen (1971), see bureaucrats as being both opportunistic in pursuit of their self-interests and influential in shaping policy away from what was desired by the president and the Congress. The implication is that reforms are needed to increase political control over the bureaucracy (see also Borcherding 1977). A similar conclusion is drawn by students of public administration, such as Frederick Mosher (1982), Hugh Heclo (1977), James Wilson (1989), and Herbert Kaufman (1965). In that literature, career federal bureaucrats are described as having different objectives from those of either political appointees, who are nominally their superiors, or elected officials. As career officials have become increasingly professional, scientific-management principles and discipline solidarity have provided a protective veil for increasing bureaucratic autonomy. Because monitoring and enforcement by the Congress and the president are costly activities, senior bureaucratic officials are assumed to be able to alter policy to better fit their own preferences. Moreover, it is argued that the agency-review process is too limited and perfunctory to provide an effective constraint. Instances of federal agencies acting as if they were autonomous are interpreted as supporting evidence of this view. For example, activist regulatory policies taken by the Federal Trade Commission (FTC) in the 1970s to restrict television advertising aimed at children and to engage in antitrust investigations of horizontal mergers generated complaints that the agency was operating beyond congressional control.[4]

Contrasting assessments, however, are made by those, such as Sam Peltzman (1976) and Gary Becker (1983), who see nonelected bureaucratic officials as more or less passive respondents to the desires of politicians. Although this assumption does not appear to be based on an extensive analysis of bureaucratic behavior, policy analyses in this literature focus almost solely on the actions of politicians, not on those of bureaucrats.[5]

Bureaucrats are given a more active role in yet another literature, characterized by the work of Matthew McCubbins, Roger Noll, and Barry Weingast (1989), but these officials are assumed to be constrained by Congress through budget appropriations, monitoring by oversight committees, and tight administrative rules. Administrative rules approved by the president and the Congress limit bureaucratic discretion by requiring public participation in the design of new policies and in mandating that agencies give notice before carrying out policy changes. In one of the few empirical cases to test these assertions, Barry Weingast and Mark Moran (1983) argue that controversial FTC decisions in the 1970s were influenced by the composition and demands of congressional subcommittees for consumer affairs and that little opportunity existed for independent action.[6] Wilson (1989, 256), however, objects to this assessment of FTC behavior. He contends that exclusive reliance on congressional oversight ignores the fact that agencies must be responsive to both the president and the Congress, each of whom will attempt to influence agency actions. As a consequence, bureaucratic officials will often be subject to conflicting signals that both will obscure policy directions from politicians and may allow for greater improvisation by the agency.[7] Further, the general conclusion reached that independent bureaucratic behavior is tightly constrained through congressional oversight seems unwarranted by this limited evidence. Showing that Congress had sufficient power to control a "runaway" agency does not deny the existence of independent bureaucratic behavior.

It is clear from this short review of the literature on bureaucracy that there is no consensus on the role that bureaucrats play in policy formation and implementation or on the need for further reform in civil service rules. Any resolution, however, requires an understanding of the institutions in which bureaucratic decisions are made. Virtually all the authors cited in this section, regardless of their views on agency accountability, largely ignore the effects of civil service rules on bureaucratic incentives and the ability deliberately to alter policy. This is a serious omission. The civil service system operates in an environment where there is no clear structure of political control over the federal bureaucracy. These conditions complicate the principal/agent problem in the federal government beyond that generally encountered by firms in the private sector and allow for more bureaucratic discretion in policy matters than is generally recognized in the literature.

7.3   Federal Employees and the Principal/Agent Problem

Consider the three-tier principal-supervisor-subordinate model commonly used to analyze behavior within hierarchical organizations.[8] In the context of the firm, the principal can be thought of as the owner, supervisors as managers, and subordinates as workers. The owners (assuming that there are more than one) generally are considered to be a relatively homogeneous group in terms of their underlying objectives, which we take to be the maximization of the residual (profits). The objectives of workers, however, generally will not coincide with those of the owners. Lacking the time (relatively high opportunity costs), knowledge, and skill to manage workers directly, the owners hire managers to supervise workers. The standard principal/agent problem arises because monitoring, even of supervisors, is costly and incentive contracts may not foreclose all margins for deviation from the owners' objectives. Accordingly, owners are confronted with the potential for opportunistic behavior on the part of both managers and workers. Nevertheless, with clear property rights and a well-defined principal, monitoring will be directed toward maximizing firm profits. Hence, the principal/agent model provides a framework for analyzing the divergent interests of the principal and its agents and how they might be brought into reasonable alignment.[9]

In the federal government, however, the analogous forces leading to a joining of the interests of the principal and the agent are much weaker. To see why, we denote voters as the principal, elected officials (the president and members of the Congress) as supervisors, and bureaucrats as the agents. The first complication is that, unlike owners of a firm, voters are unlikely to possess a distinct common objective, and this situation affects the ability of voters to organize effectively to monitor both politicians and bureaucrats. Thus, the latitude available to supervisors and agents in the federal government is likely to be greater than that which exists in private firms. Voter interests vary across districts, a condition that largely explains why members of the Congress have different role-call voting records (Peltzman 1984). The president's district is the entire country, a far larger and more heterogeneous constituency than that found for members of Congress. Since elected officials, acting as supervisors, do not represent the same set of principals, reaching agreement on a particular policy requires compromise between the president and members of the Senate and the House to form a winning coalition. Once having agreed on legislation, there remains the problem of actually implementing policy within federal agencies in a manner that follows the agreement.

A second complication is that the agents (bureaucrats) are subject to two supervisors since under the Constitution both the president and the Congress have authority over the federal bureaucracy. Under these conditions, there will be competition among the supervisors to influence bureaucratic implementation of policy. That is, the president and members of Congress have incentives to manipulate the bureaucracy in the delivery of government goods and services to meet the preferences of their respective constituents.[10] The potential for such opportunistic behavior by the president and members of Congress in implementing policy, however, can destroy the coalition that led to the initial legislative agreement. Because such actions will be predicted, the costs of negotiating and enforcing policy compromises will be increased. Accordingly, the president and the Congress are motivated to find ways of limiting competitive manipulation of the bureaucracy.

This particular problem has been recognized by McCubbins, Noll, and Weingast, who argue that administrative procedures are designed by politicians to confine agent discretion and to force their decisions to be consistent with the enabling legislation. Elaborate procedural requirements are designed to safeguard against most deviant behavior. Undesirable policy drift is avoided by forcing agencies to move slowly and publicly. Delay gives politicians time to hear from and to mobilize constituents. In essence, with a protracted administrative process in executing policy, elected officials can use their constituents to monitor the actions of both other politicians and bureaucrats.[11] The administrative structure, then, may serve to reduce defection from legislative coalitions.

Competition over the bureaucracy has important implications for understanding the civil service system and the special principal/agent problems that exist within the federal government. As such, it deserves more attention in the literature.[12] Within this competitive environment, the roles played by political appointees and career civil servants are quite different.[13]

7.3.1 The Rivalry for Control of the Bureaucracy and the Roles of Political Appointees and Career Officials

Alone among Western democracies, the American system relies on the use of political appointees to head most federal agencies. Elsewhere, these same positions would most likely be held by senior career civil servants.[14] Wilson argues that the reason for this difference is the separation of powers described in the Constitution, which makes the president and the Congress "rivals for control of the American administrative system" (1989, 257). Contributing to the potential competition over the bureaucracy is the failure of the Constitution to provide a sharp delineation between the authority of the president and that of the Congress in administrative matters. The Constitution instructs the president to execute the law faithfully, but it also grants legislative power to Congress to fund administrative agencies.[15] In fact, the notion that the president is the chief executive officer of the United States, who administers the law and manages executive branch agencies, is a relatively recent one. Before 1921, bureaus and departments could submit bills directly to Congress without clearing them with the president. In the past, both the Congress and the president have claimed the power to remove administrative officials, and Congress has repeatedly challenged the president on the use of the White House staff, which itself dates only from the 1930s.[16] In contrast, under a parliamentary system, such as that which exists in Great Britain, the power to supervise the civil service is assigned to the prime minister, and the House of Commons has no significant authority over it.

The rivalry between the president and the Congress over the career bureaucracy fosters an atmosphere of distrust, whereby presidents view bureaus as unaccountable and the Congress sees them as unresponsive, and these conditions further politicize the administrative process. Such an environment has made a relatively neutral career bureaucracy difficult to achieve.[17]

As we have shown, conflict between the president and the Congress over the career civil service has existed for a long time. In the post–World War II period, however, the rivalry seems to have intensified.[18] With the growing role of government in the economy, deep divisions have occurred between the president and the Congress. Policy issues have become more complex, and the costs of monitoring agency behavior have risen. The administration of Richard Nixon is illustrative of the tensions that exist between the president and the Congress. In President Nixon's view, the permanent bureaucracy was aligned with the Democratic-controlled House of Representatives and, generally, was not responsive to the president. Nixon responded by creating an advisory council to redesign the executive branch with the aim of gaining greater control over the bureaucracy. The Congress reacted by charging that these proposals were mere attempts to bolster the role of the presidency and to weaken the constitutional authority of Congress (U.S. House of Representatives 1976, 489–92).

Similarly, as one of the goals of his administration, President Jimmy Carter promised to improve the performance and accountability of the federal bureaucracy. The focus was on senior career officials, who were most able to affect policy execution and, probably more than incidently, were not represented by federal unions, which would oppose any major restructuring of lower-level positions.[19] The centerpiece of Carter's Civil Service Reform Act of 1978 was the establishment of the Senior Executive Service (SES). Positions in the SES were to be filled by the federal government's top management personnel, usually those who had held GS-16–GS-18 positions, who were to participate more in policy-making activities in addition to more traditional administrative duties. Performance appraisals and merit pay were to be integral parts of the Senior Executive Service, in exchange for which individuals gave up certain civil service protections that allowed them to be transferred to other units or even to be removed.[20] These reforms later proved useful to President Reagan, who replaced a number of SES managers with officials thought to be more loyal to his administration. Nevertheless, the president continued to view contact between representatives of government bureaus and Congress with distrust.

At least on the surface, however, it is difficult to see why the president would not hold an advantage over the Congress in managing the actions of career employees within an agency.[21] The president can alter administrative procedures by executive order, reorganize agencies, and, through the Office of Management and Budget, has the initiative in regulating agency resources.[22] Another important advantage that the President has is the power to select and to discharge the most senior agency officials because they are political appointees. These individuals owe their positions and loyalty to the president.

In 1883, there were 130,000 federal employees, and the president had the authority to appoint and to remove the majority of them.[23] The number of political appointments available to the president today is much reduced, approximately 5,800, not including federal judgeships.[24] These, however, are not the clerks and postal workers of the late 1800s. Today's political appointees hold top management positions. Of the total slots available to the president, about 1,500 are appointments that require the advice and consent of the Senate. Included in this category are department secretaries, federal commissioners, and agency directors and deputy directors. There are another 1,900 positions, including those on the White House staff, that the president can fill without the consent of the Senate. In addition, there are about 700 noncareer SES positions available to agency heads. By law (5. U.S.C. 3134), no more than 10 percent of all SES positions can be filled by political appointees. Finally, there are some 1,800 Schedule C positions that are considered to be of a confidential or policy-determining character and are exempt from the competitive civil service. The selection of individuals for these positions is usually left to agency heads, although the president has the right to make the appointment. Schedule

C appointments are important because they include such positions as confidential assistant to the agency director and regional director. Accordingly, the highest echelon in most federal agencies is staffed by the president's political appointees. Since loyalty to the president is explicit when an individual accepts a political appointment to a senior position, the potential for the agency to "drift" toward the policy preferences of the president seems apparent. An appointee who does not follow the administration's agenda can be removed quickly.[25]

The problem, of course, faced by top administration officials is in obtaining the compliance of career civil servants, who have tenure and a sheltering array of civil service rules. Moreover, not all policy-making positions are held by political appointees. Career civil servants within the Senior Executive Service or those who have high-ranking GS (GM if managerial) positions also are employed near the top of various bureaus within federal agencies. These individuals can affect the administration and enforcement of policy in important ways. For example, at the FTC and in the Department of Justice, lawyers and economists, who are neither political appointees nor in the Senior Executive Service, often make decisions about whether a case is worth pursuing and whether a particular piece of evidence is relevant (see Katzman 1980; Eisner and Meier 1990). Similarly, at the Environmental Protection Agency, field investigators have considerable leeway in the enforcement of the clean air and other environmental regulations authorized by Congress (Wood 1988).[26]

As a result, career civil servants play a central role in the competition between the president and the Congress over control of the bureaucracy. They can be valuable political assets. Career officials can testify before Congress about administration policies and let Congress know if legislated rules are being broken.[27] Because of their day-to-day contact with political appointees within agencies, senior career officials will be among the first to know when the administration is attempting to change policy in a clandestine manner by not first consulting with Congress. Knowledge that agency policy is undergoing change is essential if Congress is to enforce legislative agreements and maintain its authority with respect to the president. Bureaucrats, who have regular contact with client groups, are also in a position to sense shifts in constituents' demands.

The widespread concern over bureaucratic accountability, however, suggests that career officials may also act in ways that are distinct from the objectives of *both* the Congress and the president. They can elect to withhold information or to provide it with a particular slant if it is in their self-interest to do so.[28] Because they are often professionals with specialized education, training, and occupational experience, career bureaucrats have the potential to shape information and to guide opinions. This possibility adds yet another complication to the principal/agent problem within the federal government. Indeed, asymmetric information and the associated management of information on bureau performance that is released to the president and the Congress can provide career bureaucrats with significant advantages over both sets of supervisors. Before we can assign career officials a major role in influencing policy in their self-interest, however, we need to consider what incentive they would have to do so and under what conditions they might take independent action.

7.3.2   The Budget-Maximizing Bureaucrat

One of the best-known hypotheses about bureaucratic behavior is that of Niskanen (1971), who assumed that bureaucrats act to maximize their budgets. The rationale offered was straightforward. Senior bureaucrats maximized budgets because the opportunities for promotion and higher salaries, as well as for greater prestige and power, depended on the size and growth of their agencies.[29] Bureaucrats were able to accomplish their objective because they controlled the information used by the Congress in deciding agency appropriations.

Niskanen was one of the first to apply standard economic behavioral assumptions to the analysis of bureaus, and his work was a respite from much of the early bureaucracy literature, which had portrayed public servants as selfless administrators of the public weal. The notion that bureaucrats would seek to maximize their agency's budget, however, has been challenged.[30] André Blais and Stéphane Dion have summarized the evidence on whether bureaucrats are budget maximizers, and there is only limited empirical support for the hypothesis. One reason for that finding is that the link between a budget-maximizing strategy and bureaucratic self-interest is thin (see Blais and Dion 1991, 355–61).

Our research shows why there is little tie between salary growth and agency size. Faced with a potential for bureaucrats to expand the size of their agency deliberately, Congress could either increase its monitoring and data collection regarding the bureaucracy or sever any link between salaries and agency size. The latter response seems to be the option chosen by Congress. As we discussed in chapter 5, the salaries of senior career officials are restricted by law (5 U.S.C. 5308), and they may not exceed those paid to officials in Executive Level V, who are generally political appointees.[31] These salary caps for top management officials are low, compared to compensation in the private sector. Because salary limits apply to all agency managers and are relatively inflexible, they largely remove any incentives that senior officials might otherwise have had to expand their agency to facilitate promotion and higher salaries.[32]

Moreover, the national pay plan for all GS workers seems empirically to have removed any association between bureaucratic compensation and agency growth or decline. In chapter 6, we presented evidence indicating that agency growth had little effect on the salaries of white-collar federal employees. The reported tests, however, were for all GS employees, not just the senior bureaucrats to whom Niskanen implicitly referred. Nevertheless, restricting the sample to just senior administrative and professional employees, who are best positioned to promote agency growth, produced even smaller and less significant effects of agency growth on salaries.[33] The coefficient on the agency growth variable for this restricted sample is only .033, implying that an agency must more than double its size in order for salaries to increase by 3.3 percent, relative to an agency that did not grow. Further, introducing an agency-size variable in the standard wage regressions for GS employees revealed a negative relation between agency size and salary, although the effect was small.[34] The coefficient on the size variable for both the 1980 and the 1985 samples indicated that salaries in the smallest agencies (fewer than 1,000 employees) were approximately 1 percent higher than those in larger agencies (over 100,000 employees) (see Johnson and Libecap 1989a, 72). The results of these various tests suggest that bureaucratic salaries are largely determined independently of either agency growth or agency size.[35] As we have stressed, salaries are standardized within the national civil service structure and are not agency specific.[36]

Constraints on bureaucratic behavior are also evident in the structure of the appropriations process. Niskanen's portrayal of federal government agencies, attempting to maximize their budgets by making essentially all-or-nothing offers of a promised output in exchange for a particular budget allocation, ignores the institutional constraints that greatly limit what an agency can do with its funds.[37] In the appropriations process, Congress budgets an amount for salaries and expenses, and it specifies a number of full-time-equivalent positions that cannot be exceeded. These procedures limit the ability of an agency to trade off personnel for higher salaries. Agency budgets, however, are sufficiently fungible to cover most promotions and associated salary increases (Hartman 1983, 108; U.S. Classification Task Force 1981, 106).

The salary caps for senior officials also serve another purpose. In an environment of competition between the president and members of Congress to influence the bureaucracy, salary limits make it more difficult for politicians to reward agency officials who are especially responsive to their demands to adjust policy. The restrictive effects of salary caps are complemented by a national system of uniform position classification, a corresponding national pay plan, and fixed promotion schedules, all supervised by a separate agency (the Office of Personnel Management). The need to restrain political manipulation of the bureaucracy and thereby to maintain legislative coalitions also explains why the president and the Congress have been unwilling to allow supervisors much discretion in rewarding or disciplining their subordinates. Moreover, it explains why only marginal funding has been provided for the performance pay schemes authorized by law and why only meager amounts can be paid to any individual.[38] Further, the authority granted federal supervisors, who may be political appointees, in performance evaluations of subordinates appears to be less than that delegated in the private sector. In the private sector, performance rewards to motivate employees appear to be much more widespread, larger, and more frequently used than in the federal government (Milkovich et al. 1991). For government employees, the evaluation process is more formal and the rewards smaller.[39] Additionally, performance evaluations are almost always satisfactory or better for most federal employees, with the result that promotion within a job ladder is usually routine.[40] In sum, civil service pay plans tend to reduce the ability of politicians to entice agency officials to alter policy toward designated constituents.[41] It seems likely that, through these constraints on their ability to influence the bureaucracy in implementing policy, politicians are better able to reach and to enforce legislative agreements.

Although there is a growing recognition that civil service rules play a critical role in salary determination, in setting promotions, and in limiting the overall discretion available to agency managers in personnel issues, the benefits that such an arrangement provides to elected officials are much less appreciated.[42] These benefits also help explain why the civil service system has been maintained, despite voter complaints about poor performance and responsiveness by the federal workers who are protected by it. In addition to constraining opportunistic behavior by politicians and bureaucrats, the compensation and promotion practices of the civil service system appear to lower the political costs of implementing organizational and policy changes by reducing potential bureaucratic opposition.

With no firm link between salary growth and agency expansion or contraction, bureaucrats have less of a stake in the maintenance of a particular organization. Consider, for example, the termination of the Civil Aeronautics Board (CAB) on 1 January 1985, as authorized by Congress. There was no entrenched and sustained resistance from career agency officials or appeals by them to constituents to derail the process of airline deregulation. Civil service rules contributed to a smooth transition because they offered job protection to career employees. Under uniform systemwide pay policies, individual salaries or promotions were not placed at serious risk. Beginning in 1980, budgets and staffing levels were gradually reduced at the CAB, with employment falling from 734 in 1980 to 367 in 1984 through attrition and without the need of a potentially disruptive reduction in force. At the end of 1984, most of the remaining CAB functions and personnel, including division chiefs and staffs, were transferred to the Department of Transportation, with many offices remaining essentially unchanged.[43]

The civil service system, then, provides substantial benefits to the president and the Congress, especially as it pertains to senior career officials who are in a position to influence the administration of policy. As we have argued, however, the protections and privileges granted by the system are not restricted to top officeholders. Tenure guarantees, relatively high levels of compensation, inordinate weight on seniority for promotion, and other benefits are granted to the rank and file, with less obvious parallel benefits to federal politicians. These aspects of the civil service system have been added at the behest of federal unions.

There are, of course, trade-offs from a strictly formalized compensation and promotion system that provides few opportunities for political intervention.

Under the civil service system, the effectiveness of the delivery of government goods and services hinges less on factors easily adjusted by politicians and more on other factors, such as identification with agency mission or professional ties, that are not under the direct control of the president or the Congress.

7.3.3   A Professional Bureaucracy

The real control problems that Congress and the president face with the federal bureaucracy are not those of bureaucrats seeking to expand the size of their agencies in order to increase their salaries. Instead, the problems are how to direct and to motivate a professional bureaucratic labor force within the very protective structure of civil service rules. These rules reduce the authority held by politicians over the bureaucracy and allow bureaucrats to engage in independent, nonneutral activities that are motivated by professional goals.

Professionalism has expanded rapidly in the federal government during the post–World War II period. As government services have become more complex in nature, there has been greater reliance on professional training and certification of federal employees. The changing composition of federal jobs illustrates the pattern. In 1973, for example, 15.0 percent of total General Schedule employment was in professional occupations. By 1983, however, the proportion had risen to 22.4 percent.[44] Working for professional objectives with which one agrees would seem to be especially important in an environment where financial incentives are largely absent. Heclo (1977), for instance, noted that career civil servants often associate closely with the historical mission of their agencies. These ties provide an important motivation for implementing policy. For example, in his case study, Jerry Mashaw (1983) emphasized the role of administrators' personal values and identification with the goals of the agency in analyzing the performance of the Social Security Administration (SSA) in processing disability claims.[45] Further, professional and career links between government employees and outside groups can also give job performance incentives through peer group pressure and greater employment opportunities in the private sector.

Professional relationships, however, are likely to lead to bureaucratic behavior that is not desired generally by the Congress or the president. Indeed, the growing professionalism of the federal labor force and the problems that it poses for presidential and congressional control have long been a concern to those who study the federal bureaucracy.[46] To be in good standing within a particular professional group requires investment in education and a dedication to the codes of conduct, goals, and methods of analysis of the discipline. Hence, professional ties often involve the use of discipline-based methodologies for accomplishing agency objectives.[47] Government employees whose goal is professional advancement tend to promote structural changes within agencies that enhance their own autonomy and ability to pursue their objectives (Mosher 1982). They encourage further professionalism within their agencies and the hiring of those with similar credentials. The professional ties of government employees may go beyond the agency, and the potential for related job opportunities in the private sector can make individuals more sympathetic to the interests of certain clients in executing policy (Spiller 1990).

We recognize that professionalism and a close association with the interests of a client group do not, by themselves, present an administrative problem to politicians. Indeed, when the president and the Congress both agree on policy, and when that course of action fits well with the agenda of professional groups within an administrative agency, there is no reason to expect policy drift.[48] Moreover, since under the civil service system supervisors have only limited means for addressing shirking, it can be reduced when there is substantial professional agreement by all parties, politicians and bureaucrats alike, on the agency's mission and the direction of its policies.[49]

The problems that most analysts see with professionalism occur when these conditions are not met. When an agency is relatively new, the professionals hired are likely to meet the various litmus tests that match them with the agency's political sponsors. Indeed, civil servants may seek and even help secure the expansion of their agency, if they closely identify with its output. In the face of changing conditions and political uncertainty, however, politicians must be flexible in responding to new demands and influential constituents. Agency officials with close professional ties to old constituents are less likely to be willing to adapt to new circumstances and, hence, likely to engage in tactics that delay or limit the adjustment of policy. Further, if agency personnel disagree with the new policy orientation, their enthusiasm and work effort may decline. Alternatively, agency employees who are associated with a new policy may seek to move away from old constituents more rapidly than is desired by politicians.

The conflict between the new Reagan administration and the EPA over environmental policy (see Wood 1988, 1989; Cook 1989) presents an illustrative case study of professional career officials who attempt to maintain policies with which they identify even though political conditions have changed. Under political appointee Ann Burford, and with OMB cost-benefit reviews of regulatory policy, the administration attempted to slow or block the implementation of environmental restrictions enacted under the Carter administration. As B. Dan Wood shows, career program and enforcement officials in the EPA, who had professional and personal goals that required more activist regulation, attempted to resist these changes by doing their jobs "regardless" (1989, 973). Wood argues that their active resistance helped undermine Burford.

The incentives of bureaucrats to resist or, alternatively, to promote policy change are increased because of the very nature of many government services. Federal agencies often administer policies regarding the environment, health care, and defense, and people hold intense preferences about what the government's role in these areas should be. Professionals seeking employment with the government are often attracted to a particular agency because of its stated mission or because of the opportunity offered to help change the way in which it operates.

The problems that an identification with an agency's mission can bring for presidential and congressional control are noted by Samuel Beer (1976). Beer argues that close links develop between the professional bureaucracy in Washington, D.C., and their colleagues at the state and local level, with federal officials becoming inside lobbyists for their programs. Beer asserts that this bureaucratic coalition not only promotes the expansion of federal programs but leads to greater decentralization as well, with actual implementation shifted to state and local agencies that are beyond the direct control of federal politicians.[50]

An example of the effects of changing political conditions and apparent independent behavior on the part of agency personnel, sheltered by civil service rules, is provided by the U.S. Forest Service (USFS). Herbert Kaufman (1960) once described USFS personnel as being highly motivated and dedicated to the agency's main mission. Throughout much of its history, the Service's mission largely centered on providing services and commodities to the timber and grazing industry.[51] In the 1960s and 1970s, the professional staff of the agency was composed largely of people trained in timber management and harvesting, foresters and engineers who supervised timber sales and road construction to access sites. The political success of the environmental movement greatly changed the mission of the agency and pitted interest groups against one another. These conflicts resulted in a change in the types of professionals employed by the USFS. Individuals trained in wildlife management, biologists, and specialists in recreation became much more common. For example, in 1972 there were 4,945 professional foresters and only 121 wildlife biologists in the Department of Agriculture, with almost all employed by the USFS. In comparison, the number of foresters in 1991 was 5,399, while the number of wildlife biologists had expanded to 1,159.[52]

With the change in professional orientation within the USFS, there has been a growth in the number of employees who actively challenge agency policy. These individuals want the Forest Service to move more completely toward environmental goals, such as wilderness preservation, and away from past policies in support of the timber industry. Politicians bear the political costs of such policy adjustments and, hence, must act more judiciously and more slowly. Agency employees, on the other hand, with professional ties to new policies and strongly held beliefs about their implementation have latitude within the civil service system to act as advocates. For instance, the Association of Forest Service Employees for Environmental Ethics, with a claimed membership of 2,000, openly encourages employee opposition to timber sales.[53]

Although in the 1960s expanding the agency's budget and harvesting more timber blended with the Forest Service's notion of its mission as well as with the background of top staff members who were trained in timber management, more recent events suggest that top officials are willing to sacrifice their budgets and even their jobs rather than expand timber harvesting. John Mumma, a SES employee and the first wildlife biologist in the history of the USFS to have risen to the level of regional forester, openly resisted Bush administration demands to expand harvests on the fifteen national forests in his jurisdiction. Because of his actions, he was asked to resign his position.[54]

In the private sector, actions such as those taken by the Association of Forest Service Employees for Environmental Ethics would likely bring dismissal. Although career federal employees can be, and occasionally are, dismissed, civil service rules offer them greater protections than are available to private-sector employees.[55]

Accordingly, the civil service system provides the opportunity for discretionary behavior by career federal employees, and their motivation for doing so is more likely due to their professional beliefs and preferences than to a conspiratorial attempt to increase salaries by expanding agency size. In situations where government employees hold strong personal preferences, the notion that they will be neutral civil servants is a naive one. In those cases where federal employees are most likely to be neutral, however, the problems of motivating productivity and encouraging responsibility are apt to be the greatest. In the absence of pecuniary rewards or a professional interest in agency policy, bureaucrats have little reason to perform or to be overly responsive to politicians or their constituents.

As a result, the civil service system has evolved into an institution that provides neither strong incentives for performance nor a policy-neutral workforce. Since federal employees have had a major role in the design of the system, especially as it applies to the rank and file, the outcome should not come as a surprise. Nor should it come as a surprise that the president and the Congress have managed to do so little to change the institution as its defects have become apparent. As we have suggested, the principal/agent problem encountered within the federal bureaucracy is a complex one. Voters, as the principals, are heterogeneous with conflicting political objectives, and the supervisors of their agents, the president and the Congress, have unclear political property rights over the bureaucracy. They compete as rivals, and, with different constituents, the president and the Congress are motivated to direct the bureaucracy in different ways. By limiting competition to entice senior career employees to alter policies, the civil service system can reduce the dissipation of political rents. Because the system provides important benefits to federal politicians, they are reluctant to make major changes without other safeguards to take their place.

7.4   Conclusions

The problems of bureaucratic productivity and accountability associated with the current federal civil service system are in contrast with the reforms initiated by the Pendleton Act. The Pendleton Act instituted merit hiring, and it did not grant tenure or address dismissal. Dismissal, of course, became an issue, but the limited tenure guarantees granted by President McKinley in 1897 allowed for firing for just cause. The overriding emphasis in the early administration of the civil service system was efficiency. More iron-clad tenure rules, as well as salary and promotion provisions that heavily weigh time over productivity, were added later at the behest of federal employee unions, who could appeal to the Congress.[56] For rank-and-file career employees, however, complete tenure guarantees make little political sense for the president and the Congress. More remote from policy determination and management, lower-level workers are less susceptible to (and less valuable for) political manipulation than are those at more senior policy-administration levels. Further, it is in the interest of politicians to have federal employees perform effectively in the delivery of services to constituents. The issue is less clear for senior career employees. The president and the Congress have perceived collective gains from limiting their ability to influence senior career officials in policy administration to prevent political opportunism. Tenure provisions and salary caps make it difficult for politicians to intervene at the agency level to pressure senior officials, either through threats of dismissal or through promises of salary increases, in order to influence policy administration. Although there are benefits from this arrangement, these constraints shield senior career officials, along with their rank-and-file colleagues, from direct political control.[57]

Some actions have been taken in an effort to reform the federal bureaucracy through system reorganization and adoption of performance pay. Indeed, the promise of civil service reform was an integral part of President Jimmy Carter's 1976 election campaign. Under his administration, the Civil Service Reform Act of 1978 (92 Stat. 1111) was passed. A major provision of the law was the establishment of merit pay for certain middle-level managers (GS-13–GS-15 supervisors and management officials) and performance pay for members of the newly created Senior Executive Service (formerly GS-16–GS-18). Although these pay plans were designed to provide work incentives, they quickly succumbed to pressures on supervisors to rate employee performances uniformly high and to an unwillingness on the part of Congress to provide sufficiently large rewards to provide a credible incentive structure (see Milkovitch et al. 1991, 18–33). For example, the average reward to middle-level managers in 1985 was around 3 percent of base pay.[58] For these reasons, most authors have concluded that the 1978 law did little to institute pay-performance incentives (see Wilson 1989; Milkovich et al. 1991).

Meaningful bureaucratic reform has been difficult to achieve for two fundamental reasons. First, federal unions have resisted it, especially attempts to replace seniority in pay determination with performance-related measures for general employees. The second reason is that, since the structure of protective bureaucratic rules also guards against political opportunism, members of Congress are not apt to make adjustments that would give advantages to the president. Nor is it in the president's interest to grant more authority over the bureaucracy to the Congress. Not only would this dilute the president's constitutional powers, but, since members of Congress have much narrower constituencies, greater congressional control over the bureaucracy would direct policy away from the president's constituents. Under current conditions, there is a standoff between the president and the Congress that will block major changes in the civil service system, at least as they affect senior career officials.

In countering civil service reform efforts, federal unions can resort to the use of popular myths about patronage. That is, any effort to reduce the privileges held by rank-and-file employees and to strengthen political control of the bureaucracy can be cast as a return to patronage. In this way, the bureaucracy is attempting to control or to mold the flow of information in the debate over civil service reform. By raising the "devil" of patronage, the discussion is diverted from an analysis of the private benefits received by career employees under the current system to a debate over the risks of dismantling civil service protections and reinstating patronage.

The notion is that, left to their own devices, politicians will readily reinstate the spoils system and that only the efforts of public-minded citizens and the courts prevent them from doing so.[59] Although such a characterization is useful to federal unions, it ignores the interests of federal politicians that we have emphasized in this volume. There is no returning to patronage. Since 1883, the President and the Congress have had important reasons for limiting patronage, and those reasons remain today. Nevertheless, the belief that politicians would readily return to the days of patronage has contributed in important ways to institutional change in the civil service, an issue that we deal with in the next and concluding chapter.

Notes

1. The history of the federal civil service is replete with examples of commissions established to study the performance of the federal government workforce. One recent study that attempted to identify particular areas of waste and inefficiency is the Grace Commission, appointed by President Ronald Reagan. Its report (Grace Commission 1984) claimed that more than $400 billion could be saved over a three-year period by eliminating waste and inefficiency. The commission listed numerous practices that could be eliminated or changed to achieve savings, including excessive compensation of federal workers. The commission's report, of course, was not well received in all quarters, but it reflects a general consensus that the federal bureaucracy has become increasingly unmanageable. A more popular view of the problems of bureaucracy is provided in Haas (1990) and Osborne and Gaebler (1992). DiLulio, Garvey, and Kettl (1993) provide an academic discussion of ways to improve the performance of the federal bureaucracy, and the most recent political effort is made by the National Performance Review of the Clinton administration (Gore 1993).

2. Cain, Ferejohn, and Fiorina (1987, 1–16) point to the absence of details in the

Constitution on the duties and powers of members of Congress in implementing policy and to the necessity of bargaining with the president.

3. An example of the belief that politics and administration not only can be but should be separated is Pisani's (1992) analysis of water law and policy in the American West. He is critical of existing water use and allocation practices and argues that the problems are due to the intrusion of politics over sound administration. Had water been allocated by a technically proficient planning agency, according to Pisani, many of the historical and current problems of water use would have been avoided. Given the value of water in arid regions, the view that it could be neutrally allocated by disinterested administrators is unrealistic. Further, the decisions of an autonomous bureaucracy on the allocation and use of an extremely valuable asset are unlikely to result in a welfare improvement over the existing situation. For another historical discussion, in this case the delegation of New Deal regulatory policies to autonomous agencies, see Irons (1982).

4. The FTC is an independent commission headed by five commissioners, who are appointed by the president with the consent of the Senate. The main mechanism available to the Congress for influencing the behavior of FTC personnel is the agency's budget appropriations.

5. Becker (1983, 396) acknowledges that bureaucrats may, on occasion, influence the content and direction of policy.

6. Weingast and Moran use roll-call voting scores of committee members, as measured by Americans for Democratic Action (ADA), to identify changes in their preferences. One problem with these so-called ideology measures is that they are very broadly based and may include only a few votes that have anything directly to do with FTC operations or policy.

7. Moe (1982) has also analyzed the behavior of the FTC as well as a number of other federal agencies. His findings suggest that agency actions vary with changing presidential administrations.

8. For elaboration, see Tirole (1986).

9. For discussion of the agency problem in the firm and the various ways in which it is addressed, see Williamson (1985) and Fama (1980).

10. Concerns about the appropriateness of the standard principal/agent model for analyzing bureaucratic control issues in the federal government are raised by Cook (1989). In his investigation of Environmental Protection Agency (EPA) responsiveness to the president and Congress, he argues that these competing political principals made separate and conflicting demands on the agency, possibly allowing for more agency discretion.

11. The description of this progress by McCubbins, Noll, and Weingast (1989, 439) is similar to that of a cartel attempting to enforce its agreement by use of devices that signal cheating.

12. Macy (1992) argues that the "tug of war" over the federal bureaucracy is beneficial, reducing the likelihood that an agency will be captured by special interests.

13. Kiewiet and McCubbins (1991, 22, 182) discuss the principal/agent problem that arises with congressional delegation of policy implementation to federal bureaus. Although they point out that the government is divided between the president and the Congress, they do not develop the implications for the principal/agent problem. As we argue, with no clear principal/supervisor, the agency problem in managing the federal bureaucracy is more complicated than that found in private firms. For reference to the agency problem in the federal government, see also Mashaw (1983, 72).

14. For a comparison of civil service systems in other countries, see U.S. House of Representatives (1976), Smith (1984), and Peters (1991).

15. The Constitution (art. 1, sec. 8) grants the Congress budget and oversight author-

ity over the federal bureaucracy. Presidential oversight over the executive department agencies grew during Franklin Roosevelt's administration, following the report of the President's Committee on Administration and Management.

16. For a history of some of these conflicts, see U.S. House of Representatives (1978a), Sundquist (1981), and Wilson (1989, 258).

17. For discussion, see Kaufman (1965, 55).

18. Conflicts over the control of the civil service described in this section are similar to the discussions in Heclo (1977), Sundquist (1981), Knott and Miller (1987), and Wilson (1989).

19. As we pointed out earlier, senior officials may belong to professional groups, but they do not generally belong to the major government unions, whose memberships are largely from the rank and file. Federal unions did oppose provisions of the Civil Service Reform Act, which they saw as threatening the position of their members (see U.S. Senate 1978; and U.S. House of Representatives 1978a).

20. Reassignment and transfer to another agency is allowed with fifteen days advance notification (see 5 U.S.C. 3395).

21. Fitts and Inman (1992) describe the ability of presidents to constrain the actions of Congress in determining levels of domestic spending and tax favors.

22. For discussion of Reagan administration actions regarding the EPA, see Cook (1989).

23. Since the Tenure of Office Act of 1867 was still in effect, the removal of any officer first confirmed by the Senate required the approval of that body. The act was repealed in 1887 (see Van Riper 1958, 67).

24. The figures presented on the distribution of political appointment positions were provided by James Pfiffner of George Mason University and are based on data obtained from the executive clerk to the president, as of February 1992. See also the so-called Plum Book (U.S. House of Representatives 1988).

25. The appointment process can fail, and some appointees may set off on a path that deviates from that desired by the president. It may well have been that both the president and the Congress wished for a much earlier departure of FBI chief J. Edgar Hoover but were unable to achieve that result. Hoover appears to have lasted as long as he did because he was able to play the president and the Congress off against one another and kept "secret files" on members of Congress (Knott and Miller 1987, 169–70).

26. Cook (1989) describes the conflicting actions and tools available to President Reagan and the Congress in their separate efforts to influence EPA policy in the early 1980s. The president relied on Office of Management and Budget reviews and presidential appointments to slow environmental policy. Congress, however, relied on its past legislative authorizations and links between key committees and EPA officials.

27. Congress encourages these exchanges and can grant protection to employees under the so-called Whistleblower Protection Act (see 5 U.S.C. 1201).

28. Wood (1989) argues that career officials of the EPA who strongly identified with an activist environmental policy engaged in guerrilla action to leak selected information to the press to undermine Reagan's political appointee, Ann Burford, who attempted to restrain EPA actions.

29. Niskanen was not alone in making this argument. For example, Arnold stated, "The income incentive is probably their most important personal goal . . . . Ordinarily, promotions can be obtained only when others resign or retire; however, they are considerably easier to obtain if the organization grows and new positions are created. It is, therefore, in the bureaucrat's self-interest to promote organizational growth by working for budgetary increases" (1979, 22).

30. Migué and Bélanger (1974) argued that bureaucrats would act to maximize the bureau's discretionary budget, not its total budget. Breton and Wintrobe (1975) pointed

out that bureaucrats, on occasion, move to smaller units from larger ones. Niskanen has been influenced by these arguments and has changed his views on the budget-maximizing hypothesis. He now suggests that the assumption that bureaucrats maximize their budgets be dropped in favor of the assumption that they maximize their discretionary budget (Niskanen 1991, 28).

31. For a discussion of the problems that salary caps pose for the recruitment of top-level personnel, see Hartman (1980).

32. Indeed, pay compression problems for senior employees are often emphasized in hearings on federal salary legislation (see chap. 5; and U.S. Senate 1962).

33. These results are based on wage regressions that provided estimates of individual agency salary growth over the five-year period 1980–85 while controlling for changes in characteristics of the agency's workforce (see Johnson and Libecap 1989a, 445).

34. The results were obtained by estimating the same wage regression reported in app. C, but replacing the agency identifiers with a variable measuring the size (number of GS employees) of the individual's agency. For both the 1980 and the 1985 data sets, the estimated coefficients on the agency-size variable were negative and statistically significant at better than the 1 percent level (Johnson and Libecap 1989b, 72).

35. It is not a contradiction to claim that agency growth can have a positive and agency size a negative effect on salaries. As we argue below, the contracting environment in larger agencies is different than it is in smaller ones.

36. For additional evidence that direct benefits accruing to bureaucrats who manage to increase the size of their staff are few, see Young (1991).

37. These budget constraints are often overlooked. Borjas (1980), e.g., offers a model wherein federal agencies are assumed to have been given a fixed budget and are then free to spend it on hiring a workforce. His model implies a direct trade-off between employment and the agency wage rate, with the wage rate falling as the agency hires more staff. Because Congress allocates a fixed number of positions to each agency and there exists a position classification scheme, we do not see support for a wage/employment trade-off within a particular agency.

38. It is important to note that the merit pay system for middle managers, GS-13–GS-15, was to be revenue neutral. No additional monies were appropriated. Limitations on how much an individual can receive also exist. For example, performance pay for SES personnel is not to exceed 20 percent of base pay. See the discussion by Milkovich et al. (1991, 18–30) and Johnson and Libecap (1989b).

39. There is some evidence of possible managerial discretion in the setting of salaries within the limitations of the civil service system (Johnson and Libecap 1989b). As shown in app. C, wage estimates, using the 1985 data set for 16,616 federal employees, reveal differences across the agencies, controlling for socioeconomic and occupational factors. Such variation across the agencies in what is otherwise a national pay plan with uniform position classifications and salaries may reflect, in part, the actions of supervisors to bend the rules in order to reward selected individuals. One might expect that discretionary activities like these are influenced by agency size. Although personnel rules are the same in large and small agencies, the informal structure of smaller organizations may foster cooperation among employees, supervisors, and those who classify job positions within an agency. These conditions could explain why agency size would have a negative effect on salaries. As mentioned above, however, the effect of size on salaries is small, no doubt reflecting the constraints imposed on managers and supervisors by civil service rules. Another reason for differences across agencies is the use of special pay rates. By law (5 U.S.C. 5303), the Office of Personnel Management is allowed to establish special rates where the government encounters difficulty in recruiting and retaining personnel in certain occupations and locations.

40. Appraisals of job achievements carry more weight for senior employees seeking promotion across occupational job ladders than they do for rank-and-file employees within a specific job ladder.

41. Horn also argues that the organizational features of the civil service system reflect a deliberate attempt by legislators to guard against opportunism: "The merit system undermines the ability of a political faction to entice officials out of their neutrality" (1988, 271). He also suggests that certain aspects of the civil services rules such as tenure provisions reduce agency problems. In contrast, we argue that there are opposing effects to granting tenure that lead to a new set of agency problems and that these problems are not overcome by an incentive structure that fosters what Horn calls "competition among officials for promotion" (p. 279).

42. Blais and Dion (1991), e.g., discuss some of the constraints that the current system imposes on managerial discretion.

43. See the discussion in "Where to Find CAB Functions" (1985).

44. Professional job categories have been defined by the Civil Service Commission and the Office of Personnel Management using such criteria as the need for specialized training and the existence of professional standards (see U.S. Civil Service Commission 1973; and U.S. Office of Personnel Management, *Federal Civilian Work Force Statistics: Monthly Release* [July 1984]).

45. Indeed, Mashaw describes how SSA administrators create a culture wherein there is reliance on the professional judgment of agency employees in administering benefits.

46. For discussion, see the papers in Sayre (1965).

47. How professional differences can alter the implementation of policy was illustrated when a large number of economists were added to the staff of the Federal Trade Commission (FTC). The economists often disagreed with the agency's lawyers on whether an antitrust case should be pursued (Katzman 1980). Coate, Higgins, and McChesney (1990) present empirical evidence that the Bureau of Economics, staffed mainly by economists, and the Bureau of Competition, staffed mainly by lawyers, view merger cases differently. Coate et al. attribute this result to different incentives faced by economists and lawyers. The latter's human capital is benefited more by litigation as it raises subsequent returns in both the private and the public sectors, thus providing the incentive to file a complaint. For an analysis of antitrust policy at the Department of Justice that also emphasizes the composition of the personnel who make up the bureaucracy, see Eisner and Meier (1990).

48. There is an extensive literature that addresses the desire of elected officials to have policy implementation bureaucratized (see Fenno 1978; Fiorina and Noll 1978; Cain, Ferejohn, and Fiorina 1987; and Fiorina 1989).

49. Shirking by government officials can take a variety of forms, including low productivity and selectively directing effort to those projects that blend well with bureaucratic preferences and away from others. McCubbins, Noll, and Weingast also offer a distinction as to the different forms that deviant bureaucratic behavior can take: "One is simple shirking: an agency becomes a Club Med for government officials who undersupply policy decisions. Another is corruption: agency officials allow the bureau to be 'captured' by selling out to an external group. Still another is oligarchy: the peculiar political preferences of the agency override democratic preferences" (1987, 247).

50. Inman (1988) provides some econometric evidence of the political pressures by local constituents for greater federal expenditures under federal revenue sharing.

51. For a brief history of the USFS and how its past behavior fit the budget-maximization hypothesis, see Johnson (1985).

52. Data on employment by occupation and selected agencies is available from Office of Personnel Management.

53. The actions of these employees are supported by environmental groups. See the discussion offered by Schneider (1992). The fact that they appeal to only one of the affected interest groups is clear evidence of their nonneutrality.

54. This particular case attracted considerable attention, and Congress held hearings on the reassignment of John Mumma (see U.S. House of Representatives 1992).

55. See our discussion of the cost of dismissals to supervisors presented in chap. 5. See also Wilson (1989, 145–46).

56. For discussion of efficiency goals and the growing conflict between the Bureau of Efficiency and federal postal unions, see, e.g., Spero (1927).

57. One problem faced in civil service reform at the senior level, then, is that it must be shown that the costs associated with the problem of bureaucracy exceed the gains of restricting opportunism.

58. This figure was supplied by the Office of Personnel Management. The total amount available for awards is limited to the amount that Congress appropriates for salary increases for mid-level managers. This is generally equivalent to the across-the-board GS increase.

59. The bogey of patronage is not always explicitly introduced, but federal unions can exploit the threat of political coercion to argue that existing protections and personnel rules are in place to guard against such behavior. See, e.g., the claims made by the president of the AFGE regarding the existing civil service system and why its protections would allow for the repeal of the Hatch Act (U.S. Senate 1989, 136, 146–49).

8   The Economics and Politics of Institutional Change in the Political Arena

8.1   Introduction

By any measure, the federal government and its role in the development of the American economy have grown dramatically in this century. While there were some 100,000 federal civilian employees in 1880, by 1990 there were over 3 million. Concomitantly, federal government outlays, as a share of GNP, rose from approximately 2.4 percent in 1880 to nearly 23 percent in 1990 (U.S. Department of Commerce 1975, 224, 1114; U.S. Department of Commerce 1991, 315, 330). These numbers certainly understate the influence of government in the economy because regulatory policies and transfer programs affect economic behavior far beyond what budgets and staffing levels alone would indicate. It is natural, then, for economists, economic historians, and political scientists to be concerned about the performance of government. Persistent and widespread complains about a lack of effectiveness and responsiveness on the part of the federal civilian bureaucracy suggest that all is not well in this vital sector of the economy. In this final chapter, we place civil service reform into the broader context of institutional change in the political arena. We argue that transactions costs are a more serious problem for political institutional change than they are for institutional change in the private sector. This condition has important implications if the civil service system is to be made more productive and accountable to voters.

Despite its problems, meaningful reform in the civil service system appears to be an elusive objective.[1] To understand why the federal bureaucracy is so resistant to change, we have analyzed the forces behind the emergence of the civil service institution and identified the key attributes of it that contribute to the current problems of bureaucratic accountability and performance.

Through most of the nineteenth century, federal workers were employed under a system of political patronage. Patronage was a popular institution, one that carried none of the negative connotations that are associated with it today. Misgivings began to arise after the Civil War as the size of the patronage workforce grew and it became more difficult to manage. With growing scandals and allegations of inefficiency that embarrassed federal politicians, the president and certain members of Congress passed the Pendleton Act in 1883, authorizing merit employment. The gradual replacement of patronage with merit employees illustrates the response of elected officials to an institution that was costing them electoral support.

The development of the federal civil service system, creating a permanent bureaucracy and a vast array of bureaucratic rules, was the result of conscious decisions by successive politicians. The system has, in part, evolved in the way it has because of the objectives of elected officials and the confused political property rights that exist over the federal bureaucracy. As more and more federal workers were placed into the merit service, rules and sanctions had to be devised to limit political conflict over the federal labor force. Bit by bit, federal workers were placed off limits to direct partisan use by politicians. As a consequence, attempts to restructure the civil service that would entail a shift of power either to or from the president will be met by opposition in Congress.

We also have emphasized that institutional adjustments made by the president and the congress to shield federal workers from political manipulation to lessen competition over the bureaucracy have had other important consequences. The emerging structure of the civil service system set the stage for federal workers to emerge as a powerful interest group, one that will, unless sufficiently compensated, resist changes that are not in its interests. In this chapter, we examine another factor that limits the prospects for further civil service reform—incomplete information among voters about patronage and the effects of modifications of the current system of protective bureaucratic rules. Popular perceptions about the evils of patronage have contributed to beliefs about he undesirability of weakening civil service protections, thus aiding the cause of federal unions and contributing to the establishment of an organization that is now resistant to change. As we discuss in the following section, perceptions matter because they affect the cost of transacting. Indeed, consideration of transaction costs is key for understanding the economics and politics of institutional change.

8.2   Transaction Costs and Institutional Change in the Private Sector and in the Political Arena

If we are correct that the civil service system contributes directly to the problem of bureaucracy, then a question immediately arises about the potential for and consequences of institutional change in the political arena. Does the process lead to efficient outcomes as envisioned, for example, by Richard Posner's (1980) description of the development of the common law or by Gary Becker's (1983) analysis of government transfer programs? The claim that the political process will favor efficient institutional choice is a natural application of the standard Pareto conditions. Assuming, for instance, that the political process mandates the transfer of wealth to a particular interest group, policy instruments that generate wealth transfers at the least cost to voters would seemingly be favored over those that impose higher costs. Indeed, absent transaction costs, this is a perfectly reasonable prediction. But information is incomplete and costly to obtain, making transaction costs positive. This problem is compounded by the incentive that interest groups have to mold information made available to voters in self-serving ways. These conditions suggest that the political process will lead to institutional choices that differ from what one would expect if the notion of neoclassical economic efficiency were the dominating criteria. Moreover, as argued by Douglass North (1981, 1990), institutions that inhibit economic growth and development can persist for long periods of time. These different views of institutional change in the political arena raise important questions because they bear not only on our understanding of the process of institutional change but also on discussions of the functioning of representative democracy and of reforming government (see Wittman 1989; and Osborne and Gaebler 1992).

The literature on institutional change in the private sector provides some guidance on this issue. It is generally argued that market forces, arising from changes in relative prices, will lead to the beneficial creation or modification of institutional structures.[2] That is, markets will erode those institutions that are out of step with the economic environment. In this setting, institutional change occurs through negotiations among self-interested parties, each seeking to maximize the attainment of particular goals within the new structure. Since it takes resources to create, utilize, and guarantee institutions, modifications will be made only when the affected parties anticipate individual net gains from doing so. Lance Davis and Douglass North described the motivation for private institutional change as follows: "It is the possibility of profits that cannot be captured within the existing arrangemental structure that leads to the formation of new (or the mutation of old) institutional arrangements" (1971, 59; see also Demsetz 1967).

Even so, the process of private institutional change is complex and can be derailed by high transactions costs. The bargaining underlying the creation or modification of institutions involves debate over the aggregate benefits of the new arrangement and the distribution of those benefits among the various interested parties. Negotiations can break down if there are serious disagreements about either the net benefits of institutional change or their allocation. Conflicts, blocking cooperative solutions, can arise from, among other things, serious information asymmetries among the parties, bounded rationality, and an inability to devise side payments to compensate those who believe that they will be harmed by institutional change.[3] These problems increase with the size and heterogeneity of the bargaining group. As a result, institutional changes that would be anticipated in an environment free of transactions costs do not take place, or they emerge only in abbreviated form.[4] Nevertheless, it can be predicted that institutional change in the private sector will most often foster aggregate wealth maximization. It is our contention, however, that this is often not the case for political institutional change.

Although institutional change takes place both in private settings and in the political arena, the literature has not focused enough on the details of political bargaining to explain observed outcomes or to indicate why the process will likely vary between the two settings. North (1981, 1990) has been one of the leaders in analyzing institutional change, particularly as it involves government. He has described a theory of the state that emphasizes the importance of its coercive power for promoting or for hindering socially beneficial institutional adjustments. North has stressed the potential use of government by special interests and politicians to create local monopolies and other institutions that retard economic progress, but he has not addressed the particulars of the political process by which certain groups and institutions predominate.[5]

A key difference between institutional change in the private and political arenas is the lack of a clear principal or residual claimant in politics, who can direct the process toward efficient outcomes. In negotiations for private institutional change, such as the restructuring of a firm, the parties must reach agreement on the size and nature of the aggregate gains from the proposed reorganization and on the effect of the change on the relevant principals, in this instance, equity- and debtholders. If property rights are complete, the negotiating parties represent the residual claimants, and they have incentives to collect data effectively for forecasting the effects of the restructuring. Stock and bond markets provide mechanisms for evaluating the effect of the proposed reorganization on the principals and for determining their incentives for supporting or modifying the plan.

In the political arena, however, there are few parallels to this process.[6] Political institutional change has economic consequences, but there are fewer opportunities for the types of market trades that in private settings sort out the economic effects and channel the process in a wealth-maximizing way. Politicians are the agents of institutional change in the political arena, and they must be responsive to the demands of their constituents if they are to be reelected. Neither politicians nor the organized interests to which they respond, however, bear the full social costs of their actions. Accordingly, constituents are motivated to demand and politicians to provide government services and transfers beyond what is socially optimal.

Although interest groups will not get all that they demand, the costs imposed on others can be significant. The general electorate is usually considered to be so widely dispersed and the effect of transfers for a single interest group so broadly spread that political opposition from taxpayers will be limited. Given organizing costs, there may be no effective means of assembling the political trades needed for socially beneficial policy adjustments. These conditions facilitate the development of powerful interest groups.[7] Moreover, once interest groups succeed in securing initial legislation, they will be able to seek additional legislation to reinforce their political influence.[8] Importantly, limited or asymmetric information about policy effects can be especially beneficial to an interest group's objective. Indeed, in the case at hand, it is through the selective use of information to influence popular conceptions about patronage that federal unions have been able to strengthen their position and make further civil service reform more costly for politicians.

8.3   The Legacy of Patronage

An example of the importance of molding information to affect popular images is the widely held opinion, promoted by federal unions, that patronage is an inherently evil institution that would be quickly reinstated by politicians given the slightest opportunity. Federal employee unions are not the originators of this view. It comes from histories of the progressive era that discuss patronage. As we show, however, federal employee unions have been skillful in capitalizing on public fears of patronage by labeling reforms of the civil service as returns to the spoils system. Further, these views of patronage have been incorporated into judicial opinions that constrain the actions that politicians might take with regard to government employees. Such judicial rulings serve to raise the political costs of addressing the problems of bureaucratic accountability and productivity.

In histories of the progressive era, the shift to merit is portrayed as a moral crusade (see, e.g., Hoogenboom 1968). Civic reformers fought corrupt politicians, who used patronage to ensure their own and their party's reelection and continued access to the spoils. The overriding goal of reformers was the depoliticization of the federal workforce. Achievement of this goal was possible by eliminating the tie between government employment and party affiliation and creating a politically neutral labor force, with the result that policy administration could be based solely on expertise and professionalism.

Although this is a popular conception of civil service reform, it carries with it a number of myths that federal workers as an interest group have found useful. First, it ignores the fact that patronage was not always considered a problem. The spoils system was popular for a long time. It was viewed as a means of promoting democratic access to government and ensuring accountability between government employees and their political mentors. Those who strayed from the desires of politicians could be (and were) fired. It is true that the institution began to exhibit management problems with the growth of the federal labor force after the Civil War. Even after the Pendleton Act was passed in 1883, however, patronage did not disappear in the federal government. It remained sufficiently popular among enough voters that it was replaced by the merit system only gradually over the following fifty years.

Second, the popular view of civil service reform fails to recognize the incentives that elected officials had to replace patronage when it no longer generated electoral support. If representative democracy works as efficiently as some claim, then those civil service reformers, who receive so much emphasis in the historical literature, were merely messengers of constituent interests to politicians (see Wittman 1989). As we have pointed out, the constituents involved, urban business groups, were well organized and were particularly affected by inefficiencies and scandals in the large post offices and custom houses in the late nineteenth century. These were also the groups that were providing new sources of campaign funds. Accordingly, federal politicians had incentives to be responsive to the demands of these constituents for institutional change.

Third, the popular assessment of patronage, which is also emphasized by a number of students of public administration, suggests an inherent tension between politicians (especially the president) and bureaucrats over civil service protections and an irrepressible tendency of politics to intrude with a return to the spoils (see Lane and Wolf 1990; Levitan and Noden 1983). As we have argued, the reasons that the Congress and the president replaced patronage with merit after 1883 remain in force today. Although patronage may be effective for relatively small government units, the problems of managing a large patronage labor force are too great, relative to any political benefits that might be obtained from abandoning a merit system.

Finally, the belief that a politically neutral, professional bureaucracy could be installed if patronage were removed and politicians held at bay remains an attractive, if naive, notion. What would motivate bureaucrats to be responsive to constituent demands under those sheltered circumstances remains a mystery. It would seem that accountability and productivity would become even greater problems if political control were further weakened. Nevertheless, the view that political preferences, like gender and race, should not be a factor in government hiring or removal decisions is now part of case law.

These four myths about patronage have helped shape the current institutional environment, and their legacy limits the types of reforms that are possible when dealing with the problem of bureaucracy. The fear of patronage is a convenient ploy to which federal employee unions can turn in responding to criticisms about the performance of the bureaucracy. For example, the National Federation of Federal Employees opposed provisions of the Civil Service Reform Act of 1978 granting supervisors authority to award merit pay. Union representative Sam Silverman claimed that the bill "allows for the ready politicization of the civil service. The bill, in short, represents a return to the conditions of 1883, prior to the enactment of the first civil service legislation" (U.S. Senate 1978, 407). In another example, the 1988 annual report of the American Federation of Government Employees (AFGE 1988, 53), the largest federal union, emphasized that politicians would take away the benefits granted to federal employees under the civil service system if they had the opportunity to do so.

8.4   Judicial Interpretations of Patronage and the Costs of Further Institutional Change in the Political Arena

Misconceptions about patronage have been incorporated in important court rulings that have further weakened the control of politicians over the bureaucracy. These rulings have been generated by cases involving state and local governments, but they have set precedents for what would be possible for civil service reform at the federal level. Although by the early 1950s patronage control over rank-and-file positions in the federal government had essentially been eliminated, it remained a fact of political life at the state and local level until the 1980s. Indeed, while many states and cities passed laws restricting patronage hiring, smaller jurisdictions seemed to function well with patronage (Wolfinger 1972). Nevertheless, the notion that patronage was inconsistent with good government led to judicial challenges to political hiring and firing in many jurisdictions.

Patronage practices were addressed by the U.S. Supreme Court in *Elrod v. Burns* (47 U.S. 347 [1976]) and *Branti v. Finkel* (445 U.S. 507 [1980]), where the Court decided that the First Amendment protects individuals from discharge or threats of discharge solely because they did not support the political party in power.[9] An exception to the judgment was made for positions that involved policy making. Although employees were not to be fired for their political party affiliation, hiring or promotion on the basis of party was not explicitly ruled out by the Court. Nevertheless, these rulings largely abolished the established practice of new administrations coming into office, ousting government workers, and replacing them with party members.

In 1989, the Supreme Court was asked to determine the constitutionality of other patronage practices involving the hiring, promotion, transfer, and recall of rank-and-file government employees on the basis of party affiliation and support. The complaint in *Rutan v. Republican Party of Illinois* (497 U.S. 62 [1989]) involved an executive order issued by the Republican governor of Illinois proclaiming a hiring freeze. No exceptions were to be made without the expressed permission of the governor, and state agencies were to submit hiring requests to an office established by him. The complaint asserted that, in these hiring requests, applicants were screened for their vote in Republican primaries or for contributions to the party. Five individuals who brought the suit alleged that they had been discriminated against because they had not supported the Republican party. In a 5 to 4 decision, the Supreme Court held that such practices violated the First Amendment guarantee of freedom of speech.

The *Rutan* ruling is important because it virtually ended patronage hiring and promotion for most government jobs at all levels. It is also important because the Court's arguments clearly reflected a general distrust of patronage, a lack of understanding of current civil service constraints on politicians, and a failure to appreciate the problems of extending tenure guarantees for employees in the public sector. Consider the statements of Justice Brennan, who delivered the majority opinion of the Court: "A government's interest in securing effective employees can be met by discharging, demoting, or transferring staff members whose work is deficient. A government's interest in securing employees who will loyally implement its policies can be adequately served by choosing or dismissing certain high-level employees on the basis of their political views." Brennan went on to argue that "the First Amendment is not a tenure provision, protecting public employees from actual or constructive discharge" (497 U.S. 74, 76 [1989]). In a concurring opinion, Justice Stevens went even further in asserting a distinction between politics and administration when he stated that "this defense of patronage obfuscates the critical distinction between partisan interest and the public interests" (497 U.S. 88 [1989]).

Justice Brennan was incorrect in stating that firing civil servants for cause was a readily available management tool. As we have shown, this is not the case at the federal level. Both Brennan and Stevens were also incorrect in arguing that there is a clear distinction between politics and administration, that a few political appointees could ensure that the administration's policies would be implemented by neutral, career employees. The statements by the two justices ignored the agency problems face by politicians and securing the compliance of government workers in molding and administering policy. Moreover, they did not consider that senior career civil servants are involved in policy determination and that even lower-level career employees are in a position to channel the administration of policy toward particular constituents or toward professional goals that can be inconsistent with the interests of politicians.

Justice Stevens was responding to the dissent of Justice Scalia, who argued that the Court's opinion assumed away the possibility that the benefits of patronage could ever outweigh its coercive effects, "not merely in 1990 in the State of Illinois, but at any time in any of the numerous political subdivisions of this vast country. It seems to me that categorical pronouncement reflects a naive vision of politics and an inadequate appreciation of the systemic effects of patronage in promoting political stability and facilitating the social and political integration of previously powerless groups" (497 U.S. 103–4 [1989]).[10] Scalia went on to argue that: "[t]he whole point of my dissent is that the desirability of patronage is a policy question to be decided by the people's representatives" (497 U.S. 104 [1989]).

The Court's majority differed from Justice Scalia in its view of the responsiveness of politicians to the demands of voters regarding the desirability of patronage. The history of the extension of the federal civil service system, however, seems to make it clear that politicians will choose to reduce patronage whenever they perceive it to be in their political interests to do so. In 1883, the president and the Congress agreed to decrease patronage without any prodding from the Court.

There is another aspect of the *Rutan* case that illustrates a misunderstanding by the justices both of patronage and of the relative benefits of a very protective merit system. Under patronage, federal employees were forced to pay political assessments. Such practices, however, did not imply that the net income of patronage workers was reduced below what they could earn elsewhere. The evidence presented in chapter 4 indicates that patronage workers were compensated for those contributions in the form of higher salaries, and, when the composition of the federal workforce began to shift toward merit employees, the federal wage fell until the 1920s. In the nineteenth century, political assessments were condemned as unfairly forcing government employees to pay for the campaign costs of their mentors. This view of campaign assessments on government workers remains today, and it was reflected in the *Rutan* opinion. Indeed, Justice Brennan claimed that "political parties [today] are nurtured by other, less intrusive and equally effective methods" (497 U.S. 74 [1989]).

In the late nineteenth century, political parties did have other sources of campaign funding, and that undoubtedly made giving up patronage easier.[11] The suggestion that these other methods of funding are "less intrusive" ignores what politicians are expected to do in exchange for contributions. Special interest-group legislation, as a payback, likely intrudes on the interests of taxpayers. This point seems to have been missed by the Court. Moreover, the Court neglected the role played by public employee unions in providing campaign funds to candidates. At the federal level, patronage may be gone, but federal workers remain a major source of campaign funds. In fact, there may be little difference between patronage assessments and PAC contributions by civil service employees. Rank-and-file federal employees pay for their documented salary advantages through union dues and PAC contributions arranged by their unions. Even though it may have been that politicians were able to extract a greater percentage of any given wage premium under patronage than they are under the current civil service system, federal employees were then, and remain today, a major source of campaign funding.

8.5 Concluding Remarks

In an environment of interest-group politics and vague lines of authority over the federal bureaucracy, reform of the civil service system has become exceedingly difficult. For example, one remedy for the problems of accountability and productivity among rank-and-file employees is more hierarchical control. Such changes would allow supervisors more discretion in rewarding and punishing subordinates. Although these incentive structures are common in the private sector, there are obstacles for their adoption in the federal government. Indeed, such arrangements have been proposed, tried temporarily, and then severely curtailed. For example, the Civil Service Reform Act of 1978 authorized performance pay arrangements. Merit pay, however, was opposed by federal unions, and, when it was implemented for senior officials, politicians failed to provide sufficient funds to make the rewards meaningful.[12] Hence, under the existing incentive structure for career employees, the motivation to be very responsive to voters is quite limited. Ironically, under patronage, voters at least had an opportunity to remove bureaucrats from office every few years.

Other popular reform proposals have been superficial. Although David Osborne and Ted Gaebler argued that "we obviously need some protection against patronage hiring and firing" (1992,130), they also recommended that the current civil service system be scrapped and replaced by a new one. They provided no details about the proposed institution, nor did they recognize that the civil service system developed as politicians and labor unions alike sought to replace patronage with merit hiring and other bureaucratic protections. Many parties have a stake in the current arrangement, and significantly changing it will be costly.

Some reform of the civil service system in response to the problem of bureaucracy is possible. The historical record is clear that institutions are modified, usually slowly, in response to changes in the benefits and costs of the groups directly affected by them. In the case of the federal bureaucracy, the existing arrangement is imposing increased costs on politicians. Despite opposition from federal unions, politicians have contracted out to the private sector an increasing amount of goods and services formerly provided by the federal civil service. Moreover, the size of federal bureaucracy has shown only modest growth in the past twenty years. As we have argued, organizational size increases the costs of managing the labor force, and the federal bureaucracy has become one of the largest in the world. There is a growing sense that smaller government units work better and are more responsive to the demands of voters.

Even though politicians will respond in some way to demands for institutional change, that does not suggest that the outcome in the political arena will closely reflect standard economic efficiency criteria. Since there are high organization costs for effective and persistent lobbying, some groups are better able to exert political influence than are others. We have already stressed that federal employee unions are a well-organized and impressive lobbying force. They have succeeded in establishing an institutional structure that benefits their members, and they will devote resources to protect their gains. Added to this is the widely held belief that any major change in the current arrangement invites a return to patronage. If reforms to improve the productivity and accountability of the federal bureaucracy are portrayed as weakening the protections available to government workers, then they will be even more difficult to enact. Although it is always possible to imagine institutional alternatives whereby all parties could be made better off, in practice such outcomes may be impossible in a world of high information and transactions costs.[13] Given the presence of transaction costs that are particularly apparent in the political arena, institutions that inhibit economic growth and reduce welfare can and will persist.

Notes

1. The most recent attempt at restructuring the federal bureacracy is that of the Clinton administration (see Gore 1993).

2. For a summary of a broader literature on institutional change and the role of institutions in economic and political decison making, see Furubotn and Richter (1991). Specific work includes that by Williamson (1975, 1985), North (1981, 1990), Eggertsson (1990), Ostrom (1986, 1990), and Libecap (1989a).

3. For a discussion of some of the issues involved, see Libecap (1989b).

4. Johnson and Libecap's (1982) and Wiggins and Libecap's (1985) analyses of generally unsuccessful private efforts to change property rights in fisheries and oil fields to reduce rent dissipation are cases in point.

5. In their examination of efforts to secure government intervention for unitization of oil fields, Libecap and Wiggins (1985) do examine how private conflicts over the distribution of the gains of unitization spill over and impede political action.

6. In the most extreme case, politics is viewed like a market, and vote-maximizing politicians are viewed like utility- or profit-maximizing individuals in a private setting. Although there are important insights to be gained from modeling politicians as self-interested actors and from incorporating economic theory into analyses of the political process, there are limits to the analogy. The key problem is the lack of a clear principal or residual claimant in political negotiations. At least among some authors, there is a sense that political institutions are an extension of private ones. The notion is one of progression from private negotiations to ones that involve government, whenever private agreements break down. For example, the power of the state to reduce transactions costs through new institutional design has been used by Goldberg (1976) and Williamson (1976) to explain the development of certain kinds of regulatory policies. We, however, emphasize that, in the political process, new transactions costs are introduced that critically affect the outcome of institutional change.

7. The implication is that institutional change in the political arena is unlikely to have the inherent efficiency attributes often associated with organizational change in a private market setting (see Williamson 1985).

8. Johnson (1990) describes efforts that resulted in limited entry regulations in the Alaskan salmon fishery. The irony is that such regulations also created a group that was more effective at exerting political pressure. This group succeeded in restricting the development of a competing sector that had the potential to yield an even more efficient outcome.

9. An implication that follows from these rulings and the discussion presented in chap. 6 is that voter participation rates for state and local employees should decline relative to that of their private-sector counterparts. Johnson and Libecap (1991) provide evidence that those rates have fallen over time.

10. As we pointed out in chap. 2, patronage served a variety of goals, one of which was to democratize government employment. It is likely that civil service reform worked against immigrants and other unorganized groups, who were denied access to government jobs. The tests that were subsequently adopted at the behest of influential business groups emphasized expertise and professionalism, and they likely served the interests of these groups.

11. Moreover, today both members of Congress and the president have their own staffs, and these are large.

12. Moreover, as we have argued, Congress would be wary of providing new opportunities for the president and department heads to influence the bureaucracy in policy administration.

13. As Ronald Coase explains, "The reason why some activities are not the subject of contracts is exactly the same as the reason why some contracts are commonly unsatisfactory—it would cost too much to put the matter right" (1960, 39).

Appendixes

Appendix A
Appendix to Chapter 2

This appendix offers a simple model that more formally characterizes the trade-offs facing members of Congress and the president on the issue of patronage. In particular, the model illustrates why the growth of the federal labor force contributed to the adoption of a merit system, why the president was likely to lead efforts to control the volume of patronage, and which members of Congress were most likely to support passage of the Pendleton Act. In generating these results, it will be assumed that individual members of Congress and the president are all vote maximizers.

Following Denzau and Munger (1986) and others, we divide the voting population into two groups: informed and uninformed voters. The former group compares the receipt of government services with taxes levied and, hence, is concerned about the productivity of the federal workforce. In addition, informed voters monitor the voting record of elected officials and keep track of the positions taken by them on various issues. The closer this voting record is to the preferences of the informed voters, the more likely it is that this group of voters will vote in favor of the elected official. In contrast to informed voters, uninformed voters pay no attention to these issues and instead are influenced by campaign advertising, electioneering, canvassing by patronage workers, and, in some cases, the promise of a federal job.

The foregoing discussion suggests a model of vote maximization of the form

$$(A1) \qquad V = nF(Q, I) + (N - n)H(\alpha W, C).$$

This equation is designed to capture the behavior of a given member of Congress; a similar model will be constructed for the president. In line with the approach taken by Peltzman (1976), we have two separate probability functions: F is the probability that a member of the informed group votes for the legislator, while H is the probability that a member of the uninformed group votes in favor. The number of informed voters in the legislator's district is denoted by n and the total number of voters by N. The probability that an informed voter grants support is a positive function of the productivity, or performance, of the federal workforce, Q, and the voting record of the legislator, I. In the relevant range, it is assumed that both Q and I are subject to decreasing returns so that

$$F_Q > 0, \quad F_{QQ} < 0, \quad F_I > 0, \quad F_{II} < 0.$$

(Unless specified otherwise, subscripts refer to either partial or, where appropriate, total derivatives.) We also assume that, in the relevant range, Q and I are independent factors in the vote function so that the cross-effects are zero (i.e., $F_{QI} = 0$). While this assumption is not tenable when F approaches unity, most election outcomes in the late 1800s were substantially less than unity, around 0.7. The campaign services rendered by patronage workers are denoted by W, where α is a productivity coefficient. In addition, legislators can devote their own time and resources, C, to campaign activities. Both W and C are assumed to be subject to decreasing returns so that

$$H_W > 0, \quad H_{WW} < 0, \quad H_C > 0, \quad H_{CC} < 0.$$

Although not explicitly included in equation (A1), it is assumed that vote maximization is conditional on the probable reactions of an opponent.

To include explicitly the trade-offs facing an individual member of Congress in bargaining for patronage, we set

(A2) $Q = Q(r, L),$

(A3) $I = X - P(\bar{W})W,$

(A4) $\alpha = \alpha(m) = \alpha(e/W),$

(A5) $C = \bar{e} - e.$

Equation (A2) indicates that the productivity of federal workers is a function of two variables, r and L. One of the main objectives of the Pendleton Act was the separation of the civil service into two components: classified (merit) and unclassified (patronage) employees. To account for this delineation, r is defined as the ratio of merit system employees to total federal employment. As explained in the text, productivity differed between patronage and merit workers. Thus, holding the total number of federal workers, L, constant, an increase in r will increase Q (i.e., $Q_r > 0$). In contrast, given the arguments presented in the text on control and increasing organizational size, an increase in L holding r constant should lower productivity (i.e., $Q_L < 0$). These conditions also suggest that expanding the merit system will have a greater effect on productivity the larger is the federal labor force (i.e., $Q_{rL} > 0$).

Because legislators engage in trades with the president for the rights to patronage positions, equation (A3) provides a means for incorporating the costs of obtaining patronage positions into the model. Under the Constitution, it is the president who in general holds the initial rights to allocate patronage. As described in the text, the president would exchange these rights for support on various programs In essence, there is a market for patronage, wherein the president acts as the seller of patronage and members of Congress are the demanders. Within this framework, there is both a quantity and a unit price. Here, the going price for a patronage position, P, can be thought of in terms of roll-call votes promised the president. Although in actual practice this price will likely vary across bills, the purpose here is to incorporate into the model the notion that the president trades patronage for congressional support. Accordingly, we simplify the analysis and assume that there is a single price in terms of roll-call votes that each member of Congress pays in order to buy a patronage position. The price is a function of the total amount of patronage offered by the president, $\bar{W}$, and W is the quantity of patronage purchased by the member of Congress. Since the president is using patronage to buy favorable roll-call votes that he would not otherwise have, and since members of Congress are vote maximizers, these exchanges have their costs to legislators. To illustrate the cost to a legislator of buying patronage, we simplify and assume that each legislator can be thought of as having a preferred roll-call voting record, assumed to be single dimensional, that reflects his or her vote-maximizing position on the issues, absent any trades with the president. This point is denoted as X in equation (A3). When buying patronage, the legislator moves away from that point, with the decline measured by the unit price of patronage times the quantity purchased.

In the text, it was argued that patronage workers had to be monitored else local party officials would exercise control over their activities and the provision of campaign services to the legislator would decline. To incorporate this aspect into the model, let m denote monitoring activity by the legislator, and allow for increases in m to increase the productivity of patronage workers (i.e., $\alpha_m > 0$). Monitoring requires that the legislator devote effort, e, to that activity. How effective each unit of effort is in raising m depends on the number of patronage workers the legislator has; the larger is W, the less effective is each unit of e. These concepts are contained in the definition of α in equation (A4). The opportunity cost for e is embodied within the model via equation (A5). Here, $\bar{e}$ is the legislator's total stock of effort that can be devoted to nonpatronage provided campaign activities, C.

The objective function for the president is very similar to that of a member of Congress and is written as

(A6) $$\hat{V} = \sum n\hat{F}(Q, \hat{I}) + \sum(N - n)\,\hat{H}(\hat{\alpha}\hat{W}, \hat{C}).$$

Here, the ^ identifies the particular function or variable as referring to the president. With the following exceptions, these variables and functions have the same general purpose and form as those in equation (A1):

(A7) $$\hat{I} = \hat{X} + P(\bar{W})\bar{W},$$

(A8) $$\frac{dP(\bar{W})\bar{W}}{d\bar{W}} = \mathrm{MR}(\bar{W}) = P(\bar{W})(1 + 1/\varepsilon_d),$$

(A9) $$\bar{W} = (1 - r)L - \hat{W}.$$

In equation (A7), the term $P(\bar{W})\bar{W}$ is the total number of roll-call votes obtained by the president in exchange for patronage positions. By exchanging patronage for roll-call votes, the president attains a more preferred policy position, which in turn will increase the support received from informed voters. Since we assume price-taking behavior for each member of Congress, $P(\bar{W})$ is the aggregate inverse demand function for patronage. Thus, $P(\bar{W})\bar{W}$ is analogous to total revenue in standard market analysis, and, as shown in equation (A8), the derivative of $P(\bar{W})\bar{W}$ with respect to $\bar{W}$ yields the marginal revenue function, MR. In turn, MR is a function of the elasticity of demand for patronage, ε_d. Given a negatively sloped demand curve for patronage, the price elasticity will be negative.

A key variable in the president's objective function is $\hat{W}$. As shown in equation (A9), the number of patronage positions that the president chooses to exchange for roll-call votes is equal to the total number of unclassified positions available, $(1 - r)L$, less $\hat{W}$. The latter variable measures the number of patronage positions that the president keeps for his own dispensation. These patronage workers are selected by the president and, as shown in the second term in equation (A6), provide campaign and constituency services that generate direct support for the president. In actual practice, the president can also benefit from having political appointees in the various agencies to monitor and effectuate policy, implying that $\hat{I}$ could be a positive function of $\hat{W}$. The analysis offered here, however, is meant to apply to rank-and-file federal employees, not to high-ranking political appointees, whose selection was and remains largely unaffected by civil service reform. As with members of Congress, the productivity of the president's own patronage workers is a function of his monitoring activity, with $\hat{m}$ equal to $\hat{e}/\hat{W}$.

Consider first the optimization problem faced by the president. Prior to passage of the Pendleton Act, r was equal to zero, leaving the president with the choice variables $\hat{e}$ and $\hat{W}$. Optimizing with respect to these two variables yields the following first-order conditions:

(A10) $$\hat{V}_{\hat{e}} = \hat{H}_{\hat{W}}\alpha_{\hat{m}} - \hat{H}_{\hat{C}} = 0,$$

(A11) $$\hat{V}_{\hat{W}} = \hat{F}_{\hat{I}}(-\mathrm{MR}) + \hat{H}_{\hat{W}}(\hat{\alpha} - \hat{m}\hat{\alpha}_{\hat{m}}) = 0.$$

To reduce the amount of notation, voter population numbers are not shown. Equation (A10) indicates that effort will be devoted to monitoring activity until the marginal returns to effort in the two types of campaign activities are equal. Now consider the implications embodied in equation (A11). The sign of the first term in equation (A11) depends on whether marginal revenue, MR, is positive or negative. If the president could effectively monitor and utilize an unlimited number of patronage workers, $\hat{W}$, the quantity of patronage workers exchanged for roll-call votes, $\bar{W}$, would always be located within the elastic proportion of the demand function. But there are limitations on the president's ability to utilize a large number of patronage workers effectively. Indeed, the description offered in the text suggests a president who was overwhelmed with the problem of managing patronage. Within the context of the model, notice that the term $(\hat{\alpha} - \hat{m}\hat{\alpha}_m)$ in equation (A11) could be negative, with the likelihood of that outcome increasing with increases in $\hat{W}$. Basically, if $\hat{W}$ is too large, there is a loss of control, implying that the per unit decline in productivity dominates the benefits of increasing $\hat{W}$. While the president would prefer to avoid such an outcome, prior to the Pendleton Act the only alternative was an increase in $\bar{W}$, and that would lead to a decrease in the price of patronage. Thus, the optimal choice of $\hat{W}$ could be such that the demand for patronage, $\bar{W}$, is inelastic in the relevant range. Under these conditions, the net benefits derived by the president from patronage will deteriorate if the federal labor force continues to expand.

Before showing why the net benefits from patronage will eventually decline with the growth of the labor force, it is important to emphasize that we are treating L as an exogenous variable. In actual practice, the size of the federal labor force is collectively determined by the president and the Congress. Moreover, elected officials can be expected to have their own preferred level of L that maximizes the number of votes they receive. Increases in demand for government services will likely increase the demand for L, and, when viewed in the aggregate, voter support can increase with the expansion of the labor force. However, the major emphasis of the analysis offered here is on changes in voter support due to changes in the size of the patronage pool, not on the aggregate effect of expanding the size of government.

To show why voter support for the president will eventually decline as the patronage pool expands, evaluate the president's objective function, $\hat{\phi}$, at its optimal values, $\hat{e}^*$ and $\hat{W}^*$, and differentiate with respect to L:

$$(A12) \qquad\qquad \hat{\phi}_L = \hat{F}_Q Q_L + \hat{F}_i MR.$$

With increases in L, productivity declines, implying that the first term in equation (A12) is negative. The sign of the second term depends on whether MR is positive or negative. If there are limitations on the ability of the president to utilize patronage workers effectively, then $\bar{W}$ must eventually increase as L increases. Since equation (A4) also suggests that there is a maximum number of patronage workers that a member of Congress can effectively handle, there will be a quantity beyond which no additional patronage will be demanded. Given this cutoff point, MR must eventually turn negative. But, if MR turns negative as L expands, the president will not only be confronted with a decline in productivity, a lower Q, but actually desire a smaller patronage pool since that would raise price and increase the returns from exchanging patronage. Thus, sufficiently high levels of L will induce the president to promote civil service reform aimed at reducing the number of patronage positions.

The provisions of the Pendleton Act essentially called for a small increase in r. If MR were negative, the president would gain from implementation of the act. To show this, evaluate the president's objective function at its optimal values, and differentiate with respect to r:

$$(A13) \qquad \hat{\phi}_r = \hat{F}_Q Q_r + \hat{F}_f(-L\text{MR}).$$

When MR is negative, both terms in equation (A13) are positive, indicating that the president would gain if the total number of patronage positions were reduced.

Now consider the optimization problem for a member of Congress. Collectively, the members of Congress could, with sufficient support, change r, as they did with the passage of the Pendleton Act. Individually, however, they take r as given and maximize with respect to e and W. The first-order conditions are

$$(A14) \qquad V_e = H_W \alpha_M - H_C = 0,$$

$$(A15) \qquad V_W = -F_f P + H_W(\alpha - m\alpha_m) = 0.$$

The above conditions are similar to those for the president except that a member of Congress would not obtain more patronage than he or she could effectively manage. That is, the term $(\alpha - m\alpha_m)$ in equation (A15) would not be negative. We have asserted throughout that the demand curve for patronage is negatively sloped. Since the problem is not identical to a standard factor demand analysis, it is noteworthy that the structure of the model does yield a negatively sloped demand curve for patronage. From the envelope theorem (see Silberberg 1990), we know that the following condition must hold:

$$(A16) \qquad V_{WP} \frac{\partial W^*}{\partial P} > 0.$$

Here, $\partial W^*/\partial P$ is the slope of the demand curve. From the first-order conditions we obtain

$$(A17) \qquad V_{WP} = -F_f + F_{ff} P W^* < 0,$$

implying that the demand curve for patronage is negatively sloped.

As we argue in the text, not only did the growth of the federal labor force have an important effect on the president's willingness to support civil service reform, but it also influenced members of Congress. However, because an increase in L will lower the price of patronage, the incentive to support reform as the labor force expanded was not as strong for members of Congress as it was for the president. To show why, consider the situation prior to the Pendleton Act, where r is equal to zero. Setting e and W at their optimal values, e^*

and W^*, the legislator's objective function, ϕ, can be differentiated with respect to L to yield

(A18)
$$\phi_L = F_Q Q_L + F_I \left(\frac{\partial \hat{W}^*}{\partial L} - 1 \right) P_{\overline{W}} W.$$

Because of the negative effect that growth has on productivity, the first term is negative. The second term in equation (A18), however, is positive for the following reasons. First, note that, since the demand curve is negatively sloped, $P_{\overline{W}}$ is negative. Now consider $(\partial \hat{W}/\partial L - 1)$, and recall that equation (A9) reflects both the direct and the indirect effects of a change in L on the quantity of patronage offered to the Congress. The indirect effect accounts for the change in the president's own use of patronage, $\hat{W}$, as L increases (we are assuming that each member of Congress correctly anticipates how the president will react to a change in L). Again using the envelope theorem, we know that the following condition must hold:

(A19)
$$\hat{V}_{\hat{W}L} \frac{\partial \hat{W}^*}{\partial L} > 0.$$

From the first-order condition, equation (A11), we obtain

(A20)
$$\hat{V}_{\hat{W}L} = \hat{F}_I(-MR_{\overline{W}}) + \hat{F}_{II}(-MR^2) > 0.$$

Accordingly, as L expands, the president will increase the amount of patronage that he utilizes in his own campaign, and that action will temper the decline in P. But for the term $(\partial \hat{W}/\partial L - 1)$ in (A18) to be positive, $\partial \hat{W}^*/\partial L$ would have to be greater than unity. Since $\hat{W}$ cannot exceed L, it is not possible for this effect to be greater than unity except in some local area. Thus, in contrast to the results for the president, the price effect of an increase in L can continue to temper the negative effect that the growth of the federal labor force has on productivity even as L gets very large.

Consider now the likelihood that a particular member of Congress will vote for the Pendleton Act. If an increase in r increases support from the electorate, the legislator will vote in favor. Differentiating the legislator's objective function with respect to r yields

(A21)
$$\phi_r = F_Q Q_r + F_I \left(\frac{\partial \hat{W}^*}{\partial r} + L \right) P_{\overline{W}} W.$$

Because increasing r will improve productivity, $Q_r > 0$, the first term in the above equation is positive. The second term, however, is negative. Even though the sign of $\partial \hat{W}^*/\partial r$ is negative (with the increase in r due to passage of the Pendleton Act, the president will reduce $\hat{W}$), the magnitude of the change cannot exceed L. Thus, equation (A21) captures the basic trade-off facing members of Congress when voting on the Pendleton Act. Establishing a merit system would increase the productivity of the federal workforce, but it would also decrease the size of the patronage pool, leading to an increase in the price of patronage. Of course, Congress was not monolithic, and the benefits of improving productivity relative to the negative effects of a price increase for patronage will vary across members. For example, in districts where the productivity of the federal labor force, Q is relatively more important to voters, it is more likely that the first term in equation (A21) will dominate the second. The evidence presented in the text indicates that the share of federal output tended to be the highest in the areas where commercial activity was greatest. The quality of federal services, such as postal and customs, was particularly important to voters in those districts. Thus, the importance of Q in the informed-voters probability function would likely increase with increases in the share of federal output in the congressional district.

The above model was also employed in chapter 3 to show why, once having adopted a merit system, the proportion of merit system employees to total employment would expand with increases in total federal employment, why the president would take the lead in expanding merit system coverage, and why there would be continuing conflict between the president and the Congress over patronage issues.

Appendix B
Appendix to Chapter 3

In the text, it is argued that, once having adopted a merit system, the proportion of merit system employees to total employment would expand with increases in total federal employment. In particular, it is argued that the president would be in the vanguard to expand coverage. To show why, recall that, in passing the Pendleton Act, Congress gave the president the authority to expand coverage of the merit system. In effect, the president was given the power to control r, the ratio of merit system workers to total federal civilian employment. Using the same assumptions and notation as in appendix A, recall that the president's objective function is

(B1) $$\hat{V} = \sum n\hat{F}(Q, \hat{I}) + \sum (N - n)\,\hat{H}(\hat{\alpha}\hat{W}, \hat{C}).$$

Given the power to control r, the president maximizes support by choosing $\hat{e}$, $\hat{W}$, and r. The first-order conditions are

(B2) $$\hat{V}_{\hat{e}} = \hat{H}_{\hat{W}}\hat{\alpha}_{\hat{m}} - \hat{H}_C = 0,$$

(B3) $$\hat{V}_{\hat{W}} = \hat{F}_I(-\mathrm{MR}) + \hat{H}_{\hat{W}}(\hat{\alpha} - \hat{m}\hat{\alpha}_{\hat{m}}) = 0,$$

(B4) $$\hat{V}_r = \hat{F}_Q Q_r + \hat{F}_I(-\mathrm{LMR}) = 0.$$

Equations (B2) and (B3) are the same as before. But now equation (B4) indicates that the ability to control r gives the president the option of placing federal workers off limits to partisan use, and that can benefit the president in two distinct ways. First, increases in r raise productivity. Second, the ability to reduce the number of patronage positions means that the president can effectively control $\bar{W}$ ($\bar{W} = [1 - r]L - \hat{W}$) at a lower cost, and that means that he will always operate in the elastic proportion of the demand function (i.e., MR > 0).

Now consider the effect of a change in L on r. Once the Pendleton Act was passed, the president was in a position to control r. Evaluating the president's objective function at $\hat{e}*$, $\hat{W}*$, and $r*$, we know from the envelope theorem that the following condition must hold:

$$\text{(B5)} \qquad \hat{V}_{\hat{W}L} \frac{\partial \hat{W}*}{\partial L} + \hat{V}_{rL} \frac{\partial r*}{\partial L} > 0.$$

From the first-order conditions, equations (B2) and (B4), we obtain

$$\text{(B6)} \qquad \hat{V}_{\hat{W}L} = F_r[-(1 - r)\text{MR}_{\bar{w}}] + F_{rl}[-(1 - r)\text{MR}^2] > 0,$$

$$\text{(B7)} \qquad \hat{V}_{rL} = \hat{F}_Q Q_{rL} + \hat{F}_{QQ} Q_r Q_L + \hat{F}_{rl}[-(1 - r)L\text{MR}^2]$$
$$- \hat{F}_r[\text{MR} + (1 - r)L\text{MR}_{\bar{w}}].$$

Given the underlying assumptions, the expression in equation (B6) is unambiguously positive. In equation (B7), the first three terms are positive, while the sign of the fourth term depends on the magnitude of MR. If productivity, Q, was not affected by changes in r or was not important in influencing votes, $\hat{F}_Q = 0$, then the first-order conditions indicate that the president would choose $\hat{W}$ so that MR would be equal to zero. In that case, the fourth term in equation (B7) would also be positive, and the sign of $\partial r*/\partial L$ would be unambiguously positive. When productivity of the federal workforce is important and affected by the level of r, as we have argued that it is, MR will be positive. But, here again, the expression in equation (B7) is positive. Using equation (B4) to rewrite (B7) yields

$$\text{(B8)} \qquad \hat{V}_{rL} = \hat{F}_{QQ} Q_r Q_L + \hat{F}_{rl}[-(1 - r)\text{MR}^2] - \hat{F}_r(1 - r)L\,\text{MR}_{\bar{w}}$$
$$+ \hat{F}_Q\left(Q_{rL} - \frac{Q_r}{L}\right).$$

The first three terms in equation (B8) are all positive. The sign of the fourth term depends on the underlying functional form of Q. However, we have argued that $Q_L < 0$ and that $Q_{rL} > 0$. The rationale is that loss of control over the labor force increases with organizational size and, thus, that converting to a merit system will have a greater effect on productivity the larger is the size of the federal labor force. Given these functional relations, it follows that $\partial Q_{rL}/\partial L > 0$, indicating that the average function, Q_r/L, lies below the marginal, Q_{rL}. Accordingly, $\hat{V}_{rL}$ is positive, implying that an increase in the federal labor force will induce the president to expand coverage of the merit system such that r will be a positive function of L. This implication was examined in chapter 3.

Appendix C
Appendix to Chapter 5

The data used to estimate the earnings profile for federal workers were obtained from a random sample of individual General Schedule (GS) employees. The samples were taken from the Central Personnel Data File, March 1985. The number of observations is 16,616. The sample includes forty-eight federal agencies. For the larger agencies, a 1 percent random sample of full-time GS employees was obtained, whereas, for the smaller agencies, 10 percent samples were used, excluding those agencies with fewer than 200 employees. The agencies in the samples account for 98.5 percent of all GS employees. Table C.1 reports the OLS regression estimates. In addition to the estimated coefficients on the total experience and tenure variable, table C.1 contains the estimated effects on salary of minority status, veterans' preference, sex, handicap status, employment location, education, occupation, and agency variables. The variables are defined as follows (the definitions and codes used to generate the variables are from U.S. Office of Personnel Management [1985b]):

Minority status. The minority vector comprises three dummies representing basic racial and national origin and an excluded category (white, not of Hispanic origin):

MINORITY 1 = black, not of Hispanic origin;
MINORITY 2 = Hispanic;
MINORITY 3 = all other groups.

Veterans' preference categories. The veterans' preference vector is composed of two dummies plus an excluded category (no veterans' preference):

VET 5 = a veteran entitled to a five-point preference;
VET 10 = a veteran entitled to a ten-point preference.

Other socioeconomic variables.

FEMALE   = one if female, zero otherwise;
HANDICAP = one if no reported history of physical or mental disabilities, zero otherwise.

Employment location. The regional variables are composed of six dummies plus an excluded category (the states of Virginia, West Virginia, Maryland, Pennsylvania, New Jersey, and Delaware excluding the Washington, D.C., SMSA):

PACIFIC   = Washington, Oregon, and California;
MOUNTAIN = Montana, Idaho, Wyoming, Nevada, Utah, Colorado, Arizona, and New Mexico;

Table C.1   **Earnings Regression for Individual Federal White-Collar Workers: Dependent Variable = ln W_i.**

	Coefficient	t-statistic
Constant	10.109	282.78
Total experience:		
E	.008	11.14
E2	−.0002	−10.89
Tenure:		
T	.03	42.82
T2	−.0004	−16.37
Interaction:		
ET	−.00008	−2.27
Minority status:		
MINORITY 1	−.08	−20.99
MINORITY 2	−.03	−3.35
MINORITY 3	−.028	−3.83
Veterans' preference categories:		
VET 5	−.018	−4.43
VET 10	−.035	−4.93
Other socioeconomic variables:		
FEMALE	−.096	−24.14
HANDICAP	.032	5.58
Employment location:		
PACIFIC	−.003	−.55
MOUNTAIN	−.022	−3.26
NORTHCENT	.006	1.26
SOUTHERN	−.009	−1.85
NORTHEAST	−.003	−.43
DC	.11	21.08
Education variables:		
ED 1	.043	4.28
ED 2	.037	3.43
ED 3	.06	5.96
ED 4	.091	8.27
ED 5	.174	16.39
ED 6	.219	18.66
ED 7	.408	27.69
ED 8	.279	9.13
ED 9	.273	22.86
ED 10	.294	18.68
ED 11	.359	9.3
ED 12	.369	8.95
ED 13	.431	27.54
ED 14	.433	14.9
YHDO	−.004	−11.16
Occupational groups:		
Social science, psychology, and welfare	−.012	−1.38
Personnel management & industrial relations	.04	5.44
Biological sciences	−.124	−11.18
Accounting and budget	−.026	−4.56

(continued)

Table C.1 (continued)

	Coefficient	*t*-statistic
Medical, hospital, dental, and public health	−.077	−9.49
Veterinary medical science	−.113	−3.58
Engineering and architecture	.095	13.49
Legal and kindred	.002	.28
Information and arts	.013	1.14
Business and industry	.021	3.36
Copyright, patent, and trademark	−.002	−.54
Physical sciences	−.001	−.14
Library and archives	−.137	−7.09
Mathematics and statistics	−.002	−.15
Equipment, facilities, and service	.023	1.61
Education	−.058	−4.57
Investigation	.062	7.04
Quality assurance, inspection, and grading	−.014	−.98
Supply	−.036	−4.59
Transportation	.083	7.95
Miscellaneous	−.078	−6.27
PATCO classification:		
Professional	.09	15.48
Technical	−.257	−54.76
Clerical	−.419	−88.86
Other	−.373	−27.4
Supervisory position	.142	32.12
Managerial position	.287	29.62
Agency identifiers:		
Agriculture	−.046	−4.82
Commerce	.016	1.26
Defense	−.035	−5.26
Justice	.061	5.33
Labor	.071	4.77
Energy	.065	4.02
Education	.07	6.78
Equal Employment Opportunity Commission	.04	3.35
Federal Emergency Management	.05	3.55
Environmental Protection Agency	.081	3.96
Federal Communications Commission	.023	1.63
Federal Home Loan Bank	.048	2.85
Federal Trade Commission	.108	5.82
General Services Administration	−.024	−1.6
Housing and Urban Development	.049	2.69
Interior	−.031	−2.93
National Labor Relations Board	.087	6.84
National Aeronautics and Space Administration	.057	3.9
Office of Personnel Management	−.062	−6.13
Railroad Retirement Board	−.033	−1.9
Small Business Administration	.09	8.03

Table C.1   (continued)

	Coefficient	t-statistic
Securities and Exchange Commission	.075	5.18
Smithsonian Institution	−.034	−2.61
State	.009	.86
Transportation	.092	8.57
Treasury	.001	.07
Veterans Administration	−.056	−6.92
National Foundation on Arts and Humanities	−.027	−1.05
Federal Labor Relations Authority	.164	4.73
Merit Systems Protection Board	.109	3.8
Pension Benefit Guaranty Corporation	−.004	−.13
Office of Management and Budget	.228	8.14
Commission on Civil Rights	.074	1.48
Commodity Futures Trading Commission	.067	2.71
National Credit Union Administration	−.007	−.27
Export-Import Bank of the United States	.038	1.07
Farm Credit Administration	.149	4.81
Federal Mediation and Conciliation Service	.218	7.65
Interstate Commerce Commission	.026	1.23
ACTION	.101	3.4
Federal Maritime Commission	−.054	−1.37
National Science Foundation	.067	3.58
U.S. Soldiers' and Airmen's Home	−.207	−7.68
Consumer Product Safety Commission	.036	1.38
Selective Service System	.07	1.99
National Transportation Safety Board	.055	1.66
U.S. International Trade Commission	.025	.78

Note: The excluded agency is the Department of Health and Human Services.

NORTHCENT = North Dakota, South Dakota, Nebraska, Kansas, Montana, Iowa, Missouri, Wisconsin, Illinois, Indiana, Ohio, and Michigan;

SOUTHERN = Texas, Oklahoma, Arkansas, Louisiana, Mississippi, Tennessee, Kentucky, Alabama, Florida, Georgia, South Carolina, and North Carolina;

NORTHEAST = New York, Connecticut, Rhode Island, Massachusetts, New Hampshire, Maine, and Vermont;

DC = Washington, D.C., SMSA.

Education. The vector of education variables is composed of fourteen dummies plus an excluded category (individuals without a high school diploma). The variables included are as follows:

ED 1   = graduated from high school;
ED 2   = attended an occupational training program;
ED 3   = attended college but for less than eighty-nine semester hours;
ED 4   = three to four years of college, but did not obtain a bachelor's degree;
ED 5   = bachelor's degree;
ED 6   = postbachelor's work but no additional higher degree;
ED 7   = first professional degree (e.g., dentistry, law, medicine);
ED 8   = post–first professional degree work but no additional degree;
ED 9   = master's degree;
ED 10 = postmaster's but no additional higher degree;
ED 11 = sixth-year degree (e.g., advanced certificate in education or other areas):
ED 12 = some work beyond a sixth-year degree but no additional degree;
ED 13 = doctorate degree;
ED 14 = postdoctorate;
YHDO = calendar year in which highest degree was obtained; if no degree, for the 1985 data set YHDO was set equal to 1985 minus age plus six years of schooling.

Occupational variables. For a listing, see table C.1.
Agency variables. For a listing, see table C.1.

Appendix D
Appendix to Chapter 6

Tables D.1 and D.2 present the full set of variables and probit estimates used in obtaining the results reported in tables 6.1 and 6.2.

Table D.1   **Variable Definitions**

Variable	Description
1. Education 12	Equal to one if completed high school
2. Education 14	Equal to one if completed one or two years of college
3. Education 15	Equal to one if completed three years of college
4. Education 16	Equal to one if completed four years of college
5. Education 17	Equal to one if completed five or more years of college
6. Age	Individual's age in years
7. Age squared	Variable 6 squared
8. Male	Dummy variable equal to one if male
9. Marital status	Dummy variable equal to one if married
10. SMSA	Dummy variable equal to one if residence is in an SMSA
11. Union	Dummy variable equal to one if a member of a union

Table D.1   (continued)

Variable	Description
12. Earnings	Weekly earnings in dollars
13. Black	Dummy variable equal to one if race is black
14. Hispanic	Dummy variable equal to one if ethnic background is Hispanic
15. Manager	Managerial and executive positions
16. Administrative	Administrative support, including clerical supervisory positions
17. Professional	Includes lawyers, engineers, and other professionals
18. Teacher	Primary and high school teachers
19. College	College teacher
20. Technical	Technicians
21. Service	Service workers
22. Production	Factory and agricultural workers
23. Federal	Dummy variable equal to one if employed by the federal government
24. State	Dummy variable equal to one if employed by a state government
25. Local	Dummy variable equal to one if employed by county, city, or municipality

Note: There are five dummy educational achievement variables, variables 1–5. The excluded category consists of those individuals who did not complete high school. Variables 6–14 describe other socioeconomic characteristics. There are also eight dummy occupational variables, variables 15–22. The excluded category consists of those in sales. Variables 23–25 designate government employment at the federal, state, and local levels, respectively. The excluded category is private-sector employment. Included with the twenty-five variables listed above were fifty state dummy variables, including the District of Columbia. The omitted state was Pennsylvania. The estimated coefficients on state dummies are available on request.

Table D.2   **Probit Estimates of the Effect of Public Employment on Voting**

Variable	1984 Elections	1986 Elections
Education 12	.424	.386
	(8.25)	(6.40)
Education 14	.675	.616
	(11.20)	(9.06)
Education 15	.795	.679
	(8.98)	(7.08)
Education 16	1.096	.800
	(14.78)	(10.37)
Education 17	1.19	.831
	(13.51)	(9.40)
Age	.031	.051
	(3.95)	(5.67)
Age squared	−.00005	−.0002
	(−.51)	(−1.90)
Male	−.121	−.039
	(−3.14)	(−.97)
Marital status	.203	.209
	(6.03)	(6.08)

(continued)

Table D.2   (continued)

Variable	1984 Elections	1986 Elections
SMSA	−.069	−.188
	(−1.70)	(−4.32)
Union	.133	.181
	(2.88)	(3.71)
Earnings	.00033	.000077
	(3.10)	(.79)
Black	.212	.178
	(3.71)	(3.24)
Hispanic	.020	.116
	(.25)	(1.39)
Manager	.161	.119
	(2.10)	(1.66)
Administrative	.172	.038
	(2.82)	(.63)
Professional	.067	.118
	(.86)	(1.52)
Teacher	.034	−.006
	(.28)	(−.06)
College	−.044	.129
	(−.19)	(.60)
Technical	.053	−.075
	(.56)	(−.77)
Service	−.141	−.244
	(−2.21)	(−3.69)
Production	−.174	−.216
	(−2.97)	(−3.44)
Federal	.058	−.032
	(.73)	(−.38)
State	.160	.282
	(1.88)	(3.74)
Local	.279	.312
	(4.32)	(4.85)
Constant	−1.510	−2.360
	(−8.46)	(−11.28)

Note: *t*-statistics are given in parentheses.
Source: Johnson and Libecap (1991).

References

Adie, Douglas K. 1977. *An evaluation of Postal Service wage rates.* Washington, D.C.: American Enterprise Institute.

Alexander, Herbert E. 1971. Financing presidential campaigns. In *History of American presidential elections: 1789–1968,* vol. 4, ed. Arthur M. Schlesinger, Jr. New York: McGraw-Hill.

American Federation of Government Employees (AFGE). 1988. *Report of the national officers to the 31st convention.* Miami Beach.

Arnold, R. Douglas. 1979. *Congress and the bureaucracy.* New Haven, Conn.: Yale University Press.

———. 1987. Political control of administrative officials. *Journal of Law, Economics, and Organization* 3, no. 2:279–86.

Atack, Jeremy. 1985. Industrial Structure and the emergence of the modern industrial corporation. *Explorations in Economic History* 22, no. 1:29–52.

Bagnoli, Mark, Stephen W. Salant, and Joseph E. Swierzbinski. 1989. Durable-goods monopoly with discrete demand. *Journal of Political Economy* 97, no. 6:1459–78.

Baruch, Ismar. 1941. *History of position-classification and salary standardization in the federal service.* Washington, D.C.: U.S. Civil Service Commission.

Becker, Gary S. 1983. A theory of competition among pressure groups for political influence. *Quarterly Journal of Economics* 68, no. 3:371–400.

Becker, William H. 1982. *The dynamics of business-government relations: Industry and exports, 1893–1921.* Chicago: University of Chicago Press.

Beer, Samuel H. 1976. The adoption of general revenue sharing: A case study in public sector politics. *Public Policy* 24, no. 2:127–95.

Bennett, James T., and William P. Orzechowski. 1983. The voting behavior of bureaucrats: Some empirical evidence. *Public Choice* 41, no. 2:271–83.

Benson, B. L., and R. N. Johnson. 1986. The lagged impact of state and local taxes on economic activity and political behavior. *Economic Inquiry* 24, no. 3:389–401.

Bentley, Arthur F. 1908. *The process of government.* Chicago: University of Chicago Press.

Biographical directory of the American Congress: 1774–1971. 1971. Washington, D.C.: U.S. Government Printing Office.

Biographical directory of the United States Congress: 1774–1989. 1989. Washington, D.C.: U.S. Government Printing Office.

Blais, André, Donald E. Blake, and Stéphane Dion. 1991. The voting behavior of bureaucrats. In *The budget-maximizing bureaucrat: Appraisals and evidence,* ed. André
Blais and Stéphane Dion. Pittsburgh: University of Pittsburgh Press.

Blais, André, and Stéphane Dion, eds. 1991. *The budget-maximizing bureaucrat: Appraisals and evidence.* Pittsburgh: University of Pittsburgh Press.

Borcherding, Thomas E., ed. 1977. *Budgets and bureaucrats: The sources of government growth.* Durham, N.C.: Duke University Press.

Borcherding, Thomas E., Winston C. Bush, and Robert Spann. 1977. The effects of
public spending of the divisibility of public outputs in consumption, bureaucratic
power, and size of the tax-sharing group. In *Budgets and bureaucrats: The sources
of government growth,* ed. Thomas E. Borcherding. Durham, N.C.: Duke University Press.

Borjas, George J. 1980. Wage determination in the federal government: The role of
constituents and bureaucrats. *Journal of Political Economy* 88, no. 6:111–47.

———. 1982. Labor turnover in the U.S. Federal bureaucracy. *Journal of Public Economics* 19, no. 2:187–202.

Brady, David W., Joseph Cooper, and Patricia A. Hurley. 1979. The decline of party in
the U.S. House of Representatives, 1887–1968. *Legislative Studies Quarterly* 4, no.
3 (August): 381–407.

Breton, Albert, and Ronald Wintrobe. 1975. The equilibrium size of a budget-
maximizing bureau: A note on Niskanen's theory of bureaucracy. *Journal of Political
Economy* 83, no. 1:195–207.

———. 1982. *The logic of bureaucratic conduct.* Cambridge: Cambridge University
Press.

Bronars, Steven G., and John R. Lott. 1989. Why do workers join unions? The importance of rent seeking. *Economic Inquiry* 27, no. 2:305–24.

Brooks, Thomas R. 1971. *Toil and trouble: A history of American labor.* New York:
Delacorte.

Buchanan, James M. 1977. Why does government grow? In *Budgets and bureaucrats:
The sources of government growth,* ed. Thomas E. Borcherding. Durham, N.C.: Duke
University Press.

Burton, John F., and Terry Thomason. 1988. The extent of collective bargaining in the
public sector. In *Public-Sector Bargaining,* 2d ed., ed. Benjamin Aaron, Joyce M.
Najita, and James L. Stern. Washington, D.C.: Bureau of National Affairs.

Bush, Winston C., and Arthur T. Denzau. 1977. The voting behavior of bureaucrats and
public sector growth. In *Budgets and bureaucrats: The sources of government
growth,* ed. Thomas E. Borcherding. Durham, N.C.: Duke University Press.

Cahill, Marion Cotter. 1968. *Shorter hours: A study of the movement since the Civil
War.* New York: AMS.

Cain, Bruce, John Ferejohn, and Morris Fiorina. 1987. *The personal vote: Constituent
service and electoral independence.* Cambridge, Mass.: Harvard University Press.

Campbell, Alan K., and Linda S. Dix, eds. 1990. *Recruitment, retention, and utilization
of federal scientists and engineers.* Washington, D.C.: National Academy Press.

Caplow, Theodore. 1957. Organizational size. *Administrative Science Quarterly*
1:484–505.

Case, H. Manley. 1986. Federal employee job rights: The Pendleton Act of 1883 to the
Civil Service Reform Act of 1978. *Howard Law Journal* 29, no. 2:283–306.

Chambers, William N. 1975. Party development and the American mainstream. In *The
American party systems: Stages of political development,* 2d ed., ed. William N.
Chambers and Walter D. Burnham. New York: Oxford University Press.

Civil service retirement and old-age pensions. 1916. *Monthly Labor Review,* June,
101–13.

Coase, Ronald H. 1960. The problem of social cost. *Journal of Law and Economics* 3:1–44.

———. 1972. Durability and monopoly. *Journal of Law and Economics* 15, no. 1:143–49.

Coate, Malcolm, B., Richard S. Higgins, and Fred S. McChesney. 1990. Bureaucracy and politics in FTC merger challenges. *Journal of Law and Economics* 33, no. 2:463–82.

Commons, John R. 1935. *History of labor in U.S., 1896–1932.* New York: Macmillan.

Commons, John R., and John B. Andrews. 1936. *Principles of labor legislation.* New York: Harper & Bros.

Congressional Quarterly Almanac. Various years. Washington, D.C.: Congressional Quarterly.

Congressional Quarterly's guide to U.S. elections. 1985. Washington, D.C.: Congressional Quarterly.

Conyngton, Mary. 1920. Separations from the government service. *Monthly Labor Review* 11:1131–44.

———. 1926. Industrial pension for old age and disability. *Monthly Labor Review* 22 (January): 21–56.

Cook, Brian J. 1989. Principal-agent models of political control of bureaucracy. *American Political Science Review* 83, no. 3:965–70.

Council of State Governments. 1942. *The book of the states, 1941–1942.* Chicago.

Courant, P. N., E. M. Gramlich, and D. L. Rubinfeld. 1979. Public employees market power and the level of government spending. *American Economic Review* 69, no. 5:806–17.

———. 1980. Why voters support tax limitation amendments: The Michigan case. *National Tax Journal* 33:1–20.

Cox, Gary, and Matthew McCubbins. 1989. Parties and the congressional committee system. Working paper. University of California, San Diego.

Craig, Lee. 1992. The federal regulation of workers' pensions and the provision of retirement income insurance. Working paper. North Carolina State University, Department of Economics.

Curtis, George. 1887. The last assault upon reform. *Harper's Weekly,* 21 May.

Dankert, Clyde E., Floyd C. Mann, and Herbert R. Northrup. 1965. *Hours of work.* New York: Harper & Row.

David, Paul A. 1985. CLIO and economics of QWERTY. *American Economic Review* 75, no. 2:2–7.

Davis, James J., Harry M. Daugherty, and Hubert Work. 1923. Cabinet officers suggest changes in civil service system. *Congressional Digest* 2, no. 7 (April): 204–5.

Davis, Lance E. 1971. Capital mobility and American economic growth. In *The Reinterpretation of American Economic Growth,* ed. Robert Fogel and Stanley Engerman. New York: Harper and Row.

Davis, Lance E., and Douglass C. North. 1971. *Institutional change and American economic growth.* New York: Cambridge University Press.

Demsetz, Harold. 1967. Towards a theory of property rights. *American Economic Review* 57, no. 2:347–59.

Denzau, Arthur T., and Michael C. Munger. 1986. Legislators and interest groups: How unorganized interests get represented. *American Political Science Review* 80, no. 1:89–106.

DiIulio, John J., Jr., Gerald Garvey, and Donald F. Kettl. 1993. *Improving government performance: An owner's manual.* Washington, D.C.: Brookings.

Doeringer, Peter B., and Michael J. Poire. 1971. *Internal labor markets and manpower analysis.* Armonk: Sharpe.

Donoian, Harry A. 1967. Organizational problems of government employee unions. *Labor Law Journal* 18, no. 3:137–44.

Douglas, Paul R. 1930. *Real wages in the United States, 1890 to 1926.* Boston: Houghton Mifflin.

Downs, Anthony. 1957. *An economic theory of democracy.* New York: Harper and Row.

———. 1967. *Inside Bureaucracy.* New York: Little, Brown.

Eaton, Dorman. 1880. *The civil service in Great Britain.* New York: Harper and Bros.

Eccles, James R. 1981. *The Hatch Act and the American bureaucracy.* New York: Vantage.

Eggertsson, Thrainn. 1990. *Economic behavior and institutions.* New York: Cambridge University Press.

Ehrenberg, Ronald G., and Joshua L. Schwarz. 1986. Public-sector labor markets. In *Handbook of labor economics,* vol. 2, ed. O. Ashenfelter and R. Layard. Amsterdam: North-Holland.

Eisner, Marc Allen, and Kenneth J. Meier. 1990. Presidential control versus bureaucratic power: Explaining the Reagan revolution in antitrust. *American Journal of Political Science* 34, no. 1:269–87.

Epstein, Abraham. 1928. *The challenge of the aged.* New York: Vanguard.

———. 1933. *Insecurity: A challenge to America.* New York: Harrison Smith & Robert Haas.

Fabricant, Solomon. 1952. *The trend of government activity in the United States since 1900.* New York: National Bureau of Economic Research.

Fama, Eugene F. 1980. Agency problems and the theory of the firm. *Journal of Political Economy* 88, no. 2:288–310.

Farber, Henry S., and Daniel H. Saks. 1980. Why workers want unions: The role of relative wages and job characteristics. *Journal of Political Economy* 88, no. 2:349–69.

Faught, Albert S. 1915. Civil service legislation—1915. *American Political Science Review* 4, no. 3:549–55.

Feldman, Herman. 1931. *A personnel program for the federal civil service.* 71st Cong. 3d sess. H. Doc. 773. Washington, D.C.: U.S. Government Printing Office.

Fenno, Richard F., Jr. 1966. *The power of the purse: Appropriations politics in Congress.* Boston: Little, Brown.

———. 1973. *Congressmen in committees.* Boston: Little, Brown.

———. 1978. *Home style: House members in their districts.* Boston: Little, Brown.

Ferejohn, John A. 1977. On the decline of competition in congressional elections. *American Political Science Review* 71, no. 1:166–76.

Fiorina, Morris P. 1974. *Representatives, roll calls, and constituencies,* Boston: Lexington.

———. 1977. The case of the vanishing marginals: The bureaucracy did it. *American Political Science Review* 71, no. 1:177–81.

———. 1989. *Congress: Keystone of the Washington establishment.* 2d ed. New Haven, Conn.: Yale University Press.

Fiorina, Morris, P., and Roger G. Noll. 1978. Voters, bureaucrats, and legislators. *Journal of Public Economics* 9, no. 2:239–54.

Fish, Carl R. 1905. *The civil service and the patronage.* New York: Longmans, Green.

Fitts, Michael, and Robert Inman. 1992. Controlling Congress: Presidential influence in domestic fiscal policy. *Georgetown Law Journal* 80, no. 5:1737–85.

Foulke, William Dudley. 1925. *Roosevelt and the spoilsmen.* New York: National Civil Service Reform League.

Fowler, Dorothy G. 1943. *The cabinet politician: The postmaster general, 1829–1909.* New York: Columbia University Press.

Freeman, Richard B. 1980. Unionism and the dispersion of wages. *Industrial and Labor Relations Review* 34, no. 1:3–23.

———. 1986. Unionism comes to the public sector. *Journal of Economic Literature* 24, no. 1: 41–86.

———. 1987. How do public sector wages and employment respond to economic conditions? In *Public sector payrolls,* ed. D. A. Wise. Chicago: University of Chicago Press.

Freeman, Richard B., and Casey Ichniowski. 1988. *When public sector workers unionize.* Chicago: University of Chicago Press.

Freeman, Richard B., and James L. Medoff. 1984. *What do unions do?* New York: Basic.

Frey, Bruno S., and Weiner W. Pommerehne. 1982. How powerful are public bureaucrats as voters. *Public Choice* 38:253–62.

Furubotn, Eirik G., and Rudolf Richter, eds. 1991. *The new institutional economics.* College Station: Texas A&M University Press.

Galambos, Louis. 1987. *The new American state: Bureaucracies and policies since World War II.* Baltimore: Johns Hopkins University Press.

Garand, James C., and Donald A. Gross. 1984. Changes in the vote margins for congressional candidates: A specification of historical trends. *American Political Science Review* 78, no. 1:17–30.

Geddes, Barbara. 1991. A game theoretic model of reform in Latin American democracies. *American Political Science Review* 35, no. 2:371–92.

Gilligan, Thomas W., and Keith Krehbiel. 1989. Asymmetric information and legislative rules with heterogeneous committees. *American Journal of Political Science* 33, no. 2:459–90.

Gilligan, Thomas W., William J. Marshall, and Barry R. Weingast. 1989. Regulation and the theory of legislative choice: The Interstate Commerce Act of 1887. *Journal of Law and Economics* 32, no. 1:35–62.

Gladden, Edgar N. 1967. *Civil services of the United Kingdom 1885–1970.* London: Cass.

Goldberg, Victor P. 1976. Regulation and administered contracts. *Bell Journal of Economics* 7, no. 2:426–48.

Goldin, Claudia. 1988. Maximum hours legislation and female employment in the 1920s: A re-assessment. *Journal of Political Economy* 96, no. 1:189–205.

———. 1990. *Understanding the gender gap: An economic history of American women.* New York: Oxford University Press.

Goldstein, Judith, and Barry R. Weingast. 1991. The origins of American trade policy: Rules, coalitions and international politics. Stanford University. Typescript.

Gore, Al. 1993. *From red tape to results: Creating a government that works better and costs less.* Report of the National Performance Review. Washington, D.C.: U.S. Government Printing Office.

Grace Commission. 1984. *President's Private Sector Survey on Cost Control: A report to the president.* Washington, D.C.: U.S. Government Printing Office.

Grandjean, Burke D. 1981. History and career in a bureaucratic labor market. *American Journal of Sociology* 86, no. 5:1057–92.

Greenstein, Fred I. 1964. The changing pattern of urban party politics. *Annals of the American Academy of Political and Social Science: City Bosses and Political Machines* 353 (May): 1–13.

Griffith, Ernest S. 1974a. *A History of American city government: The conspicuous failure, 1870–1900.* New York: Praeger.

———. 1974b. *A History of American city government: The conspicuous failure, 1900–1920.* New York: Praeger.

Gyourko, Joseph, and Joseph Tracy. 1988. An analysis of public- and private-sector wages allowing for endogenous choices of both government and union status. *Journal of Labor Economics* 6, no. 2:229–53.

Haas, Lawrence J. 1990. *Running empty: Bush, Congress, and the politics of a bankrupt government.* Homewood, Ill.: Business One Irwin.

Hansen, S., Thomas R. Palfrey, and Howard Rosenthal. 1987. The Downsian model of electoral participation: Formal theory and empirical analysis of the constituent size effect. *Public Choice* 52:15–33.

Hartman, Robert W. 1980. The effects of top officials' pay on other federal employees. In *The rewards of public service: Compensating top federal officials,* ed. Robert W. Hartman and Arnold R. Weber. Washington, D.C.: Brookings.

———. 1983. *Pay and pensions for federal workers.* Washington, D.C.: Brookings.

Hartman, Robert W., and Arnold R. Weber. eds. 1980. *The rewards of public service, Compensating top federal officials.* Washington, D.C.: Brookings.

Hashimoto, Masanori, and John Raisian. 1985. Employment tenure and earnings profiles in Japan and the United States. *American Economic Review* 75, no. 4:721–36.

Hays, Samuel P. 1975. Political parties and the community-society continuum. In *The American Party systems: Stages of political development,* ed. William N. Chambers and Walter D. Burnham. New York: Oxford University Press.

Heclo, Hugh. 1977. *A government of strangers: Executive politics in Washington.* Washington, D.C.: Brookings.

Helms, Jay L. 1985. The effect of state and local taxes on economic growth: A time series-cross section approach. *Review of Economics and Statistics* 65, no. 4:574–82.

Hersch, Joni, and Patricia Reagan. 1993. Efficient gender-specific wage-tenure profiles. Working paper. University of Wyoming. Department of Economics.

Hibbing, John R. 1991. *Congressional careers: Contours of life in the U.S. House of Representatives.* Chapel Hill: University of North Carolina Press.

Higgs, Robert. 1971. *The transformation of the American economy, 1865–1914.* New York: Wiley.

Hoogenboom, Ari, 1968. *Outlawing the spoils: A history of the civil service reform movement, 1865–1883.* Urbana: University of Illinois Press.

Hoover Commission. 1949. *The Hoover Commission report on organization of the executive branch of the government.* New York: MacGraw-Hill.

Horn, Murray J. 1988. *The political economy of public administration: Organization, control and performance of the public sector.* Ph.D. diss. Harvard University.

Howlett, Robert G. 1984. Interest arbitration in the public sector. *Chicago Kent Law Review* 60, no. 4:815–37.

Hudson Institute. U.S. Office of Personnel Management. 1988. *Civil service 2000.* Washington, D.C.: U.S. Government Printing Office.

Inman, Robert P. 1988. Federal assistance and local services in the United States: The evolution of a new federalist fiscal order. In *Fiscal federation: Quantitative studies,* ed. Harvey S. Rosen. Chicago: University of Chicago Press.

Ippolito, Richard A. 1987. Why federal workers don't quit. *Journal of Human Resources* 22, no. 2:281–99.

Irons, Peter H. 1982. *The New Deal lawyers.* Princeton, N.J.: Princeton University Press.

Jaarsma, B., A. Schram, and F. Van Winden. 1986. On the voting participation of public bureaucrats. *Public Choice* 48:183–87.

Jacoby, Sanford M. 1985. *Employing bureaucracy: Managers, unions, and the transformation of work in American industry, 1900–1945.* New York: Columbia University Press.

James, John A. 1983. Structural change in American manufacturing, 1850–1890. *Journal of Economic History* 43, no. 2:433–60.

Jensen, Michael, and William Meckling. 1976. Theory of the firm: Managerial behavior, agency costs, and ownership structure. *Journal of Financial Economics* 3:305–60.

Johnson, Eldon L. 1940. General unions in the federal service. *Journal of Politics* 2, no. 1:23–56.

Johnson, Ronald N. 1985. U.S. Forest Service policy and its budget. In *Forest lands: Public and private,* ed. R. T. Deacon and M. B. Johnson. Cambridge, Mass.: Ballinger.

———. 1990. Commercial wild species rearing: Competing groups and regulation. *Journal of Environmental Economics and Management* 19, no. 2:127–42.

Johnson, Ronald N., and Gary D. Libecap. 1982. Contracting problems and regulation: The case of the fishery. *American Economic Review* 72, no. 5:1005–22.

———. 1989a. Agency growth, salaries, and the protected bureaucrat. *Economic Inquiry* 27, no. 3:431–51.

———. 1989b. Bureaucratic rules, supervisor behavior, and the effect on salaries in the federal government. *Journal of Law, Economics, and Organization* 5, no. 1:53–82.

———. 1991. Public sector employee voter participation and salaries. *Public Choice* 68, no. 1:137–50.

———. 1994. Patronage to merit and control of the federal government labor force. *Explorations in Economic History* 31:91–119.

Kappel Commission. 1968. *Towards postal excellence.* Report of the President's Commission on Postal Organization. Washington, D.C.: U.S. Government Printing Office.

Katz, Lawrence F., and Alan B. Krueger. 1991. Changes in the structure of wages in the public and private sectors. *Research in Labor Economics* 12:137–72.

———. 1992. Public sector pay flexibility: Labor market and budgetary considerations. Princeton University. Typescript.

Katzman, Robert A. 1980. *Regulatory bureaucracy: The federal trade commission and antitrust policy.* Cambridge, Mass.: MIT Press.

Kaufman, Herbert. 1956. Emerging conflicts in the doctrines of public administration. *American Political Science Review* 50, no. 4:1057–73.

———. 1960. *The forest ranger.* Baltimore: Johns Hopkins University Press.

———. 1965. The growth of the federal personnel system. In *The federal government service,* ed. Wallace S. Sayre. Englewood Cliffs, N.J.: American Assembly.

———. 1981. *The administrative behavior of federal bureau chiefs.* Washington, D.C.: Brookings.

Kiewiet, Roderick A., and Matthew D. McCubbins. 1991. *The logic of delegation: Congressional parties and the appropriations process.* Chicago: University of Chicago Press.

Knoke, David. 1982. The spread of municipal reform: Temporal, spatial, and social dynamics. *American Journal of Sociology* 87, no. 6:1314–39.

Knott, Jack H., and Gary J. Miller. 1987. *Reforming bureaucracy: The politics of institutional choice.* Englewood Cliffs, N.J.: Prentice-Hall.

Kolbe, Richard L. 1985. *American political parties: An uncertain future.* New York: Harper & Row.

Kolko, Gabriel. 1963. *The triumph of conservatism: A re-interpretation of American history, 1900–1916.* Chicago: Quadrangle.

Krueger, Alan B. 1988a. The determinants of queues for federal jobs. *Industrial and Labor Relations Review* 41:567–81.

———. 1988b. Are public sector workers paid more than their alternative wage? Evidence from longitudinal data and job queues. In *When public sector workers union-*

ize, ed. Rich B. Freeman and Casey Ichniowski. Chicago: University of Chicago Press.

Krueger, Anne O. 1991. The political economy of controls: American sugar. Reprint no. 1657. Cambridge, Mass.: NBER.

Ladd, E. C., Jr. 1970. *American political parties: Social change and political response.* New York; Norton.

Lane, Larry M., and James F. Wolf. 1990. *The human resource crisis in the public sector.* New York: Quorum.

Lazear, Edward P. 1981. Agency, earnings profiles, productivity and hours restrictions. *American Economic Review* 71:606–20.

———. 1989. Pay equality and industrial politics. *Journal of Political Economy* 87, no. 3:561–80.

Lazear, Edward P., and Sherwin Rosen. 1981. Rank-order tournaments as optimum labor contracts. *Journal of Political Economy* 89, no. 3:841–64.

Levitan, Sar A., and Alexandra B. Noden. 1983. *Working for the sovereign: Employee relations in the federal government.* Baltimore: John Hopkins University Press.

Levy, Frank, and Richard J. Murnane. 1992. U.S. earnings levels and earnings inequality: A review of recent trends and proposed explanations. *Journal of Economic Literature* 30, no. 3:1333–81.

Lewis, B. Gregory. 1986. Gender and promotions: Promotion chances of white men and women in federal white-collar employment. *Journal of Human Resources* 21:406–19.

Lewis, H. Gregg. 1990. Union/nonunion wage gaps in the public sector. *Journal of Labor Economics* 8:S260-S328.

Lewis, Meriam. 1923. Changes introduced by reclassification. *Congressional Digest* 2, no. 7 (April): 208–14.

Libecap, Gary D. 1989a. *Contracting for property rights.* New York: Cambridge University Press.

———. 1989b. Distributional issues in contracting for property rights. *Journal of Institutional and Theoretical Economics* 145, no. 1:6–24.

———. 1991. Douglass C. North. In *New Horizons in economic thought: Appraisals of leading economists,* ed. Warren Samuels. London: Elgar.

———. 1992. The rise of the Chicago packers and the origins of meat inspection and antitrust. *Economic Inquiry* 32, no. 2:242–62.

Libecap, Gary D., and Steven N. Wiggins. 1985. The influence of private contractual failure on regulation: The case of oil field unitization. *Journal of Political Economy* 93, no. 4:690–714.

Lindblom, Charles. 1959. The science of "muddling through." *Public Administration Review* 19:79–80.

Lineberry, Robert L., and Edmund P. Fowler. 1967. Reformism and public policies in American cities. *American Political Science Review* 61, no. 3:701–16.

Lohmann, Susanne, and Sharyn O'Halloran. 1992. Divided government and U.S. trade policy. Working paper. Stanford University, Graduate School of Business.

Long, James. 1982. Are government workers overpaid? Alternative evidence. *Journal of Human Resources* 17, no. 1:123–31.

Lott, John R., and Stephen G. Bronars. 1993. Time series evidence on shirking by congressmen. *Public Choice,* 76, nos. 1–2:125–50.

Lubove, Roy. 1967. Workmen's compensation and the prerogatives of voluntarism. *Journal of Labor History* 8, no. 3:254–79.

McCubbins, Matthew D., Roger G. Noll, and Barry R. Weingast. 1987. Administrative procedures as instruments of political control. *Journal of Law, Economics, and Organization* 3, no. 2:243–77.

———. 1989. Structure and process, politics and policy: Administrative arrangements and the political control of agencies. *Virginia Law Review* 75, no. 2:432–82.

Macy, Jonathan R. 1992. Separated powers and positive political theory: The tug of war over administrative agencies. *Georgetown Law Journal* 80, no. 3:671–703.

Maddala, G. S. 1983. *Limited-dependent and qualitative variables in econometrics.* New York: Cambridge University Press.

Maranto, Robert, and David Schultz. 1991. *A short history of the United States civil service.* New York: University Press of America.

Martin, R. C. 1933. The municipal electorate: A case study. *Southwestern Social Science Quarterly* 14:193–237.

Mashaw, Jerry L. 1983. *Bureaucratic justice: Managing social security disability claims.* New Haven, Conn.: Yale University Press.

Mayhew, David R. 1974a. *Congress: The electoral connection.* New Haven, Conn.: Yale University Press.

———. 1974b. Congressional elections: The case of the vanishing marginals. *Polity* 6, no. 3:295–317.

———. 1986. *Placing parties in American politics.* Princeton, N.J.: Princeton University Press.

Migué, Jean-Luc, and Gérard Bélanger. 1974. Towards a general theory of managerial discretion. *Public Choice* 17:24–47.

Milkovich, George T., and Alexandra K. Wigdor, eds., with Renae F. Broderick and Anne S. Mavor. 1991. *Pay for performance: Evaluating performance appraisal and merit pay.* Washington, D.C.: National Academy Press.

Miller, Herman P. 1960. *Income distribution in the United States.* U.S. Bureau of the Census. Washington, D.C.: U.S. Government Printing Office.

Moe, Terry M. 1982. Regulatory performance and presidential administration. *American Journal of Political Science* 26, no. 2:197–224.

———. 1989. The politics of bureaucratic structure. In *Can the government govern?* ed. John E. Chubb and Paul E. Peterson. Washington, D.C.: Brookings.

———. 1990. Political institutions: The neglected side of the story. *Journal of Law, Economics, and Organization* 6 (special issue): 213–53.

———. 1991. Politics and the theory of organization. *Journal of Law, Economics, and Organization* 7 (special issue): 106–29.

Mosher, Frederick C. 1965. Features and problems of the federal civil service. In *The federal government service,* ed. Wallace S. Sayre. Englewood Cliffs, N.J.: Prentice-Hall.

———. ed. 1975. *American public administration: Past, present, future.* University: University of Alabama Press.

———. 1979. *The GAO: The quest for accountability in American government.* Boulder, Colo.: Westview.

———. 1982. *Democracy and the public service.* 2d ed. New York: Oxford University Press.

Moulton, Brent R. 1990. A reexamination of the federal-private wage differential in the United States. *Journal of Labor Economics* 8, no. 2:270–93.

Mueller, Dennis C. 1989. *Public choice II.* Cambridge: Cambridge University Press.

Nelson, Michael. 1982. A short, ironic history of American national bureaucracy. *Journal of Politics* 44, no. 2:747–78.

Nesbitt, Murray B. 1976. *Labor relations in the federal government service.* Washington, D.C.: Bureau of National Affairs.

Newman, Robert J. 1983. Industry migration and growth in the South. *Review of Economics and Statistics* 65, no. 1:76–86.

Niskanen, William A. 1971. *Bureaucracy and representative government.* Chicago: Aldine-Atherton.

———. 1991. A reflection on bureaucracy and representative government. In *The budget-maximizing bureaucrat: Appraisals and evidence,* ed. André Blais and Stéphane Dion. Pittsburgh: University of Pittsburgh Press.

Nordlund, Willis J. 1991. The Federal Employees' Compensation Act: An overview of the Act. *Monthly Labor Review* 114, no. 9:3–14.

North, Douglass C. 1961. *The economic growth of the United States, 1790–1860.* New York: Norton.

———. 1981. *Structure and change in economic history.* New York: Norton.

———. 1990. *Institutions, institutional change, and economic performance.* New York: Cambridge University Press.

Olson, Mancur. 1965. *The logic of collective action.* Cambridge, Mass.: Harvard University Press.

Osborne, David, and Ted Gaebler. 1992. *Reinventing government.* Reading, Mass.: Addison-Wesley.

Ostrogorski, Moisei. 1974. The politicians and the machine. In *Political parties in American history, vol. 2, 1828–1890,* ed. Felice A. Bonadio. New York: Putman's.

Ostrom, Elinor. 1986. An agenda for the study of institutions. *Public Choice* 48:3–25.

———. 1990. *Governing the commons: The evolution of institutions and collective action.* New York: Cambridge University Press.

Ouchi, William G. 1977. The relationship between organizational structure and organizational control. *Administrative Science Quarterly* 22(March): 95–113.

Overacker, Louise. 1932. *Money in elections.* New York: Macmillan.

Paradis, Adrian A. 1972. *The labor reference book.* New York: Chilton.

Peltzman, Sam. 1976. Towards a more general theory of regulation. *Journal of Law and Economics* 19, no. 2:211–40.

———. 1984. Constituent interest and congressional voting. *Journal of Law and Economics* 27, no. 1:181–210.

Perlman, Selig, and Philip Taft. 1935. *History of labor in the United States, 1896–1932.* New York: Macmillan.

Peters, Guy B. 1991. The European bureaucrat: The applicability of bureaucracy and representative government to non-American settings. In *The budget-maximizing bureaucrat: Appraisals and evidence,* ed. André Blais and Stéphane Dion. Pittsburg: University of Pittsburg Press.

Pfiffner, James P. 1987. Political appointees and career executives: The democracy-bureaucract nexus in the third century. *Public Administration Review* 47:57–65.

Pisani, Donald J. 1992. *To reclaim a divided west: Water, law, and public policy, 1848–1902.* Albuquerque: University of New Mexico Press.

Polsby, Nelson W. 1968. The institutionalization of the U.S. House of Representatives. *American Political Science Review* 62, no. 1:114–68.

Posner, Richard A. 1980. A theory of primitive society, with special reference to law. *Journal of Law and Economics* 23, no. 1:1–53.

Powell, G. B. 1986. American voter turnout in comparative perspective. *American Political Science Review* 80, no. 1:17–43.

President's Pay Agent. 1980. Annual report on comparability of the federal statutory pay systems with private enterprise pay rates. 96th Cong. 2d sess. H. Doc. 281. Washington, D.C.: U.S. Government Printing Office.

Rabin, J., C. E. Teasley, A. Finkle, and L. Carter. 1985. *Personnel: Managing human resources in the public sector.* New York: Harcourt Brace Jovanovich.

Reeves, Thomas C. 1969. Chester A. Arthur and campaign assessments in the election of 1880. *Historian* 31, no. 4:573–82.

Reid, Joseph D., and Michael M. Kurth. 1988. Public employees in political firms: Part A, The patronage era. *Public Choice* 59, no. 3:253–62.

———. 1989. Public employees in political firms: Part B, Civil service and militancy. *Public Choice* 60, no. 1:41–54.

Ridley, Clarence E., and Orin F. Nolting. 1941. *The municipal year book, 1914.* Chicago: International City Managers' Association.

Roosevelt, Theodore. 1927. *Theodore Roosevelt: An autobiography.* New York: Scribner.

Rosen, Bernard. 1989. *Holding government bureaucracies accountable.* 2d ed. New York: Praeger.

Rosenbaum, James E. 1979. Organizational career mobility: Promotion chances in a corporation during periods of growth and contraction. *American Journal of Sociology* 85, no. 1:21–48.

Ross, Stephen A. 1973. The economic theory of agency: The principal's problem. *American Economic Review* 63, no. 2:134–39.

Rothman, David J. 1974. The structure of state politics. In *Political parties in American History, vol. 2, 1828–1890,* ed. Felice A. Bonadio. New York: Putman's.

Rubinfeld, Daniel L. 1977. Voting in a local school election: A micro analysis. *Review of Economics and Statistics* 59, no. 1:30–42.

Rusk, Jerrold G. 1970. The effect of the Australian ballot reform on split ticket voting: 1876–1908. *American Political Science Review* no. 4:1220–38.

———. 1974. Comment: The American electoral universe: Speculation and evidence. *American Political Science Review* 68, no. 3:1028–49.

Sageser, A. Bower. 1935. *The first decades of the Pendleton Act: A study of civil service reform.* University Studies, vols. 34–35. Lincoln: University of Nebraska Press.

Sayre, Wallace S., ed. 1965. *The federal government service.* 2d ed. Englewood Cliffs, N.J.: American Assembly.

Schneider, Paul. 1992. When a whistle blows in the forest. *Audubon* 94 (January/February): 42–49.

Scism, Thomas E. 1974. Employee mobility in the federal service: A description of some recent data. *Public Administration Review* 34:247–54.

Siedman, Harold, and Robert Gilmour. 1986. *Politics, position, and power: From the positive to the regulatory state.* 4th ed. New York: Oxford University Press.

Shepsle, Kenneth A. 1979. Institutional arrangements and equilibrium in multidimensional voting models. *American Journal of Political Science* 23, no. 1:27–59.

Shepsle, Kenneth A., and Barry R. Weingast. 1984. Political solutions to market problems. *American Political Science Review* 78, no. 2:417–33.

Silberberg, Eugene. 1990. *The structure of economics.* 2d ed. New York: McGraw-Hill.

Skowronek, Stephen. 1982. *Building a new American state: The expansion of national administrative capacities, 1877–1920.* New York: Cambridge University Press.

Smith, Bruce L. R., ed. 1984. *The higher civil service of Europe and Canada: Lessons for the United States.* Washington, D.C.: Brookings.

Smith, Sharon. 1977. *Equal pay in the public sector: Fact or fantasy?* Princeton, N.J.: Princeton University Press.

———. 1987. Comment on "Wages in the federal and private sector." In *Public sector payrolls,* ed. D. A. Wise. Chicago: University of Chicago Press.

Snowden, Kenneth A. 1990. Historical returns and security market development, 1872–1925. *Explorations in Economic History* 27, no. 4:381–420.

Sorensen, Elaine. 1989. Measuring the effect of occupational sex and race composition on earnings. In *Pay equity: Empirical inquiries,* ed. Robert Michael and Heidi I. Hartman. Washington, D.C.: National Academy Press.

Spero, Sterling D. 1927. *The labor movement in a government industry: A study of employee organization in the postal service.* New York: Macmillan.

———. 1948. *Government as employer.* New York: Remsen.

Spiller, Pablo T. 1990. Politicians, interest groups, and regulators: A multiple-principals agency theory of regulation (or "Let them be bribed"). *Journal of Law and Economics* 33, no. 1:65–101.

Spiller, Pablo T., and Santiago Urbiztondo. 1991. Political appointees vs. career civil servants: A multiple principals theory of political bureaucracies. Working paper. University of Illinois, Department of Economics.

Stahl, Glenn O. 1983. *Public personnel administration.* 8th ed. New York: Harper & Row.

Stern, James L. 1988. Unionism and the public sector. In *Public-sector bargaining,* 2d ed., ed. Benjamin Aaron, Joyce M. Najita, and James L. Stern. Washington, D.C.: Bureau of National Affairs.

Stewart, Charles H., III. 1989. *Budget reform politics: The design of the appropriations process in the House of Representatives, 1865–1921.* New York: Cambridge University Press.

Stewman, Shelby, and Suresh L. Konda. 1983. Careers and organizational labor markets: Demographic models of organizational behavior. *American Journal of Sociology* 88, no. 4:637–85.

Stokes, Donald E. 1975. Parties and the nationalization of electoral forces. In *The American party systems: Stages of political development,* 2d ed., ed. William N. Chambers and Walter D. Burnham. New York: Oxford University Press.

Stone, Alice B., and Donald C. Stone. 1968. Early development of education in public administration. In *Democracy and the public service,* ed. Frederick C. Mosher. New York: Oxford University Press.

Stratmann, Thomas. 1992. Are contributors rational? Untangling strategies of political action committees. *Journal of Political Economy* 100, no. 3:647–64.

Sundquist, James L. 1973. *Dynamics of the party system: Alignment and realignment of political parties in the United States.* Washington, D.C.: Brookings.

———. 1981. *The decline and resurgence of Congress.* Washington, D.C.: Brookings.

Sunstein, Cass R. 1987. Constitutionalism after the New Deal. *Harvard Law Review* 101, no. 2:421–510.

Thayer, George. 1973. *Who shakes the money tree: American campaign financing practices from 1789 to the present.* New York: Simon & Schuster.

Tirole, Jean. 1986. Hierarchies and bureaucracies: On the role of collusion in organizations. *Journal of Law, Economics, and Organization* 2, no. 2:181–214.

Titlow, Richard E. 1979. *Americans import merit: Origins of the United States civil service and the influence of the British model.* Washington, D.C.: University Press of America.

Tolbert, Pamela S., and Lynne G. Zucker. 1983. Institutional sources of change in the formal structure of organizations: The diffusion of civil service reform, 1880–1935. *Administrative Science Quarterly* 28:22–39.

Toppel, Robert. 1991. Specific capital, mobility, and wages: Wages rise with job seniority. *Journal of Political Economy* 99, no. 1:145–76.

Trejo, Stephen J. 1991. Public sector unions and municipal employment. *Industrial and Labor Relations Review* 45, no. 1:166–80.

Tullock, Gordon. 1965. *The politics of bureaucracy.* Washington, D.C.: Public Affairs Press.

———. 1974. Dynamic hypothesis on bureaucracy. *Public Choice* 16:127–31.

U.S. Civil Service Commission. 1941. *History of the federal civil service, 1789 to the present.* Washington, D.C.: U.S. Government Printing Office.

———. 1969. *Union recognition in the federal government.* Washington, D.C.: U.S. Government Printing Office.

———. 1973. *Occupations of federal white-collar workers.* Washington, D.C.: U.S. Government Printing Office.

———. 1978. *Study of position classification accuracy in executive branch occupations under the general schedule.* Washington, D.C.: U.S. Government Printing Office.

————. Selected Years. *Annual report.* Washington, D.C.: U.S. Government Printing Office.

U.S. Classification Task Force. 1981. *A federal position classification system for the 1980's.* Washington, D.C.: U.S. Government Printing Office.

United States Code. 1970. *Congressional and administrative news,* vol. 3, *Legislative history.* 91st Cong. 2d sess. St. Paul, Minn.: West.

————. 1978. Congressional and administrative news, vol. 4, *Legislative history.* 95th Cong. 2d sess. St. Paul, Minn.: West.

U.S. Congressional Budget Office. 1984. *Reducing grades of the General Schedule workforce.* Washington, D.C.: U.S. Government Printing Office.

U.S. Department of Commerce. 1916. *Annual report of the secretary.* Washington, D.C.: U.S. Government Printing Office.

————. 1975. *Historical statistics of the United States.* Washington, D.C.: U.S. Government Printing Office.

————. Bureau of the Census. 1983. *Congressional districts of the 98th Congress.* Washington, D.C.: U.S. Government Printing Office.

————. Bureau of the Census. 1988. *Government finances in 1986–87,* Washington, D.C.: U.S. Government Printing Office.

————. Bureau of the Census. 1991. *Statistical abstract of the United States.* Washington, D.C.: U.S. Government Printing Office.

U.S. Department of Commerce and Labor. 1921. *Workmen's compensation laws of the United States.* Labor Statistics Bulletin no. 272. Washington, D.C.: U.S. Government Printing Office.

U.S. Department of Labor. Bureau of Labor Statistics. 1981. *A decade of federal white-collar pay comparability, 1970–1980.* Washington, D.C.: U.S. Government Printing Office.

U.S. Federal Government Service Task Force. 1985. *Cumulative summary of RIF activity for fiscal years 1982–1984.* Washington, D.C.: U.S. Government Printing Office.

U.S. General Accounting Office. 1975. *Federal white-collar pay systems need fundamental changes.* Washington, D.C.: U.S. Government Printing Office.

————. 1984. *Descriptions of selected systems for classifying federal civilian positions and personnel.* Washington, D.C.: U.S. Government Printing Office.

————. 1985. *Reduction in force can sometimes be more costly to agencies than attrition and furlough.* Washington, D.C.: U.S. Government Printing Office.

U.S. House of Representatives. 1881. Civil service reform in New York City Post Office and Customs House. 46th Cong., 3d sess. H. Ex. Doc. 94. Washington, D.C.: U.S. Government Printing Office.

————. 1912a. Eight hours for drege workers. 62d Cong., 2d sess. H. Rep. 910. Washington, D.C.: U.S. Government Printing Office.

————. 1912b. Federal Employees' Compensation Bill. 62d Cong. 2d sess. H. Rep. 578. Washington, D.C.: U.S. Government Printing Office.

————. 1912c. Hearings before the Committee on Reform in the Civil Service. *Retirement of civil service employees of the classified civil service.* 62d Cong., 2d sess. Washington, D.C.: U.S. Government Printing Office.

————. 1920. Report of the Congressional Joint Commission on Reclassification of Salaries. 66th Cong., 2d sess. H. Doc. 686. Washington, D.C.: U.S. Government Printing Office.

————. 1921a. Hearings before the Subcommittee on Reform in the Civil Service. *Appeals from dismissal.* 67th Cong., 1st sess. Washington, D.C.: U.S. Government Printing Office.

————. 1921b. Hearings before the Subcommittee on Reform in the Civil Service. *Increase of annuities under retirement laws.* 67th Cong., 1st sess. Washington, D.C.: U.S. Government Printing Office.

———. 1921c. Joint hearings before the Committees on Civil Service, Congress of the United States, relative to the reclassification of salaries. 67th Cong., 1st sess. Washington, D.C.: U.S. Government Printing Office.

———. 1939. *Hearings before the Committee on the Civil Service on H.R. 960.* 76th Cong., 1st sess. Washington, D.C.: U.S. Government Printing Office.

———. 1970. *Hearings before the Subcommittee on Compensation of the Committee on Post Office and Civil Service, on H.R. 18403 and H.R. 18603.* 91st Cong., 2d sess. Washington, D.C.: U.S. Government Printing Office.

———. 1986. *Joint hearings before the Subcommittee on Civil Service and the Subcommittee on Compensation and Employee Benefits of the Committee on Post Office and Civil Service.* 99th Cong., 2d sess. Washington, D.C.: U.S. Government Printing Office.

———. 1989. *Hearings before the Committee on Post Office and Civil Service.* 101st Cong., 1st sess. Washington, D.C.: U.S. Government Printing Office.

———. 1990. *Hearings before the Subcommittee on Compensation and Employee Benefits of the Committee on Post Office and Civil Service on H.R. 3979 and H.R. 4716.* 101st Cong., 2d sess. Washington, D.C.: U.S. Government Printing Office.

———. 1992. *Hearings before the Committee on Post Office and Civil Service: The directed reassignment of John Mumma and L. Lorraine Mintzmyer.* 102d Cong., 1st sess. Serial no. 102–27. Washington, D.C.: U.S. Government Printing Office.

———. Commissions to Examine Certain Customs Houses of the United States (Jay Commission). 1877. *Letter from the Secretary of the Treasury, October 19, 1877.* 45th Cong., 1st sess. H. Ex. Doc. 8. Washington, D.C.: U.S. Government Printing Office.

———. Committee on Government Operations. 1993. *Managing the federal government: A decade of decline.* 102d Cong., 2d sess. Washington, D.C.: U.S. Government Printing Office.

———. Committee on the Judiciary. 1914. *Hearings on 15222, A bill to provide compensation for employees of the United States suffering injuries or occupational diseases in the course of employment.* 63d Cong., 2d sess. Washington, D.C.: U.S. Government Printing Office.

———. Committee on Post Office and Civil Service. 1976. *History of civil service merit systems of the United States and selected foreign countries.* 94th Cong., 2d sess. Washington, D.C.: U.S. Government Printing Office.

———. Committee on Post Office and Civil Service. 1978a. *Presidential staffing—a brief overview.* 95th Cong., 2d sess. Committee Print 95–17. Washington, D.C.: U.S. Government Printing Office.

———. Committee on Post Office and Civil Service. 1978b. Report: Civil Service Reform Act of 1978. 95th Cong., 2d sess. H. Rep. 94–1403. Washington, D.C.: U.S. Government Printing Office.

———. Committee on Post Office and Civil Service. 1988. *Policy and supporting positions.* 100th Cong., 2d sess. Washington, D.C.: U.S. Government Printing Office.

———. Joint Select Committee on Retrenchment. 1867. Civil service of the United States. 39th Cong., 2d sess. H. Rep. 8. Washington, D.C.: U.S. Government Printing Office.

———. Personnel Classification Board. 1931. Closing report of wage and personnel survey. 71st Cong., 3d sess. H. Doc. 771. Washington, D.C.: U.S. Government Printing Office.

———. U.S. President's Commission on Economy and Efficiency. 1912d. The need for a national budget. 62d Cong., 1st sess. H. Rep. 62. Washington, D.C.: U.S. Government Printing Office.

U.S. Merit System Protection Board. 1987. *Performance management and recognition system: Linking pay to performance.* Washington, D.C.: U.S. Government Printing Office.

————. 1989. *The senior executive service: Views of the former federal executives.* Washington, D.C.

————. 1990. *Why are employees leaving the federal government?* Washington, D.C.

U.S. Office of Management and Budget. 1981–86. *Object class analysis.* Washington, D.C.: U.S. Government Printing Office.

U.S. Office of Personnel Management. 1980–86. *Federal civilian work force statistics: Monthly release.* Washington, D.C.: U.S. Government Printing Office.

————. 1981–82. *Annual report of the director.* Washington, D.C.: U.S. Government Printing Office.

————. 1983. *A report on federal white-collar position classification accuracy.* Washington, D.C.: U.S. Government Printing Office.

————. 1984. *Federal personnel manual.* Washington, D.C.: U.S. Government Printing Office.

————. 1985a. *Issue analysis: Government management of position classification and position management programs.* Washington, D.C.: U.S. Government Printing Office.

————. 1985b. *Personnel data standards, FPM supplement 292–1.* Washington, D.C.: U.S. Government Printing Office.

————. 1985c. *Union Recognition in the federal government.* Washington, D.C.: U.S. Government Printing Office.

————. 1986. *Qualification standards for positions under the General Schedule, handbook X-118.* Washington, D.C.: U.S. Government Printing Office.

————. 1989. *Pay structure of the federal civil service.* Washington, D.C.: U.S. Government Printing Office.

U.S. Post Office Department. Selected Years. *Annual report of the postmaster general.* Washington, D.C.: U.S. Government Printing Office.

U.S. Senate. 1881. The regulation and improvement of the civil service: The merit system substituted for the partisan spoils system. 46th Cong., 3d sess. S. Rep. 872. Washington, D.C.: U.S. Government Printing Office.

————. 1882. Report to accompany Bill S. 133. 47th Cong., 1st sess. S. Rep. 576. Washington, D.C.: U.S. Government Printing Office.

————. 1922. *Hearings before the Subcommittee of the Committee on Appropriations on HR 8928, A bill to provide for the classification of civilian positions within the District of Columbia and in the field service.* 67th Cong., 2d and 4th sess. Washington, D.C.: U.S. Government Printing Office.

————. 1937. *Joint hearings before the Committee on Education and Labor, U.S. Senate and Committee on Labor, House of Representatives* (on 52474 and H.R. 7200, Bills to provide for the establishment of fair labor standards in employments in and affecting interstate commerce and for other purposes). 75th Cong., 1st sess. Washington, D.C.: U.S. Government Printing Office.

————. 1949. *Hearings before a Subcommittee of the Committee on Post Office and Civil Service.* 81st Cong., 1st sess. Washington, D.C.: U.S. Government Printing Office.

————. 1962. *Hearings before the Committee on Post Office and Civil Service on S2712.* 87th Cong. 2d sess. Washington, D.C.: U.S. Government Printing Office.

————. 1965. *Hearings before the Committee on Post Office and Civil Service on legislation pertaining to federal employees' compensation, H.R. 10281.* 89th Cong., 1st sess. Washington, D.C.: U.S. Government Printing Office.

————. 1976. *Documentary history of federal pay legislation: 1975.* 94th Cong., 2d sess. Washington, D.C.: U.S. Government Printing Office.

————. 1978. *Hearings before Committee on Governmental Affairs: Civil Service Reform Act of 1978 and Reorganization Plan of 1978.* 95th Cong. 2d sess. Washington, D.C.: U.S. Government Printing Office.

————. Committee on Civil Service and Retrenchment. 1882. Statements on Bill S. 133. 47th Cong., 1st sess. Washington, D.C.: U.S. Government Printing Office.

————. Committee on Civil Service and Retrenchment. 1918. Retirement of Classified Civil Service Employees. 65th Cong., 2d sess. S. Rep. 574. Washington, D.C.: U.S. Government Printing Office.

————. Committee on Civil Service and Retrenchment. 1919a. Hearings on S1699, A bill for the retirement of employees in the classified service, and for other purposes. 66th Cong., 1st sess. S. Rep. 99. Washington, D.C.: U.S. Government Printing Office.

————. Committee on the District of Columbia. 1908. Hours of Labor on contracts with the district of Columbia, on Bill S. 6414. 60th Cong., 2d sess. Washington, D.C.: U.S. Government Printing Office.

————. Committee on Governmental Affairs. 1989. Hatch Act reform amendments of 1989: Hearings on S. 135. 101st Cong., 1st sess. S. Rep. 165. Washington, D.C.: U.S. Government Printing Office.

————. Committee on Governmental Affairs. 1993. *Government Performance and Results Act of 1993.* Report to accompany S. 20. 103d Cong., 1st sess. Washington, D.C.: U.S. Government Printing Office.

————. Committee on the Reform of the Civil Service. 1919b. Retirement of employees in the classified civil service. 66th Cong., 1st sess. S. Rep. 120.Washington, D.C.: U.S. Government Printing Office.

Van Riper, Paul P. 1958. *History of the United States civil service.* Evanston, Ill.: Row Peterson.

Venti, Steven F. 1987. Wages in the federal and private sectors. In *Public sector payrolls,* ed. David A. Wise. Chicago: University of Chicago Press.

Volcker, Paul A. 1988. *Public service: The quiet crisis.* Washington, D.C.: American Enterprise Institute.

Wachter, Michael L., and Jeffrey Perloff. 1992. A comparative analysis of wage premiums and industrial relations in the British post office and the U.S. postal service. Discussion Paper no. 98. University of Pennsylvania, Institute for Law and Economics.

Walker, Harvey. 1941a. Employee organizations in the national government service: 1. The period prior to the world war. *Public Personnel Studies* 10:67–73.

————. 1941b. Employee organizations in the national government service: 2. The formation of the national federation of federal employees. *Public Personnel Studies* 10:130–35.

Walker, Jack L. 1969. The diffusion of innovations among the American states. *American Political Science Review* 63, no. 3:880–99.

Walsh, John, and Garth Mangum. 1992. *Labor struggle in the post office.* Armonk, N.Y.: Sharpe.

Weber, Max. 1979. *Economy and society.* Edited by Guenther Roth and Claus Wittich. Berkeley and Los Angeles: University of California Press.

Weingast, Barry R. 1989. The political institutions of representative government: Legislatures. *Journal of Institutional and Theoretical Economics* 145, no. 4:693–703.

Weingast, Barry R., and William J. Marshall. 1988. The industrial organization of Congress; or, Why legislators, like firms, are not organized as markets. *Journal of Political Economy* 96, no. 1:132–63.

Weingast, Barry R., and Mark J. Moran. 1983. Bureaucratic discretion or congressional control? Regulatory policymaking by the Federal Trade Commission. *Journal of Political Economy* 91, no. 5:765–800.

Weingast, Barry R., Kenneth A. Shepsle, and Christopher Johnsen. 1981. The political economy of benefits and costs. *Journal of Political Economy* 89, no. 4:642–64.

Weinstein, James. 1967. Big business and the origins of workmen's compensation. *Journal of Labor History* 8, no. 2:156–74.

Wessels, Walter J. 1991. Do unions contract for added employment? *Industrial and Labor Relations Review* 45, no. 1:181–93.

Wiebe, Robert. 1967. *The search for order, 1877–1920.* New York: Hill & Wang.

Where to find CAB functions at DOT. 1985. *Air Transport World,* March, 68–69.

White, Leonard D. 1954. *The Jacksonians: A study in administrative history.* New York: Macmillan.

Wiggins, Steven N., and Gary D. Libecap. 1985. Oil field unitization: Contractual failure in the presence of imperfect information. *American Economic Review* 75, no. 3:368–85.

Wildavsky, Aaron. 1979. *The politics of the budgetary process.* 3d ed. Boston: Little, Brown.

———. 1988. Ubiquitous anomie: Public Service in an era of ideological dissensus. *Public Administration Review* 4:753–55.

Williamson, Oliver E. 1967. Hierarchical control and optimum firm size. *Journal of Political Economy* 75, no. 1:123–38.

———. 1970. *Corporate control and business behavior.* Englewood Cliffs, N.J.: Prentice-Hall.

———. 1975. *Markets and hierarchies.* New York: Free Press.

———. 1976. Franchise bidding for natural monopolies—in general and with respect to CATV. *Bell Journal of Economics* 7, no. 1:195–223.

———. 1985. *The economic institutions of capitalism.* New York: Free Press.

Wilson, James Q. 1961. The economy of patronage. *Journal of Political Economy* 69, no. 4:369–80.

———. 1989. *Bureaucracy: What government agencies do and why they do it.* New York: Basic.

Wilson, Rick. 1986. An empirical test of preferences for the political pork barrel: District level appropriations for river and harbor legislation, 1889–1913 *American Journal of Political Science* 30, no. 4:729–54.

Wilson, Woodrow. 1887. The study of administration. *Public Science Quarterly* 2:197–222.

Wittman, Donald. 1989. Why democracies produce efficient results. *Journal of Political Economy* 97, no. 6:1395–1424.

Wolfinger, Raymond E. 1972. Why political machines have not withered away and other revisionist thoughts. *Journal of Politics* 34, no. 2:365–98.

Wolfinger, Raymond, and John Field. 1966. Political ethos and the structure of city governments. *American Political Science Review* 60, no. 2:306–26.

Wolfinger, Raymond, and S. J. Rosenstone. 1980. *Who votes?* New Haven, Conn.: Yale University Press.

Wood, B. Dan. 1988. Principals, bureaucrats, and responsiveness in clean air enforcements. *American Political Science Review* 82, no. 1:213–34.

———. 1989. Reply: Principal-agent models of political control of bureaucracy. *American Political Science Review* 83, no. 3:970–78.

Young, Robert A. 1991. Budget size and bureaucratic careers. In *The budget-maximizing bureaucrat: Appraisals and evidence,* ed. André Blais and Stéphane Dion. Pittsburgh: University of Pittsburgh Press.

Zax, Jeffrey S., and Casey Ichniowski. 1988. The effects of public sector unionism on pay, employment, department budgets, and municipal expenditures. In *When public sector workers unionize,* ed. Richard B. Freeman and Casey Ichniowksy. Chicago: University of Chicago Press.

Index

Accountability: of civil service, 2, 154–58, 162; with growth of federal labor force, 28; under patronage system, 4

Agencies: bureaucratic promotion of growth, 2; effect of growth on salaries, 133–34; influence of civil servants in, 162–66; mission as motivation, 166–69; problem in patronage system, 19–21; questions of accountability, 154–58. *See also* New Deal agencies

Alexander, Herbert E., 23t

American Federation of Government Employees (AFGE), 78, 182

American Federation of Labor (AFL), 78–79, 80, 87–88

Arnold, R. Douglas, 2

Arthur, Chester A., 15

Autonomy, bureaucratic, 156–57

Baruch, Ismar, 85

Becker, Gary S., 138, 157, 178

Beer, Samuel, 168

Bennett, James T., 126, 128, 133

Biemiller, Andrew, 100

Blais, André, 136, 163

Blake, Donald E., 136

Blanketing in tenure, 38, 49, 60–61

Borcherding, Thomas E., 157

Brady, David W., 41

Branti v. Finkel, 183

Brennan, William J., 184–85

Brotherhood of Railway Postal Clerks, 78, 80

Brown, Joseph, 32

Brownlow Committee, 1

Buchanan, James M., 126

Bureaucracy: achieving reform, 170–71; competition over, 3, 160–63; components of, 154–55; effect of change on control of, 8–9; in principal/agent analysis of behavior, 158–59; problems of performance and accountability, 1–2, 4, 28, 154–58, 162; promotion of budget maximization, 2; role in policy formation and implementation, 2, 156–58; undefined property rights linked to, 6, 18–19, 26–28, 155, 178, 180

Burton, John F., 102t, 120

Bush, George, 143

Bush, Winston C., 126

Campaign expenses: financing from assessments on patronage employees, 15–16, 23–25, 185; growth (1860–1904), 23–25

Carter, Jimmy, 1, 161, 170

Chambers, William N., 22

Civil servants: function and goals of career, 7; role in competition over civil service, 3, 162; salary caps for senior, 148, 163–64

Civil Service Commission: creation and duration (1871), 20, 31; under provisions of Pendleton Act, 33–34, 51, 78

Civil service reform: attempts, 1–2; congressional committee support, 142; as election issue, 25; Jenckes bill (1867, 1868, 1870, 1871), 30–31; lack of progress in, 155; state and local level: late nineteenth

223